Edward E. Hale

The Story of Spain

Edward E. Hale

The Story of Spain

ISBN/EAN: 9783337239893

Printed in Europe, USA, Canada, Australia, Japan

Cover: Foto ©ninafisch / pixelio.de

More available books at **www.hansebooks.com**

The Story of the Nations

THE
STORY OF SPAIN

BY

EDWARD EVERETT HALE
AND
SUSAN HALE

NEW YORK AND LONDON
G. P. PUTNAM'S SONS
The Knickerbocker Press
1887

COPYRIGHT
G. P. PUTNAM'S SONS
1886

Press of
G. P. Putnam's Sons
New York

INTRODUCTION.

Spain has held, for two thousand years, an interesting and important position among the states of Europe. She is of Europe and she is not. For the Pyrenees separate her so far from the continent, that her people have always had characteristics of their own, more deeply stamped upon them than those of any other European nation. Yet the Pyrenees are not impassable, and the Mediterranean is easily traversed. So that Spain has been no separated Japan, but she has had to give and take in the international courtesies, exchanges, and conflicts of the western world. There have been times when the monarchs of Spain gave the law to Europe. Even the Greek emperor once owed his crown to the succor of Catalonia. There have been times, again, when none have been so poor as to render to Spain any reverence. There are spots in Spain where a year may pass without a drop of rain. But within a few hundred miles the rainfall of the same year is all that is needed for the most successful agriculture, and these regions are rich and beautiful, while the others are arid deserts. The history of Spain shows contrasts which are as strong. It is hard to believe that we are reading of the same nation, when we follow the history of the great expeditions of discovery and war by which she traversed and conquered two hemispheres; and when, within a few generations after, we drag through the wretched annals of petty court intrigues, which are all that is left of the story of the descendants of Ferdinand and Isabella.

To write every detail of such a history for English readers, would literally not be worth the ink and the paper which it would cost. Of what is forgotten in it, much is well forgotten, and no writer need attempt to raise it from its grave. But we have thought that the reader of to-day ought to know what are the successive steps by which the Iberia, which was almost a fabled country to the Romans of the time of the Consuls, has become the Spain of to-day, with the proud record of Spain in literature, in adventure, in discovery, in statesmanship, and in war. The book which the reader holds undertakes to show these important steps. We pass, intentionally and without a word, much of the detail of long periods, that we may have the more space and chance to describe the essential movements of history, on which the real fortunes of Spain have depended, and, in many instances, the fortunes of the world. What is left out is by no means without interest, and we do not pretend that it is without importance. We shall be glad, indeed, if in the story as we tell it, the reader shall be tempted to search for himself, in those narratives in different languages, by which he can fill out our intentional omissions.

It might probably be said that no country has furnished more fascinating subjects for literature and art than Spain. The mere contrasts of which we have spoken are such as dramatists and poets delight in; and one might almost say that the rare variety which fascinates the traveller in Spain, and the conflicts and rivalries of the five or six nations which make up the Spanish people, have given a sort of stimulus, especially to romance, which we should hardly expect where nature and life are more commonplace. From the first century, when Martial, Lucan, the Senecas, and Quintilian, all Spaniards by birth, were leaders in the literary circles of Rome, down to our days when Mr. Longfellow writes "The Spanish Student," and George Eliot "The Spanish Gipsy," the authors of every western nation have felt the Spanish fascination. The origin of modern romance might be fairly ascribed to Amadis of Gaul. It would be well indeed if some of the nineteenth-century romancers would imitate the directness of its narrative and the simplicity of its description. Though it is not to be accounted a Spanish romance originally, it owes all its early reputation to Spain; the readers of Spain knowing how to give full sympathy to the work of Lobeira, who is indeed one of their own brothers, writing in the neighboring country of Portugal and in its kindred tongue.

Within the last three months it has been said, on good authority, that among leaders of our own colored races at the South, there are traditions of the times when Islam held possession of Granada, and a vague feeling that, in the future, Africa and Africans shall regain their lost empire in Spain. This is certain, that Islam has never forgotten those glorious centuries when Cordova and the sister cities were at the head of the civilization of the world. It is not, therefore, the literature of Europe or America only which looks fondly for its subjects to Spain, but we follow her legends and her truer histories as well in the Eastern writers, so long as the East had any literature.

It has been, therefore, a part of our plan in following the Story of Spain, to refer, from chapter to chapter, to such illustrations from the writings of various authors of different countries, as might interest young readers and tempt them to follow, not only the history of Spain in its chronological order, but the series of writings which in romance, in poetry, and in other literature we owe to her suggestions.

CONTENTS.

INTRODUCTION.

PART I.

I.

PAGE

EARLY TRADITIONS 3–18

The necklace of the queen, 3—Iberians on the peninsula, 4—Thirty-seven monkeys at Gibraltar, 4—Celts from Asia migrate from the West, 5—Celts, Iberians, and Celtiberians, 5—Their arms, their food, their dress, 6—Names of the different tribes, 8—Asturians, 8—Cantabrians, 9—Vascones or Basques, 9—Basque language, or Esquera, 10—Galicians, 11—Lusitania, and the religion of the Druids, 12—Characteristics of these Northern tribes, 12—Early races of Southern Spain, 14—Phœnicians, tempted by the wealth of the country, 16—The alphabet of the Phœnicians, 17—Difference between tradition and written history, 17.

II.

CARTHAGINIANS 19–29

First acquaintance of Spain with the rest of the world, 19—The ships of Tarshish, 19—Foothold for the Carthaginians, 20—Carthage steadily gaining power, 20—Hannibal's scheme of subduing the Spaniards, 21—Hamilcar had built New Carthage, 21—The boy Hannibal and his oath, 21—War against Saguntum, 22—The Saguntines resist bravely, 24—But, left to their fate, surrender, 25—Result, described by Livy, 26—Carthaginian tinge in the blood of Spain, 27—Its mark on literature, 28—Poem of Zamora, 29.

III.

THE SCIPIOS 30–42

Rome attracted toward Spain, 30—Her conquests make of it a Roman province, 30—Scipio Africanus, the first commanding figure, 32—Publius Scipio appointed general, 33—His wise policy with the Spaniards, 33—He blockades New Carthage, 34—Surprise of Mago, the Carthaginian general, 34—Success of the attack, 34—Wealth of the city, brought to Scipio, 35—He releases the hostages, 36—Carthaginians expelled from Spain, 37—Noble character of Publius Scipio, 37—Cato the elder at Jaca, 38—Assimilation of Romans and Spaniards, 38—Latin language prevails, 38—Camilius Scipio takes control of the province, 40—Fall of Numantia, 40.

IV.

SERTORIUS 44–53

His picturesque story told by Plutarch, 44—A soldier of ability, 44—His voyage toward the Islands of the Blest, 45—Lands in Mauritania, 46—Received the white hind, 46—He is regarded as divine in Lusitania, 47—Helps the Spaniards to resist Rome, 47—Founds a university at Osca, 47—Devotion of his troops, 48—His achievement against the Characitanians, 49—Recognized master of a large part of Spain, 52—Not encouraged by Sylla; an army despatched to crush him, 52—Treaty with Mithridates, 52—Conspiracy against Sertorius; close of the episode, 53—Corneille's tragedy, 53.

V.

JULIUS CÆSAR IN SPAIN 54–69

Death of Sertorius, 54—Followed by Pompey, 54—Cæsar and Pompey at Munda, 55—Position of the armies, 56—The Waterloo of the conflict, 56—Army of Pompey broken, 57—Victory of Cæsar celebrated by a triumph, 57—Augustus Cæsar brings peace into Spain, 58—Five cities of Spain established, 60—Roman customs adopted, 61—Historians and poets born in Spain, 62—Martial's ode, 63—Ode by Prudentius, 64—His long poem, Peristephanior, 64—Roman impress upon Spanish life, 67—On language, 68.

PART II.

VI.

ATAULPHUS—EVARIC . 73-91

Northern invaders in Southern Europe, 73—Change the destinies of Spain, 73—Establishment of a Gothic dynasty, 73—Southern France, its military base, 74—Advance of its armies to the Guadalquivir, 74—Vigor infused into the Roman province, 75—Southern France overrun, and Rome powerless, besieged by Alaric, 76—Goths established in Toulouse, 77—Becoming civilized, 77—Ataulphus their king, 77; in love with Placidia, 78—Receives her as his wife from Honorius, 78—Court of Ataulphus at Barcelona, 79—Trouble with his soldiers, 80—assassinated by a dwarf, 80—Wallia chosen king, 81—Conditions of peace with Romans, 82—Hostilities against the barbarians, 84—Theodoric successor to Wallia, 84—Invasion of the Huns, 84—Attila, the Scourge of God, 85—Conquered, 85—His death, 86—Theodoric the Visigoth, 86—Evaric, king at Toulouse, 87—The founder of the Gothic kingdom in Spain, 87—Goths grown to be cultivated people, 88—Gothic language, 88—Evaric's death at Arles, 89—Government of the Visigoths, 90—Inauguration of their king, 91.

VII.

ARIANS . . . 92-105

Origin of the Goths, 92—Ulfilas converts them to the Christian religion and reduces their language to writing, 93—Their respect for the priests, 94—Their form of religion called Arianism, 95—Confronted with the dogmas of the Church, 96—Conflict between Arians and Catholics, 98—Not really a conflict as to the divine realities, 99—Most valuable gift of Arianism to Spain, 100—Muzarabic ritual, 100—Traces of the Gothic language, 101—Sermon on the Mount in four languages, 102—Resemblance of English and Spanish languages, 103—Romance authors of Spain, 104—Influence of Spanish literature, 105.

VIII.

LEOVIGILD—RECARED 106–124

Leovigild an Arian, 106—His son, Erminigild, married to a princess of France, 107—Her mother a Gothic princess, 108—Married in France, 110—Ingunda a Catholic, 111—Quarrels with her step-mother, 112—Erminigild becomes Catholic, 113—Deeply offending his father, 114—Rebels against Leovigild, 115—Punished and exiled to Valencia, 116—Thrown into prison, 117—Obstinate in his faith, 118—Executed by his father's order, 119—Death of Leovigild, 120—Recared converted from Arianism, 121—His moderate measures, 122—Catholic faith declared the religion of the state, 123—Death of Recared, 124.

IX.

TOLEDO—WAMBA 125–138

Toledo the capital of the Visigothic kings, 125—Reigning there for several centuries, 126—Catholic religion firmly established, 126—Wamba unwillingly chosen king, 127—An energetic sovereign, 128—His troops suppress a rebellion in Gothic Gaul, 129—Duke Paul its author, 130—Rebels consigned to prison, 131—Gothic Gaul pacified, 132—Wamba persecutes the Jews, 133—Defends the court from Saracens, 134—His trance, by which he was made a monk, 135—Ervigius reigns, 136—Presence of the Goths in Toledo, 137—Spirit of Roderick, 138.

X.

RODERICK, THE LAST OF THE GOTHS . . 139–151

Roderick assumes the rule of Spain, 139—Count Julian, the commander of the Spanish army in Africa, 140—Has defeated Musa, 141—Betrays to him the strongholds of the Goths, 141—Symbols of the pillars of Hercules, 142—Legend of Roderick's visit to the cave of Hercules, 143—Roderick learns of the invasion of Tarik, 145—Rallies his forces, 146—Battle of the Guadalete lost to the Goths, 146—Roderick drowned—Tarik advances to Toledo, 148—Spain reduced to a Mohammedan province, 149—" Roderick, the Last of the Goths," by Southey, 150.

CONTENTS. xi

PART III.

XI.
PAGE

THE CALIPHATE OF CORDOVA . . . 155–170
Mohammed, the founder of Islamism, 155—The triumphs of its armies, checked at Tours, 156—Moslems content themselves with Spain, 157—Abderahman, prince of the Omeyyades, 158—Entertained by Bedouins, 160—Offered sovereignty, 161—Enters Spain, 162—Resisted by Yussef, but successful, 163—Spain governed by the Omeyyades, 164—Their munificence, 165—The mosque of Cordova, 166—Cordova, centre of learning, 168—Almanza, the regent, 169—War with Christians, 169—End of the Caliphate of the West, 170.

XII.

THE SONG OF ROLAND . . . 171–186
Charlemagne at Saragossa, 171—Attacked in the Pyrenees by Basques, 172—Battle of Roncesvalles, 173—Divergence between history and legend, 173—Roland and Olivier, 174—Journey of Ganelon, 175—His treachery, 176—The rear of the army entrusted to Roland, 177—Approach of the Saracens, 178—Fearful struggle, 179—Archbishop Turpin, 180—Roland sounds his horn, 181—Too late, 182—Death of Olivier, 183—The emperor hears the horn, 184—Death of Roland, 185.

XIII.

ALMORAVIDES—ALMOHADES . . . 187–202
Christians regain some power, 187—Almoravides called to protect the Moslems, 188—Abdallah their leader, 189—Yussef ben Taxfin, 190—Takes possession of the kingdom, 191—And leads the armies to Spain, 192—Overcomes the petty princes of Andalusia, 193—Dies at Morocco, 194—Short duration of the Almoravides, 195—Mohammed the son of the lamp-lighter, 196—Becomes Mahdi, 197—Leader of the Almohades, or Unitarians, 198—His successor, Abdelmumen, victorious in Africa, 199—Becomes sovereign of all Mohammedan Spain, 200—Crusade of Christians, 200—Battle of Navas de Tolosa, 201.

XIV.

Story of the Abencerrages . . 203–212

Abencerrages, a legendary family, 203—Their rivals, the Zegris, 204—Intense jealousies, 205—Aixa, Tepi princess, bride of the king of Grenada, 206—Wedding at the Moorish court, 207—Splendors of the tribes, 208—Competition in games, 209—Abenhamet the flower of the Abencerrages, 210—Zoraïde, his beloved, married to the royal prince, 210—Interview discovered, 211—Abencerrages ordered to the palace, 211—Slaughtered in the Court of Lions, 212.

XV.

The Fall of Granada 213–228

Mohammed ben Alhamar, 213—Fortifies the kingdom of Grenada, 214—Intercourse of Christians and Moors, 215—Moors divided, and Christians united, 216—Treachery in the Alhambra, 217—End of the romantic period, 219—Isabella determined to destroy the Moors, 220—Boabdil the last prince of Grenada, 221—Situation of the Alhambra, 222—Zahara and Alhama, 223—The mother of Boabdil, 224—Grenada invested, capitulates, 225—Boabdil surrenders the keys, 226—"El ultimo sospiro del moro," 227—Moors dreaming of Granada, 228.

PART IV.

XVI.

Pelayo 231–247

Goths after their defeat, 231—Retreat to the mountains, 232—Pelayo the head of a little kingdom, 233—Alfonso el Casto, 234—Legend of Bernardo del Carpio, 235—His father imprisoned, 236—Treachery of the king, 237—Catholic faith of the early Goths, 238—Ramiro visited by Santiago, 239—Santiago at Clavigo, 240—Other legends of the saint, 241—Sancho the fat, 243—Counts of Castile, 244—Fernan Gonzalez, 245—Miracle of the grotto, 246—Successes of the Christians, 247.

XVII.

THE CID 248–261

Warfare between Mussulmans and Christians, 248—The Cid, a hero coolly doubted by critics, 249—Absolute veracity of the chronicle for us not important, 250—Single story in his life, 251—Boldness in presence of King Alfonso, 252—Kindness of the monarch, 253—Banished from Leon and Castile, 254—Attacks the Moors and becomes governor of Valencia, 256—Resists King Yussef, 257—Twenty-nine Moorish kings slain, 258—Courage of the Cid, 259—His death, 260—Translations of the chronicle and poem, 261.

XVIII.

ALFONSO X. 262–280

Seville, city of the perfect climate, 262—Won for the Christians by Ferdinand III., 264—This king a saint, 265—His son, Alfonso the Learned, 266—His claim to be Emperor of Germany, 268—Ferdinand de la Cerda, 268—Quarrels about the succession, 269—Sancho proclaimed king, 270—Pedro the Cruel adorns the Alcazar, 271—Loves Maria de Padilla, 272—Ill treats his bride, Blanche of Bourbon, 273—Kills his brother Fadrique, 274—Rouses the hostility of the French, 276—Flees before Henry at Trastamara, 277—Gains the battle of Navarrete, 278—Slain by his brother, 279—Henry of Trastamara, 280.

XIX.

ARRAGON 281–297

Occupies the northeast of Spain, 281—Successes in war, 282—John of Arragon, 283—Carlos, Prince of Viana, 284—Joan Henriques, the disagreeable step-mother, 285—Carlos in Naples, 286—Urged to return, 287—refused the title of heir-apparent, 288—Arrested, 289—Acknowledged by the insistance of the Catalans; death of the Prince of Viana, 289—Blanche, his sister, persecuted by Joan, 291—Shut up at Orthes, and poisoned, 292—Misfortunes of King John, 294—Death of Joanna, 295—Renewed courage of the old king, 296—Enters Barcelona on a white charger, 297.

XX.

FERDINAND AND ISABELLA . . . 298–320

Maria of Castile and Arragon, 298—Isabella's offers of marriage, 299—Her attractions, 300—Affianced to Ferdinand, 301—Meeting with her betrothed, 302—The marriage, 304—Proclaimed queen at Segovia, 305—Isabella strengthens the kingdom, 306—Head-quarters at Seville, 307—Soul of the war against Grenada, 308—Receives Columbus, 310—Assumes his undertaking, 311—Return of Columbus, 312—Children of Ferdinand and Isabella, 314—The Princess Joanna, 315—Illness of the queen, 316—Her death, 317—Buried in the cathedral at Grenada, 318—Effigies on the tomb, 319—The royal standard, 320.

XXI.

CHARLES I. OF SPAIN—CHARLES V. OF GERMANY 321–340

Power of Charles in Europe, 321—Tried by prosperity, 322—His endless wars, 324—Grandson of Isabella, 325—Born at Ghent, 326—Cardinal Ximenes regent, 327—Joanna, mother of Charles, insane, 328—Clemency of Charles, 329—Wars with Francis I., 330—Bravery of Spanish troops, Moorish piracy, 331—Siege of Pampeluna, 332—Loyola, 333—Society of Jesus, 334—Charles retires to Trieste, 335—His conquests at home, 336—Extent of his kingdom, 337 Reputation of Spaniards for cruelty, 339—Courage, patience, and foresight of Spain, 340.

PART V.

XXII.

THREE PHILIPS 343–357

Decline of the country, 343—Possessions of Philip II., Poem of Numantia, 345—Don Quixote, 346—Marriages of Philip II., 347—Portrait by Titian, 348—" Bloody " Mary, 348—Double marriage at the court of France, 349—Revolt of the Moriscos, 350—Their contempt for Christian forms,

351—Insurrection put down, 352—Expelled by Philip III., 353—Treasures of the Moors, 353—Another double marriage, 354—Philip III.'s death, 355—Philip IV., 356—End of the real Spanish line of sovereigns, 357.

XXIII.

THE BOURBONS 358-371

Charles II. a weak descendant of the emperor, 358—Contemporary of Charles II. of England, 359—Settlements in America, 360—War of the Spanish Succession, 361—Claimants to the throne, 362—Philip V. proclaimed, 363—Treaty of Utrecht, 365—Blow to the Jesuits, 366—United States of America, 368—Charles III., 370—Manuel Godoy, 371

XXIV.

NAPOLEON 372-378

Spain betrayed by Ferdinand, 372—Battle of Trafalgar, 373—French and Spanish fleets, 374—Death of Nelson, 375—Villeneuve a prisoner, 376—Joseph Bonaparte usurps the Spanish crown, 377—Wellesley at Salamanca; Wellington at Victoria, 378—Fall of Napoleon, 378.

PART VI.

XXV.

THE NINETEENTH CENTURY . . . 381—396

Shelley's ode to the Spaniards, 381—Return of Ferdinand VII., 382—Rebellion of the American colonies, 384—Carlist plots, 385—Isabella, heiress to the throne, 386—Her cause that of liberalism, 387—wretched failure of her life, 388—Protected by Espartero, 389—Declared queen, 390—Deposed, 391—Amadeo made king; abdicates, 392—Alfonso XII., 393—His death, 394—Birth of a prince, 395—Dirge of Larra, 395.

LIST OF ILLUSTRATIONS.

	PAGE
GATE OF THE COURT OF ORANGES, SEVILLE CATHEDRAL	*Frontispiece*
MOUNTAIN GORGE IN THE ASTURIAS	7
MONUMENT OF THE DRUIDS	13
ROMAN AMPHITHEATRE AT MURVIEDRO	23
ROMAN BRIDGE AT SALAMANCA	31
ROMAN BRIDGE AT CUENCA	39
ROMAN REMAINS AT MERIDA	43
JULIUS CÆSAR	55
CÆSAR'S METHOD OF ATTACK	59
ROMAN AQUEDUCT, SEGOVIA	65
ROMAN TEMPLE AT VIENNE	83
ROMAN GATEWAY AT TREVES	89
TOLEDO	97
THE WINDING PASS	108
PUERTA DEL SOL, TOLEDO	113
GIBRALTAR	143
MOORISH TOWER, TOLEDO	151
MOORISH MILLS, CORDOVA	159
MOSQUE AT CORDOVA	167
THE GATE OF JUSTICE, ALHAMBRA	205
VIEW OF THE ALHAMBRA	221
FOUNTAIN OF THE LIONS	228
PUERTA DI SANTA MARIA, BURGOS	253
STREET IN VALENCIA	255

xviii   THE STORY OF SPAIN.

	PAGE
TORRE DEL ORO, SEVILLE	261
GALLERY OF PEDRO I., SEVILLE	263
DIE GIRALDA	267
DOOR IN THE ALCAZAR	272
AVIGORNAGNA, BILBAO	275
SARAGOSSA	289
CHATEAU DE BELLEGARDE	293
PORTRAIT OF ISABELLA	299
CHURCH OF SAN JUAN DE LOS REYES	303
PORTRAIT OF COLUMBUS	309
DEPARTURE OF COLUMBUS	311
COLUMBUS ON THE DECK OF HIS SHIP	313
HALL OF THE TWO SISTERS, ALHAMBRA	317
TOMB OF FERDINAND AND ISABELLA	319
CHARLES THE FIFTH IN HIS THIRTY-FIRST YEAR	323
BATTLE OF PAVIA	333
VALLADOLID	343
BULL AND MATADOR, MADRID	351
MALAGA	359
CLOISTERS, TOLEDO	363
SAN SEBASTIAN	367
THE PASS OF PANCORBO	369
LEANING TOWER, SARAGOSSA	373
PALACIO REALE, MADRID	383
MADRID, GENERAL VIEW	387

CASTLES IN SPAIN.

H. W. Longfellow.

How much of my young heart, O Spain
    Went out to thee in days of yore !
What dreams romantic filled my brain
And summoned back to life again
The Paladins of Charlemagne,
    The Cid Campeador ?

And shapes more shadowy than these,
    In the dim twilight half revealed,
Phœnician galleys on the seas,
The Roman camps like hives of bees,
The Goth uplifting from his knees
    Pelayo on his shield.

    *   *   *   *   *

Yet something sombre and severe
    O'er the enchanted landscape reigned ;
A terror in the atmosphere
As if King Philip listened near,
Or Torquemada the austere,
    His ghostly sway maintained.

The softer Andalusian skies
    Dispelled the sadness and the gloom ;
There Cadiz by the seaside lies,
And Seville's orange orchards rise,
Making the land a paradise
    Of beauty and of bloom.

There Cordova is hidden among
    The palm, the olive, and the vine ;
Gem of the South, by poets sung,
And in whose mosque Almansor hung
As lamps the bells that once had rung
    At Campostella's shrine.

But over all the rest supreme,
    The star of stars, the cynosure,
The artist's and the poet's theme,
The young man's vision, the old man's dream,—
Granada by its winding stream,
    The city of the Moor.

And there the Alhambra still recalls
    Aladdin's palace of delight :
Allah il Allah through its halls
Whispers the fountain as it falls.
The Darro darts beneath its walls,
    The hills with snow are white.

    *   *   *   *   *

The Vega cleft by the Xenil,
    The fascination and allure
Of the sweet landscape chains the will,
The traveller lingers on the hill,
His parted lips are breathing still
    The last sigh of the Moor.

How like a ruin overgrown
    With flowers that hide the rents of time,
Stands now the Past that I have known,
Castles of Spain not built of stone,
But of white summer clouds and blown
    Into this little mist of rhyme.

PART I.

THE STORY OF SPAIN.

CHAPTER I.

EARLY TRADITIONS.

A CASTILIAN geographer, proud of his country, made a map of Europe representing a woman, with Spain for her head, the Pyrenees for her necklace, the Alps for her girdle. One arm was stretched out for Italy, while her feet ran off into Russia and Turkey.

The necklace of the queen forms a line of separation between her head and her body, sometimes a convenience, sometimes an obstacle to her welfare. The Pyrenees are mountains of secondary importance, compared with the Alps, but they make a strong barrier between the Spanish peninsula and the rest of Europe. On the northern or French side the descent from the summits is gradual, while on the Spanish side the valleys seem hollowed out like enormous chasms, with deep precipices and perpendicular cliffs thousands of feet high. The northern slope, exposed to the Atlantic, partakes of the European climate; the southern, influenced by Mediterranean breezes, is more like Africa than Europe.

On this peninsula, shut off from the rest of Europe by such a sharp mountain chain, long, long ago, before books were written, before people troubled themselves to make histories, there lived men called Iberians. No one can tell how they came to be living in this sunny southern corner of the continent. Probably they came across from Africa, and perhaps, when they did so, there was dry land for them to cross upon, where the narrow Straits of Gibraltar now lead the waters of the Atlantic Ocean to join those of the Mediterranean Sea. Geologists think there may once have been an isthmus at the narrowest point, at Tarifa, where the distance from one continent to the other is now but twelve miles, over which it would be easy to cross. There is a tradition of a canal being cut, with a bridge built over it by the Phœnicians. The waters of the Atlantic rushed in and widened more and more the opening, making Europe and Africa separate continents.

Thirty-seven monkeys still hold their place in the woods and among the crags of the headlands of Gibraltar. In the days of peace there is no duty more carefully impressed on the garrison than the watch over these survivors of another civilization, and in the daily report of the sentries they include the number of monkeys who have appeared. Many of the soldiers, who have watched these gentry from another country and time, will tell the traveller that there is now a subterranean passage from Europe to Africa, and that the monkeys still know the way.

This is certain, that in the early days of history

Iberians were there, and are supposed to have come from the south. Other people came from the north, around the spurs of the Pyrenees, or over them through the easier passes. These were a part of the Celtic race, who at an unknown epoch had migrated toward the west from the plains of Central Asia. These Celts are supposed to have left Asia, and in immense armies to have poured over Europe. Some of them stopped in the valley of the Danube, some of them pushed as far as Great Britain, others came into the Spanish peninsula, where they found the Iberians.

It is hard to know exactly what these people were like, and to keep any distinct idea in our minds of the difference between Celts and Iberians, or to trace the mingling of the two races into another called Celtiberians, as the historians of this early time do. We must imagine a warlike set of people, for they had to protect themselves from each other and from wild beasts. They thought every obstacle was to be overcome by fighting, so they threatened the sky with shooting arrows at it when it thundered, and drew their swords against the rising tide. They were generally friendly with each other, and often united to avenge an injustice done to one of their neighbors.

The Celts who came over the Pyrenees into Spain were tall, with white skins and light hair. Some of them shaved their beards, leaving a long mustache growing down over the lip, and wore their hair in long braids. Their voices were rough and rude, but they had among them bards who sang to them songs of praise or blame, accompanying themselves on a sort of lyre. Their arms were simple, consisting of two lances about three feet long. A short sword, a pole hooked at the end to seize the reins of horses, and a sling, were some of the weapons of foot-soldiers. The horsemen had swords, or sharp weapons which answered the purpose, and lances six feet long. They had great skill in managing horses, of which they had in early times discovered the value. Their food was frugal, a few dried acorns or chestnuts, with mead or cider, satisfied the wants of several tribes; and they were temperate and sober in their habits of eating and drinking, even in those barbarous times. They had no tables, the guests at a feast sat on benches set against the wall. At these feasts there was music and dancing, but the women were not allowed to be present.

Their dress was simple. Soldiers wore garments of linen or leather belted around the waist, with caps on their heads; in time of peace they had black woollen cloaks which fell down to their feet.

These rough people were kind to their women, but allowed them a full amount of labor, for they left the cultivation of the fields entirely to them, as their reasonable share of the burden of living, while the men were away hunting, killing wild beasts, or keeping off enemies. The women guided the oxen, held the plough, and ground the corn, besides looking after all domestic concerns.

These early tribes had a coast-trade with the countries near them, consisting in the exchange of their produce with that of the neighboring islands of

MOUNTAIN GORGE IN THE ASTURIAS.

the Mediterranean, especially for wine. They knew the properties of iron, and the swords and spears which they made of steel formed from it, were in demand wherever they were known.

Bull-fights appear to have been a favorite amusement from the earliest time in the Spanish peninsula. It is evident that this custom existed before the Romans entered Spain, for it is represented upon ancient medals of a period earlier than their arrival.

These early tribes had different names, and their characters were affected by the situations they lived in. At the present time the descendants of these early races living in the north of Spain have strongly marked traits of character which may be traced even to these remote ancestors. There are at present but few railroads or means of communication with the modern world, so that these people do not learn new fashions, and they keep up the old traditions of their fathers from year to year, even from century to century, and talk an old language not modified by words from other languages, as has happened to the Spanish now spoken in other parts of Spain.

The ASTURIANS lived in the mountain-gorges of the northwest, a region now romantic and picturesque, as it must have been in early days. It is full of steep ravines, through which foaming torrents come tumbling down on rocks from great heights. The hills are covered with great trees, oaks and beeches, for the most part. The streams come down leaping over precipices and running off into fertile valleys where fruit-trees grow, also chestnut and ash-trees.

The people are a hardy, honest, good-hearted

race, steady and industrious. They wear the same picturesque costume their great-grandfathers did, and speak the dialect which prevailed in Spain six hundred years ago.

They believe in ghosts and fairies, and fill up their simple lives, in which not many things happen during a whole year of extreme interest, with fancies and fears springing from their superstitutions.

The old women, as they sit spinning in the sun, tell long stories, over and over again, just the same as they heard them when they were little children, about the doings of the *xanas*, who are tiny fairies that come out of fountains and springs in the middle of the night, to dry their long damp hair in the moonbeams, and about the *huestes*, mischief-making imps who lurk about in the woods and marshes, only coming out when something sad or dreadful is going to happen, to foretell the misfortune.

Next the Asturians, on the east, came the Cantabrians, in a territory abounding in the precious metals, above all in iron; and beside them dwelt the Vascones or Basques. These are thought to have been Iberians, strayed up from the south, and not Celts who came from the north into Spain. This belief is founded on the peculiarity of their language, which is entirely different from Spanish, or from any other known tongue. It is impossible to understand without learning it systematically, and it is hard to learn. Only those who were born and who have grown up among the Basques can really master it.

' There are many traditions about this strange old

language, preserved unchanged since the beginning of knowledge. One legend calls it the language of the angels, with which Adam and Eve used to talk to each other. Another says that Tubal brought it into Spain, where he came, long before the confusion of tongues at the tower of Babel, so that it was not there mixed up with other languages. It is said that the devil tried to learn it, and studied it for seven years, but as he then only knew three words, he gave it up. The Andalusians say that in Basque "you spell Solomon and pronounce it Nebuchadnezzar."

It is also prevalent in Navarre, and it is still spoken by 600,000 Spaniards and French. Its native name is Esquera. It cannot be classed with any Indo-European or Semitic tongue, and appears to be of earlier origin, presenting some grammatical analogies with Mongol, North American, and certain East African languages. The forms of ordinary grammar are therefore imperfectly applicable to it. The substantive has no distinction of gender; it is made to express, by means of an extensive system of affixes, all the ordinary relations of declension and conjugations, and many which, in other languages, can only be expressed by periphrases. The termination of a word may thus express together, mood, tense, person, number, and case of the object, and also the sex, rank, and number of the individuals addressed, besides other relations. Foreign words are easily assimilated, but with such modifications as suit the Basque ear, and these vary according to local dialect. Diminutives, and other general affixes, increase the delicacy of expression, and a wide range of speech is early acquired by the natives. Compound words are readily formed by mere juxtaposition, or by elision of syllables, not peculiar modifications, for euphony. The article has two forms—*a* for the singular, *ala* for the plural—affixed to the substantive. There appears to be no genuine Basque word beginning with *r*. In the usual structure of the sentences the noun, with the article affixed, occupies the first place; it is followed by the adjective, then the adverb, next the verb, and lastly the object, with its prepositional affix. No written Basque is known of earlier date than the fifteenth century; and little genuine literature exists; the orthography is therefore arbitrary, and the earliest writings are difficult to interpret.

The Basques are very proud of their ancient language and their long descent.

The GALICIANS possessed the sea-coast in the northwest corner of the peninsula. They were like their neighbors, bold and warlike, and were prosperous on account of the abundance of fish on their coasts, which attracted merchants from other nations.

The LUSITANIANS occupied what is now Portugal, but their territory extended farther into Spain than that country does now. They had the reputation of being the most learned tribe on the peninsula. -The Romans reported in their time that for six thousand years this race had possessed poems, and laws, and grammatical rules for their language, but there is nothing now left to show that they differed from the other races in the neighborhood. -

In Cantabria and Lusitania the religion of the Druids prevailed, for in these regions are found the monuments of their strange ceremonies; there are great blocks of stone standing alone, or set in circles, sometimes marked with coarse carvings or figures in relief. Such traces of the past are more frequent in other countries where the Celts lived, but there are enough in Spain to prove that this religion was practised there. It was a worship of the forces of nature, for though the Druids believed in one Supreme God, they adored also the stars, the ocean, thunder, and wind.

Oak-forests were their sanctuaries. *Druid* means "men of oak," and in these forests they celebrated their rites. Every year, on the sixth day of the moon of Marel, the priests, dressed in a long white tunic, with their feet bare, and their heads crowned with ivy, marched with great ceremony into the forest, where they cut off mistletoe from the trees with a golden sickle.

Mistletoe is an evergreen bush with white berries which attaches itself to the trunks and branches of trees, and grows by thrusting its roots into them. The Druids considered it sacred when they found it growing upon the oak.

This part of their worship seems to us simple and graceful, but they believed in human sacrifice, and the stones which remain standing are known to be altars on which victims were killed to gratify their gods.

It is well to know something about these early Northern tribes, because as we go on with the story we shall see their descendants, the men who led the same sort of lives they did, and grew up under similar influences, under a cool mountain climate, shut off from the rest of the world, exhibiting the same brave characteristics, with temperate habits, great

MONUMENT OF THE DRUIDS.

love of country, and a superstitious faith in whatever form of religion they were led to accept by their priests.

Of the early races in the southern part of Spain it

is not easy to judge, for the population there has changed from century to century, by the invasions of other races. If the Iberians came along the shore of Africa to enter Spain by Gibraltar they were probably dark men, of Eastern characteristics, very different from the blond, hardy Celts. As they were spread over the central part of the peninsula, and mingled with the Celts who came down from the north, the two races came to live together, and to share each others habits and manners, so that in time they were a combination of both, called Celtiberians by the Romans who found them there.

The northeastern part of Spain is occupied by the Catalonians, a race with its own characteristics, as strongly marked as the races of Basques or Asturians. This part of the country seems to have been settled by the Phœnicians, a roving people who were dwelling on the sea-coast of Syria at the earliest dawn of history. Their reputation was that, having settled themselves in any country, they immediately undertook distant voyages, and carrying cargoes of goods, visited other places. They are the people called Canaanites in the Bible. They were pirates as well as merchants, for they did not hesitate to kidnap the crews of the ships they met, and to carry them off as their slaves. But although they made the nations suffer whom they visited, they also left behind them an improved civilization, and the trade they established in the ports they touched at was a benefit to these as well as to themselves.

They sailed through the Red Sea and the Persian Gulf, and thus communicated with India and the eastern coast of Africa. They searched every inlet of the Mediterranean Sea, and, passing through the Straits of Gibraltar, visited the British Isles, where they found tin.

All the sea-coast towns of Spain benefited by their commerce, and sometimes they left colonies behind them. The Catalonians are supposed to have sprung from some of these, but by the time when written history begins there is a mixture of other races in their blood. They have received additions from other nations, and their province is near enough to Gaul to have been subject to invasions from there, as well as to Gallic influence.

The Phœnicians, who were always on the look-out for trade, found Spain to be a country which promised great advantage to their commerce. Cadiz was their most powerful settlement. It is just outside the Straits of Gibraltar, and when the first enterprising Phœnician sailors reached it, they thought they had come to the very end of the world. They supplied the natives with things they had brought from the far East, and took in exchange gold, silver, and iron. 'A tradition says that they took away more silver than their ships could well carry, and that their anchors and all their common implements were made of it.' It is said that the Celts and Iberians did not know how to use their gold and silver until the newcomers taught them, but they had made themselves weapons of steel out of iron.

The Phœnicians spread all over the country, looking for mines, which they prevailed upon the natives to open and work for their benefit. Almost everywhere in Spain coins and medals bearing the mark of Phœnician workmanship have been found, and ruins of their buildings.

We can imagine that after people had learned how to make boats and to go sailing about over the sea on voyages of discovery, the news spread from country to country about what was to be found in each. The rumor that Spain was full of mines of gold and silver came back to the nations farther east, and excited the desire of adventurers there, just as when later, in Spain itself, Columbus dreamed of more gold and silver far in the West, and sailed in search of it. Such a rich field of wealth was not left to the hands of the Phœnicians; other explorers came and took what they wanted. Their successful example led the Greeks to try their luck. About eight or nine hundred years before Christ, the Rhodians arrived on the coast of Catalonia, and founded a town which they called Rhodia; and other expeditions set out from different parts in Greece, and gave names to places which may still sometimes be recognised. It does not appear that these early colonists cared to take any control of the country; probably they never thought of such a thing, but each for himself sought to get what he could and what he cared for from the inhabitants, who, for their part, welcomed the new-comers, who brought objects of luxury, new ideas and customs, into their simple lives. These Greeks, Phœnicians, and others mingled with the population, founded their own towns, and established their own industries, all for the mutual good of themselves and the original inhabitants.

One thing the Phœnicians gave to the colonies they founded,—an alphabet, for it was to this people that Western Europe—including all the races from which English-speaking people spring—owes the alphabet which we now employ. So soon as an alphabet and written language comes into use, history changes its form. Till then every thing is handed down by tradition—that is, by what is told from the old to the young for generation after generation. Now, in tradition, there is but a very indistinct notion of time. What happened to " your grandfather " is soon mixed with what happened to "your grandfather's grandfather." In the case of Spain, up to the time when the Phœnicians had settled their colonies in Spain, every thing we know about the country is vague and doubtful, but after that, the story of the land is found in the narratives that were written about what was going on in the world, and thus preserved.

The period we have been describing in this chapter lasts from the very earliest traditions of the country, down to a time about four hundred years before Christ. Some of the Iberians may have reached the north of Spain where they settled themselves, and the old Basque language may be the nearest dialect now spoken to the ancient tongue of the Iberians. Celts came from the countries north of Spain and settled in the peninsula, keeping themselves apart in some cases, sometimes wandering towards the south and mixing with the Iberians. The Phœnicians came later from the eastern shores of the Mediterranean, formed colonies, roused traffic, and introduced many features of an advanced civilization, while they were developing the resources of the country.

The fame of its mines spread abroad, and excited the desire of other nations, who came not only to share its wealth, but to conquer.

CHAPTER II.

CARTHAGINIANS.

BUT the first acquaintance which Spain made with the rest of the world, after the westward-flowing wave of Celts poured in on her, was made in her trade with Phœnicia and Carthage.

And to-day, as we of other lands read of Spain, our first glimpse of her is in the Bible language, where we read of the ships of Tarshish. Tarshish was but a vague name to the Hebrew writers, as India has been to many an English writer. But as an "Indiaman" stands in English literature for a ship of great burden which comes from a rich land far away,—and this because India is India,—so the ships of Tarshish of the Bible writers, were the Phœnician ships which dealt with Tartessus. 'Tartessus was the district west of our Gibraltar, in the south of Spain.' The traveller of to-day finds heavy English steamers there, taking in copper ore at the mouth of the River Tinto, and, if he be an American traveller, he remembers that from that same river, in other "ships of Tarshish," Columbus sailed for the discovery of lands rich with gold.

The Phœnician trade with Spain naturally gave the Carthaginians a foothold there, for Carthage was simply a Phœnician colony, which in time far outgrew the strength and empire of the northern cities of Phœnicia. Isaiah, in predicting the fall of Tyre, comes back with a steady refrain to the people of Tarshish as finding no city, no port, no welcome when they came back to Syria. In his day—that is to say, in the eighth century B.C.—the trade with Tartessus was so important for Tyre, that he brings it in in the very front of his description. Meanwhile Carthage was steadily gaining in power, and Carthaginian merchants and miners were extending the foothold which Syrian tradesmen had begun.

In what we call the first Punic war between Rome and Carthage, and in the events which led to it, Carthage had lost her hold on the great islands of Sardinia and Sicily. We owe to Niebuhr the observation, that her statesmen or her statesman resolved to repair that loss by creating a province in Spain.

"When, after the American war, it was thought in England that the ignominious peace of Paris had put an end to the greatness of England, Pitt undertook, with double courage, the restoration of his country, and displayed his extraordinary powers. It was in the same spirit that Hamilcar acted: he turned his eyes to Spain; he formed the plan of making Spain a province which should compensate for the loss of Sicily and Sardinia.

"The weakness of Carthage consisted in her having no armies; and it was a grand conception of Hamilcar's to transform Spain into a Carthaginian country, from which national armies could be obtained. His object, therefore, was, on the one hand, to subdue the Spaniards, and on the other, to win their sympathy, and to change them into a Punic nation, under the dominion of Carthage.

"The whole of the southern coast of Spain had resources of no ordinary kind; it furnished all the productions of Sicily and Sardinia, and in addition to these it had very rich silver mines, the working of which has been revived in our own days. Hamilcar was the first who introduced there a regular and systematic mode of mining, and this led him or his son-in-law, to build the town of New Carthage. While the Carthaginians thus gained the sympathy of the nation, they acquired a population of millions, which relieved them from the necessity of hiring faithless mercenaries, as they had been obliged to do in the first Punic war. They were enabled to raise armies in Spain just as if it had been in their own country."

To that province, the boy Hannibal was taken by his father, immediately after the oath by which he swore that he would always be the enemy of the Romans. This pretty story, which is cited so often, is perfectly authenticated. When Hannibal was an exile at the close of his life he told it to King Antiochus.

He said:

"When I was a little boy not more than nine years old, my father offered sacrifices to Jupiter the Best and Greatest, on his departure from Carthage as general in Spain. While he was conducting the sacrifice, he asked me if I would like to go to the camp with him. I said I would gladly, and began to beg him not to hesitate to take me. He replied: 'I will do it if you will make the promise I demand.' He took me at once to the altar, at which he had offered his sacrifice. He bade me take hold of it, having sent the others away, and bade me swear that I would never be in friendship with the Romans."

The Carthaginian faction, which opposed the family of Hamilcar, his father, opposed him also. "I think that this youth should be kept at home," said Hanno, stoutly, "and taught under the restraint of laws and magistrates, to live on an equal footing with the rest of the citizens, lest at some time or other this small fire should kindle a vast conflagration." But they could not keep him at home. He was sent into Spain, and was very soon a favorite with the army, as well he might be. No toil dismayed him. He slept and he waked when the duties of the camp required, and was satisfied with a bed on the ground. He never spared himself in any danger, and cavalry and infantry knew him as their leader before he was of the age of manhood.

So soon as he had an army under him he moved really against Rome. "From the day on which he was declared general, as if Italy had been decreed to him as a province, and war with Rome committed to him," he resolved to make war against Saguntum.

Whoever goes to find Saguntum now, finds only a town called Mur Viedro. "Mur Viedro" is what is left of the Latin words "Muri Veteres"—"Old Walls,"—and these old walls are all that is left of Saguntum. But Saguntum, in the days of Hannibal, was a strong and rich Greek city. It had been settled from Zacynthus, which is now Zante, and

ROMAN AMPHITHEATRE AT MURVIEDRO.

sends you the currants for your mince pies, and was well known to Ulysses. From Zacynthus, they say, came its name. Hannibal meant to march against Rome, and finding in his way this strong city— which had quite forgotten Greece, I think, and hoped for Roman support, because in a sense it was an ally of Rome,—he attacked Saguntum.

He made the regular approaches of those times. Protecting his troops by "vineæ," for which the ground was not unfavorable, he advanced a battering-ram' towards the wall. His army is said to have numbered one hundred and fifty thousand men. The Saguntines were heartily united. They made frequent sallies with courage, and severe engagements took place, in one of which, to the dismay of his men, Hannibal himself was wounded in the thigh. Till he recovered, the siege was little more than a blockade. But, so soon as he recovered, he pressed it eagerly. Three successive towers and the walls between were overthrown by the besiegers. But, in a pitched battle over the breach, the brave Saguntines drove the Carthaginians back to their camp. And, at this juncture, it was announced that ambassadors had arrived at the sea-shore from Rome, whence the citizens were hoping for assistance.

That assistance, alas for them, was only diplomatic! Rome was not yet aroused to a sense of the importance to her of this Spanish quarrel. The ambassadors had no army behind them. Hannibal sent word to them that he had no time to listen to embassies, and that they could not come to him through so many armed bodies of savage tribes.

They turned aside, therefore, to Carthage, and the Saguntines were left to their fate.

This fate came on with terrible certainty. In the short respite the Saguntines had repaired their wall. But Hannibal inflamed his army by the promise of the spoil of the city, and led to a new attack. He brought up a tower higher than any of the walls, and, by the catapults and balistæ upon it, cleared the walls from their defenders. With five hundred Africans at work with pickaxes, he undermined the wall itself on that side, so that it fell with a terrible crash, and the city was open again by a breach which gave space for fighting, as in the field.

Then for the first time was some offer of surrender made by the Saguntines. Alcon, one of their number, went to Hannibal's camp to offer him terms. But Hannibal's answer was so severe that Alcon did not venture to carry it back. On Hannibal's part, Alorcus carried the same terms to the Saguntine senate.

Here is the result as it is described by Livy, the Roman historian:

"He takes away from you your city," said Alorcus, "which, already for the greater part in ruins, he has almost wholly in his possession; he leaves you your territory, intending to mark out a place in which you may build a new town; he commands that all the gold and silver, both public and private, shall be brought to him; he preserves inviolate your persons and those of your wives and children, provided you are willing to depart from Saguntum, unarmed, each with two garments. These terms a victorious enemy dictates. These, though harsh and grievous, your condition commends to you. Indeed, I do not despair, when the power of every thing is given to him, that he will remit something from these terms. But even these, I think, you ought rather to endure, than suffer, by the rights of war, yourselves to be slaughtered, your wives and children to be ravished and dragged into captivity before your faces."

When an assembly of the people, by the gradual crowding round of the multitude, had mingled with the senate, to hear these proposals, the chief men suddenly withdrawing before an answer was returned, and throwing all the gold and silver collected, both from public and private stores, into a fire hastily kindled for that purpose, the greater part flung themselves into it. When the dismay and agitation produced by this deed had pervaded the whole city, another noise was heard in addition from the citadel. A tower, long battered, had fallen down; and when a Carthaginian cohort, rushing through the breach, had made a signal to the general that the city was destitute of the usual outposts and guards, Hannibal, thinking that there ought to be no delay at such an opportunity, having attacked the city with his whole forces, took it in a moment, command being given that all the adults should be put to death; which command, though cruel, was proved in the issue to have been almost necessary. For to whom of those men could mercy have been shown, who, either shut up with their wives and children, burned their houses over their own heads, or abroad in arms made no end in fighting except in death?

"The town was taken with immense spoil. Though the greater part of the goods had been purposely damaged by their owners, and resentment had made scarce any distinction of age in the massacre, and the captives were the booty of the soldiers; still it appears that some money was raised from the price of the effects that were sold, and that much costly furniture and garments were sent to Carthage."

And so Hannibal gave to Rome that affront, which was never atoned for, till he died, a fugitive,—by suicide. For nearly forty years he was the terror of Rome.

Thus is it that, as we read the story of Spain, it has mixed in with the stream this little eddy of Phœnician or Carthaginian life. What eddy, indeed, does not flow in that stream somewhere? When one reads in his Bible of Hiram, King of Tyre, or of that handsome Isabella—who has given to all jezebels of modern days her name of Jezebel,—when one reads in his Virgil of her cousin—or was it her grand-niece—the Elissa or Dido, "who wept in silence" because Æneas would not come,—one must remember that people with their names, and of their blood, came and lived, and married, and bore children, and died, in our beautiful Spain. There is their blood to-day,—all mixed in with the blood of Basques, and Celtiberians, and Galicians, and Goths, and Romans, and Moors. A bit of their language is in "Barcelona,"—which word preserves the memory of the Barca family of Carthage, to which Hamilcar and Hannibal belonged. Barca is of same root as the name of Barak—who sent Balaam on his errand,—and it means "lightning." In "Carthagena,"—both in the Old World and the New,—we have the memorial of "Carthage." And "Carthage" means "the city." Where you read, in the Book of Job, "I went out to the gate through the city,"—you read what Job wrote when he said "through *Kereth.*" And in the Book of Joshua you find that *Kartah*, in Zebulun, was one of the cities of the Levites. Kartah was the ancient godmother of Carthage, of Crita, and of the Carthagenas. Kartah-tuba, "an important city"—became the Corduba of the Romans,—and is the Cordova of to-day. From Cordovan leather, the best in the world, the workmen in leather were called cordwainers till within the memory of this generation.*

Hannibal's sway in Spain has made less mark than one might have supposed in Spanish literature. But occasionally it has furnished a subject for a picture or a poem. There is an old Spanish poem, by Lorenzo de Zamora,—called "La Saguntina,"—which, with such fact as the author has, and a sufficient addition of imagination, describes the siege of Saguntum. There is large intermixture of tournaments of the chivalric period, and of other customs which belong to the period of the Romancers. When Zamora wrote there was an enthusiasm in Spain for narrative poems. He died in 1614.

Here are two stanzas from the long poem, which will illustrate its simplicity:

* Not because they waxed their thread.

" The city chooses of its best
    Thrice five with every year ;
No one is chief above the rest
    But each with each is peer.
And five shall watch in strength and truth,
    To keep the bad in awe ;
And five shall teach the maids and youth,
    And five shall make the law.

    *   *   *   *   *   *

" Lord Hannibal upon the town
    His hirelings brings from far ;
The men of Ocaña come down,
    To serve him in the war.
With all that Andalusia yields
    Her trooping soldiers come ;
From rich Granada's fertile fields,
    From Cadiz washed with foam ;
With guards and spears, and helms and shields
    They march to fight with Rome."

CHAPTER III.

THE SCIPIOS.

Two things followed naturally from the movement of Hannibal, by way of Spain, against Rome. The first was that the attention of the Roman senate and people was attracted to a region which had, till now, only interested miners and merchants. The indifference with which the Roman senate heard the first appeal made to them by the people of Saguntum, shows that Spain was then quite outside of their world. It was not until the annihilation of Saguntum proved to be the beginning of Hannibal's march of triumph, that the government of Rome began to see the importance of Spain, and to send armies to a region which had before attracted men of commerce only.

From the armed occupation of garrisons, from the necessary invasion of provinces which must be either friends or enemies, sprang the permanent Roman occupation of Spain. Steadily, and now without any long interruption for centuries, the conquests go forward which make of Spain a Roman province. To this occupation Spain owes the basis of her language of to-day, which, as we shall see, is a language of Roman roots, handled in a Gothic or Northern gram-

ROMAN BRIDGE AT SALAMANCA.

mar. And it is to this Roman occupation that the antiquarian owes it, that he may now see in Spain traces of Roman customs, for which, sometimes, he searches unsuccessfully in Italy itself.

The first commanding figure who comes into the story of Spain in the Roman occupation is that of Scipio, the first Scipio who received the title, then honorable, of "the African,"—Scipio Africanus. Young men came to the front in trying times like those of Hannibal and his enemies. The Romans believed that the young Scipio saved his father's life at the battle of Ticinus, where Hannibal defeated him with terrible slaughter. From that time he was engaged against Hannibal, in one field or another, until he finally defeated him at Zama, sixteen years after. Of this interval much of the time was spent in Spain.

Scipio's father had been killed in battle there, and his uncle also. The family was mourning the loss of these men and of others killed in the war, when an assembly of the Roman people was called to name a general for the command in Spain. It was not the simplest thing in the world, seeing that all men knew that in a period of thirty days two generals had been killed there, and the Roman arms thoroughly defeated. No one at first volunteered for the command, though it was the custom of enterprising generals to offer themselves to the people. Then Publius Scipio appeared. He was only twenty-four years old. He took his stand in the Roman forum, where every one could see him. He asked that he might be sent to the country where his father had fallen, to take the command of the army which had been beaten. He was appointed by acclamation. Every "century" voted for him, and every man in every century. He took the command, where, as Livy says, he must carry on his work "between the tombs of his father and his uncle."

He arrived in Spain in the summer of the year 210 B.C. The whole country south of the Ebro was in possession of the Carthaginians. But the three Carthaginian generals were engaged on roving expeditions up and down in the interior, and were not on any good terms with each other.

Scipio used his time to great advantage, as it afterward proved, in conciliating the important Spaniards. They were already beginning to find that the Carthaginians were hard masters, and the courtesy and the justice of Scipio did much to detach them from their alliances. Scipio rejected all the advice which he received to attack either of the Carthaginian generals, and instead of this, marched directly upon New Carthage, which was the capital and the head-quarters of the whole Carthaginian movement. He encouraged the old soldiers, who had met so many reverses in Spain, by telling them of the Roman successes elsewhere, and by that convenient rule of life which all optimists are apt to bring forward, which he stated thus: "It has happened to us by a kind of fatality, that in all important wars we have been victorious after having been defeated." He closed his speech by saying: "Come, then, veterans, lead your new commander and your new army across the Iberus; lead us into a country with many a deed of valor." He sent his fleet around to blockade New Carthage, and moved on the city himself with such precision that the fleet arrived for a blockade and the army for a siege on the same day.

Mago, the Carthaginian general, who was in command at New Carthage, was taken by surprise. He had but a small garrison, which proved to be insufficient. Scipio did not wait for a formal siege. He attacked the city at once, attempting to scale the walls. While the enemy were engaged on this side, he pushed an attack in person on the north, and led a body of men across the lake which Mago had relied upon for protection.

"It was about mid-day, and, besides that the water was being drawn off naturally, in consequence of the tide receding, a brisk north wind rising impelled the water in the lake, which was already in motion, in the same direction as the tide, and rendered it so shallow that in some parts the water reached only to the navel, while in others it scarcely rose above the knees. Scipio, referring this discovery, which he made by his own diligence and penetration, to the gods and to miracle, which had turned the course of the sea, withdrawn it from the lake, and opened ways never before trodden by human feet to afford a passage to the Romans, ordered them to follow Neptune as their guide, and, passing through the middle of the lake, make good their way to the walls." The success of this attack quickened the assault on the walls, and the defenders, finding their lines broken in two quarters, retired into the citadel. The Roman army entered the city and put to the sword every man they found, till, as Livy says, "on a signal given they put a stop to the carnage and turned their attention to plunder."

The recapitulation of the wealth of New Carthage gives some idea of the civilization to which Spain had then attained. Two hundred and seventy-six golden bowls, almost all of which weighed a pound, were brought to Scipio; an immense number of silver vessels, and eighteen thousand pounds' weight of coined and wrought silver. One hundred and thirteen merchant ships were captured in the harbor and five ships of war. But the most valuable part of the capture, for the purposes of the victor, was to be found in his prisoners. For he took all the hostages whom the Spanish tribes had given in pledge of their fidelity to Carthage; he took two thousand artisans whom he made the slaves of the Roman people, but he held out to them a hope of emancipation if they would serve in the war loyally and strenuously. He filled up the rowers of his fleet with young men and able-bodied slaves. The proper citizens of New Carthage had their property restored to them and were recognized as freemen. It was by such a policy that he conciliated the leaders of Spain, and steadily detached them from the Carthaginian alliance. The total number of prisoners which he took by this bold push on the city was ten thousand.

The custom of giving hostages who were the relatives or dear friends of the persons bound by a treaty, was one of the wretched peculiarities of ancient warfare, from which states and statesmen are now happily set free. Here in New Carthage, Scipio found a large number of such people, all of high rank of course, who were held in captivity, however honorable that captivity might be, and whose lives would have certainly been forfeited had the Spanish allies of the Carthaginians proved false to their engagements. Some writers state the number of these hostages who fell into Scipio's hands as high as seven hundred and twenty-five. So soon as he released them, the Carthaginians lost their native allies, if they had been holding them by fear. Scipio meanwhile was doing his best to conciliate them by the courtesy and moderation of his bearing; and, in truth, he gained such an ascendancy over the Spaniards by his unselfish manliness, his courage and justice, that, on one occasion, a large body of them offered him the crown and would gladly have made him king. But with true republican dignity, Scipio refused the honor. He said to a multitude who had saluted him as king: "I think that the most honorable title is that of General. This my soldiers have given me. Other nations revere the name of King. But no Roman can endure that name. If you think a royal spirit is the noblest spirit of man, I shall be glad if you think that such a spirit is mine. But you must never call me King." The Romans called these Spaniards barbarians. But even such barbarians could feel the grandeur of such words. They brought to Scipio the best presents they could give, and did what he valued more: they entered into loyal alliances with the Romans, which they never broke, and which resulted in the expulsion of the Carthaginians from Spain. In the year B.C. 206, Gades, now Cadiz, which was their last stronghold, surrendered to the Romans, and Romans and Spaniards held the whole peninsula free from any Carthaginian army or garrison.

It ought to be said that, so far as we know, Scipio deserved this success. He is one of the noblest examples, not only of that class of the sterner virtues, which we should perhaps call Roman virtues, but of that unselfish manliness to which all virtue owes its name, and from which indeed it springs. A writer as narrow as Livy intimates that Scipio had a peculiar address in displaying his virtues, and that he did this or that for effect. But it is not fair to say that when a leader like Scipio went every day into the Capitoline temple, and spent a short period in silent meditation, he only did this to be "seen of men." This is certain, that somehow or other Publius Scipio gained that absolute self-control, which, as we have seen, won for him the admiration and even the veneration of barbarous tribes. The same self-control and the steady loyalty of the man won for him the life-long love as well as the admiration of troops of friends. It is not fair to call all this the result of that vulgar contrivance, in which a candidate for applause tries to purchase it.

One single incident of Scipio's Spanish career, in which he restored a captive lady to her lover, has often been the theme of poetry and given the subject to art.

Carthaginians and Romans had not established

their dominion over more than half of the peninsula. They seemed to have entirely subdued Catalonia, Valencia, Murcia, and Andalusia—that is, the region east and south of the mountain ranges. The Celtiberian tribes in the centre founded a republic which was in a certain alliance with the Romans, but at this time the Romans scarcely knew, even by name, the independent tribes of the north and the northwest. A few years after Scipio's success, Cato the elder took command in Spain, and there are traces of his occupancy there to-day. Whatever traveller is fortunate enough to visit in the Pyrenees, the picturesque little town of Jaca, will see walls which they say Cato built, and there he established a fortress for the protection of this defile. From that time downward the Romans steadily increased their power in Spain, until for the first four centuries of the Christian era Spain " ceased to have a place in military history," because the conquest or assimilation was so complete. Roman soldiers married Spanish women, and when their terms of service were over, they preferred, as well they might do, to remain in beautiful Spain, rather than to go back to the harder chances of Italian life. Gradually the Latin language took the place of the native dialect, and to a certain extent Latin customs took the place of native customs. Scipio adopted as his son Camilius Scipio, who was the younger son of Æmilius Paulus. It was his fortune also to will the title of "Africanus." He also volunteered to take the province in Spain when he was very young, and afterwards in repeated disasters to the Roman

ROMAN BRIDGE, CUENCA.

arms there, he was sent out to that province. This was in the year 134 B.C., after the third Punic war. It was in this consulship that Numantia fell under that terrible siege which is remembered in history by the side of the sieges of Saguntum and Saragossa, for the signal hardihood and persistency by which the beleaguered people held their own. The following passage from Cervantes' tragedy of "Numantia" recalls the story of those days of terrible suffering and brave endurance.

MORANDO.

Why so swiftly art thou flying?
  Go not, Lira,—let me still
  Taste what may my spirit fill
With glad life, even while I 'm dying.
Lira, let mine eyes awhile
  Gaze upon thy loveliness
  Since so deep is my distress,
Thus it would its pangs beguile.
O sweetest Lyre, that soundest so,
  For ever in my phantasy,
  With such delicious harmony
It turns to glory all my woe!
What now? What stand'st thou mutely thinking?
  Thou of my soul the only treasure.

LIRA.

I 'm thinking how thy dream of pleasure,
And mine so fast away is sinking:
It will not fall beneath the hand
Of him who wastes our native land;
For long, or e'er the war be o'er,
My hapless life will be no more.

MORANDO.

Joy of my soul, what hast thou said?

LIRA.

That I am worn with hunger so,
   That quickly will the o'erpowering woe
For ever break my vital thread.
   What bridal rapture dost thou dream
   From one at such a sad extreme?
   For, trust me, ere an hour be past,
   I fear I shall have breathed my last.
My brother fainted yesterday,
   By wasting hunger overborne;
   And then my mother, all outworn
By hunger, slowly sunk away.
And if my health can struggle yet
   With hunger's cruel power, in truth
   It is because my stronger youth
Its wasting force hath better met.
But now so many a day hath passed,
   Since aught I've had its powers to strengthen
   It can no more the conflict lengthen,
But it must faint and fail at last.

MORANDO.

Lira, dry thy weeping eyes;
   But, ah! let mine, my love, the more
   Their overflowing rivers pour,
Wailing thy wretched agonies.
But though thou still art held in strife
   With hunger thus incessantly,
   Of hunger still thou shalt not die,
So long as I retain my life.
I offer here, from yon high wall
   To leap o'er ditch and battlement:
   Thy death one instant to prevent,
I fear not on mine own to fall:
The bread the Roman eateth now
   I'll snatch away, and bear to thee;
   For oh, 't is worse than death to see,
Lady, thy dreadful state of woe!

LIRA.

Thou speakest like a lover :—still,
   Morando, surely, 't were not good
   That I should find a joy in food
For which thy life-blood thou mayst spill.
But little will that succor be,
   Whate'er of booty thou canst make ;
   While thou a surer way dost take
To lose thyself than win for me.
Enjoy thou still thy youthful prime
   In fresh and blooming years elate ;
   My life is nothing to the state,—
Thine, every thing at such a time.
Its noblest bulwark thou canst be
   Against the fierce and crafty foe :
   What can the feeble prowess do
Of such a wretched maid as me ?

ROMAN REMAINS AT MERIDA.

CHAPTER IV.

SERTORIUS.

THE most picturesque, perhaps, of the separate episodes in the Roman conquest is to be found in the story of Sertorius, which has accordingly been seized upon by one modern author and another for romance or drama. His life is told at length by Plutarch in his gossiping way.

Quintus Sertorius was a soldier of first-rate ability and of good education, and of Sabine birth. He served under Marius, when the German tribes first came down on Italy, and in the civil wars he took the side of Marius against Sylla. After Sylla was master of Rome, Sertorius hastened into Spain, where he had formerly served, and by his popularity with the natives, and by arming the Romans, hoped to maintain himself against any of Sylla's partisans.

Finding his force insufficient, he seized a fleet at New Carthage, our Carthagena, and crossed to Africa. It was in this escape from his enemies that he went through the Straits of Gibraltar, and sailing outward, keeping the Spanish shore on his right hand, landed a little above the mouth of the river Bætis, where it falls into the Atlantic sea, and gives the name to that part of Spain. Here he met with seamen recently arrived from the "Atlantic islands," two in number, divided from one another only by a narrow channel, and distant from the coast of Africa ten thousand furlongs. " These islands," he was told, " are called the Islands of the Blest; rains fall there seldom, and in moderate showers, but for the most part, they have gentle breezes, bringing along with them soft dews, which render the soil not only rich for ploughing and planting, but so abundantly fruitful that it produces spontaneously an abundance of delicate fruits, sufficient to feed the inhabitants, who may here enjoy all things without trouble or labor. The seasons of the year are temperate, and the transitions from one to another so moderate that the air is almost always serene and pleasant. The rough northerly and easterly winds which blow from the coasts of Europe and Africa, dissipated in the vast open space, utterly lose their force before they reach the islands. The soft western and southerly winds which breathe upon them sometimes produce gently sprinkling showers, which they convey along with them from the sea, but more usually bring days of moist, bright weather, cooling and gently fertilizing the soil, so that the firm belief prevails, even among the barbarians, that this is the seat of the blessed, and that these are the Elysian Fields celebrated by Homer.

" When Sertorius heard this account he was seized with a wonderful passion for these islands, and had an extreme desire to go and live there in peace and quietness, and safe from oppression and unending wars. But his inclinations were perceived by the

Sicilian pirates, whom he had under his nominal command. They desired not peace nor quiet, but riches and spoils, and they immediately forsook him, and sailed away into Africa to assist Ascalis, the son of Iphtha, and to help to restore him to his kingdom of Mauritania."

Sertorius was not discouraged, but landed in Mauritania, and took one side in the civil war there. He opened the grave of Antæus, which he found in the city of Tingis, and found the body sixty cubits in. length. He made himself master of all Mauritania. The Lusitanians, inhabiting the western part of the Spanish peninsula, hearing of his success, asked him to become their ruler, and he accepted the trust. It was then that he obtained possession of the famous white hind, the story of which is so closely connected with his name. "A countryman named Spanus, who lived in those parts, meeting by chance a hind that had recently calved flying from the hunters, let the dam go, and pursuing the fawn, took it, wonderfully pleased with the rarity of the color, which was all milk-white. As at that time Sertorius was living in the neighborhood, and accepted gladly any presents of fruit, fowl, or venison that the country afforded, and rewarded liberally those who presented them, the countryman brought him his young hind. Sertorius took it, and was well pleased with it at first sight. When in time he had made it so tame and gentle that it would come when he called, and follow him wheresoever he went, and could endure the noise and tumult of the camp, knowing well that uncivilized people are naturally prone to superstition, by little and little he raised it into something supernatural, saying that it was given him by the goddess Diana, and that it revealed to him many secrets."

This was one of the devices by which he recommended himself to the Lusitanian tribes. Plutarch says that they really regarded him as divine, and followed him, confident in his supernatural powers.

He had landed in Lusitania with only twenty-six hundred men, whom he called Romans, and seven hundred Africans. The Lusitanians added fifty seven hundred more. With a force so insignificant he made war against five Roman generals, who had armies amounting to nearly one hundred and thirty thousand men. In this war for a long time he was superior. He beat Cotta in a sea fight. On land he routed Aufidius, Domitius, Thoranius, and Metellus himself. Manlius came from Gaul to assist Metellus, and Pompey was sent in all haste from Rome with considerable force as an additional relief.

Sertorius held his own against these combined forces. He introduced discipline into the Spanish ranks, and taught the Spaniards that they were quite as good men as the Romans. He was not satisfied with improvements in war. He watched the training of the people in the arts, and was specially careful of their education. From all the tribes he called for the boys of good parents and placed them in a school which he founded at Osca—now Huesca—in the northeast of Spain. There is at this day a university there which preserves his name in the title of the University of Sertorius. Here they had Roman and Greek masters, so that, as he said, they might be fit when the time came to take their share in the government. Plutarch says that they were really hostages while he called them students. However this may be, the fathers were well pleased to see them dressed in the costume of young Roman gentlemen, and were not displeased at the care taken of their sons. It is certain that Sertorius is to be counted as one of the civilizers of Spain. Nor is there any history more interesting, of a great leader whose duty it has been to uplift and encourage ignorant and almost barbarous tribes.

So sagacious were his methods of elevating the fine race of men with which he had to do, that we wish we had more detail. But alas, all the archives of his government, and the accounts, said to have been considerable, of the earlier history of Lusitania, perished in the confusions which accompanied his fall. It is clear that he had the enthusiastic support of his people, and apparently this was due to hearty affection. Plutarch says it was a custom among these tribes that " when a commander was slain in battle those who attended his person fought it out till they all died with him, which the inhabitants of those countries called an *offering* or libation. There were few Spanish commanders, therefore, that had any considerable guard or number of attendants ; but Sertorius was followed by thousands who offered themselves as his body-guard and vowed to spend their blood with him. It is said that when his army was once defeated, and hard pressed by the enemy, his men took him up on their shoulders and passed him from one to another till they carried him

into the city, and only when they had thus placed
their general in safety, provided afterwards each man
for his own security."

Sertorius certainly had great resource as a commander, and knew how to use the circumstances as
well as the men with whom he had to do. He had
a singular success in his achievement against the
Characitanians. "These are a people beyond the
river Tagus, who inhabit neither cities nor towns,
but live in a vast high hill, within the deep dens and
caves of the rocks, the mouths of which open all towards the north. The country below is of a soil
resembling a light clay, so loose as easily to break
into powder, and is not firm enough to bear any one
that treads upon it, and if you touch it in the least,
it flies about like ashes or unslaked lime. In any
danger of war these people descend into their caves,
and carrying in their booty and prey along with them,
stay quietly within, secure from every attack. And
when Sertorius, leaving Metellus some distance off,
had placed his camp near this hill, they slighted and
despised him, imagining that he retired into these
parts being overthrown by the Romans. And
whether out of anger and resentment, or out of his
unwillingness to be thought to fly from his enemies,
early in the morning he rode up to view the situation of the place. But finding there was no way to
come at it, as he rode about, threatening them in
vain and disconcerted, he took notice that the wind
raised the dust and carried it up toward the caves of
the Characitanians, the mouths of which, as I said
before, opened toward the north, and the northerly

wind, which some call Cæcias, prevailing most in those parts, coming up out of moist plains or mountains covered with snow, at this particular time, in heat of summer, being further supplied and increased by the melting of the ice in the northern regions, blew a delightful fresh gale, cooling and refreshing the Characitanians and their cattle all the day long. Sertorius, considering well all circumstances in which either the information of the inhabitants or his own experience had instructed him, commanded his soldiers to shovel up a great quantity of this light, dusty earth, to heap it up together, and make a mound of it over against the hill in which these barbarous people resided, who, imagining that all this preparation was for raising a mound to get at them, only mocked and laughed at it. However, he continued the work till the evening, and brought his soldiers back into their camp. The next morning a gentle breeze at first arose, and moved the lightest parts of the earth, and dispersed it about as the chaff before the wind, but when the sun coming to be higher, the strong northerly wind had covered the hills with dust, the soldiers came and turned this mound of earth over and over, and broke the hard clods in pieces, whilst others on horseback rode through it backward and forward, and raised a cloud of dust into the air, then with the wind the whole of it was carried away and blown into the dwellings of the Characitanians, all lying open to the north. And there being no other vent or breathing-place than that through which the Cæcias rushed in upon them, it quickly blinded their eyes, and filled their lungs, and all but choked them, whilst they strove to draw in the rough air mingled with dust and powdered earth. Nor were they able, with all they could do, to hold out above two days, but yielded up themselves on the third, adding, by their defeat, not so much to the power of Sertorius as to his renown in proving that he was still able to conquer places by art, which were impregnable by the force of arms."

Sertorius was the ruler of the tribes, which he was civilizing, for nearly ten years. He was able in that time to see the fulfilment of some of the plans which he made for his people. It was one of the darkest periods of the civil wars of Rome, and many a Roman senator, obliged to flee for his life, was glad to follow Sertorius's example, and to join him among his Lusitanian admirers. The reader will understand that before the end of the success of Sertorius he was more than the ruler of the country we call Portugal. He was the recognized master of more than half of Spain. He made his new allies accept the position as he understood it. He had come there with a Roman army. They were not to suppose that they were Spanish rebels. They were to understand that he was a Roman officer, and that he was teaching them how great and how desirable a thing was the gentle sway of Rome. Had Rome only had a chief able to see the grandeur of this position, had the life of this remarkable man been spared, we should not speak of him, as we are apt to, as a sort of Robin Hood, but should rate him as he was, as one of the more remarkable leaders of mankind. But Sylla did not want to encourage other leaders, whose power might come too near his own. Army after army was despatched to crush Sertorius, and with varying success. For himself, he sent word to Metellus and to Pompey that he would lay down his arms and live a private life, if he were allowed to return home. He had rather, he said, live as the meanest citizen in Rome than be supreme commander of all other cities, if he were an exile. He was wholly attached to his mother, and when he heard of her death he almost died himself. For seven days he lay in his tent without admitting his nearest friends. It was only with the greatest difficulty that he was persuaded to resume the command of his army. Mithridates, in Asia Minor, was trying to make head again against Sylla. Hearing of the success of Sertorius, he sent an embassy to him to arrange some coöperation against their common enemy. But Sertorius answered that Mithridates might reign in Bithynia and Cappadocia, because they had never belonged to Rome; but he would have no part in assisting him to regain that part of Asia Minor which the Romans had made a province.

On this basis, Mithridates in the east and Sertorius in the west made a treaty. Sertorius was strong enough to send Marius, one of his generals, with an army to assist Mithridates, and the alliance was successful. But at this moment, unfortunately, the senators around Sertorius in Spain, who had not, it would seem, risen higher than the level of the senators left at home, became envious of his authority. They made a conspiracy against him, and assassinated him at a feast to which he had invited them. In this act of treachery closed the most interesting episode in the slow steps by which barbarous Spain became one of the most highly cultivated provinces in the Roman empire.

The story of Sertorius is so romantic that it has been eagerly seized upon by the writers of poetry in Spain and in other lands. Corneille takes from it the subject of one of his more celebrated tragedies. An English author has made it the subject of his poem called the " The White Hind of Sertorius."

CHAPTER V.

JULIUS CÆSAR IN SPAIN.

THE death of Sertorius took place in the year 72 B.C. His rule, on the whole beneficent, had lasted nearly ten years. His people in general submitted to the Romans. Pompey followed up his successes, and considered Spain as one of the provinces on which he could rely. It was nearly thirty years after the death of Sertorius that, in the great contest between Julius Cæsar and that part of the senate which adhered to Pompey and his family, the decisive battle of the world was fought out in Southern Spain. This was not much more than a year before Cæsar was killed in the senate-house at Rome. The younger Pompey was his antagonist. Cæsar was following up his own victories in Africa, and had come to Spain to end the civil war in person. The decisive battle was at Munda.

Pompey seems really to have supposed that he was superior in force,—so large a proportion of Cæsar's men were new levies. He certainly had the advantage of the ground. The narrative of the battle is not more intelligible than are the narratives of most battles where we have not the advantage of an accurate map of the place. But it is certain that

Pompey and his army had the advantage of the fortifications of the town of Munda, and apparently of considerable military stores there.* He fixed his camp about five miles from Cæsar's, where he had there advantages to rely upon. The country between

JULIUS CÆSAR.

the two armies was flat, but Pompey's front was protected by a stream, which was not easy to cross. On his left, particularly, it flowed through marshy

* Munda was not far from the city of Cordova, and the spot is to be sought for somewhere in the valley of the Guadalquiver. The author of Carmen weaves in with that story, an amusing disquisition on the discovery of the site of the city.

ground which was wellnigh impracticable. Notwithstanding this, Cæsar determined to attack him where he was, though he himself seems to have thought that this was somewhat rash. He saw that he must push his enemy in front, so well defended were both wings. The day was magnificent. "It almost seemed as if the immortal gods themselves had given such wonderful weather—just as he could have chosen it—for battle." It was early in March, and those who have travelled in Andalusia at that time can imagine what a day it was, of which a contemporary writer speaks such words. Every man knew that the final issue of the long struggle had come. An hour might decide it. It was the Waterloo of the conflict between the Senate and the Imperator.

Cæsar's men pressed forward expecting to meet their enemy. But Pompey's men did not abandon at the first their favorable position. They awaited attack. Their line of battle consisted of thirteen legions of heavy infantry, and the wings were covered by cavalry. They had six thousand light infantry beside, and almost as many native "auxiliaries." Cæsar's army was made up of eighty cohorts of infantry, and eight thousand cavalry. When he found that he could not startle Pompey's troops from their secure position, he felt himself, as has been said, how critical was his position; and for a while paused, to reconsider the ground. His men were displeased by this delay, and the enemy was encouraged. They were lured to their first mistake. They delivered an attack, while they should still have awaited it, on their left. Cæsar's extreme right was formed by the "decumani," which held their own; they were supported by the 3d and 5th legions on their left. The conflict was severe and ever wavering, but on the extreme of the wings of both armies Cæsar's veterans not only held their own, but gradually drove their enemy to give way a little. On the instant Cæsar's cavalry pounced on the shattered wing, though the rough country on which it fell back was all unfit for a charge. The army of Pompey was broken and fell back into the town of Munda.

In that fight more than thirty thousand men had fallen, among whom were Sextus Pompey, Labienus, Attius Varus, and other distinguished officers. Cæsar himself, at one moment, when he saw a legion broken, rallied it in person, and took the field as a private soldier might have done. He ran through the ranks and cried to his men: "Are you not ashamed to deliver me into the hands of boys?" And when the battle was won, he told his friends that he had often fought for victory before, but that this was the first time he had ever fought for his life. In this battle, as has been said, the war with Pompey and his army was virtually ended. It was fought on the day of the Feast of Bacchus, four years, to a day, after Pompey had left Rome to begin the war, which had cost him his life, and now virtually came to an end as Sextus Pompey died.

Julius Cæsar celebrated his victory by a triumph. This ceremonial was not very kindly taken at Rome. It was said, not unnaturally, that a victory gained over fellow-countrymen was not one which the people of Rome should be expected to rejoice in unanimously. This was not the last triumph for which Spain gave the cause. Augustus, more than once, conceded the same honor to the lieutenants to whom he entrusted its subjugation.

The Spaniards took the occasion of the civil wars of the Triumvirate to do what they could in reasserting their independence. Even when Augustus closed the gates of the Temple of Janus, it was acknowledged that Spain was not wholly at peace. But civil war was ended, and the complaints of such distant barbarians were not permitted to interfere with the rejoicing at the capital. Augustus, however, made it his first duty to go to Spain in person, and bring the peninsula to real peace. He seldom took the field himself. Indeed he spent a considerable time on his sick-bed at Tarraco, now Tarragona. The regular passage between Italy and Spain was from Rome to this seaport. The Roman lieutenants were too strong for the Spanish rebels, even when they were defending their mountain passes. By the time Augustus had recovered, peace was really secured, and he devoted himself, in person, to those arrangements which should make it permanent. He built new cities in the plains, in which he compelled the mountaineers to reside. He established military colonies for his soldiers, and gave them for their clients, the Spaniards who had been compelled to submit to him. Large numbers of the defeated were sold into captivity. It is thus that some of the finest cities of Spain were established.

CÆSAR'S METHOD OF ATTACK.

Most of them retain a memorial of their origin in their present names. Thus Saragossa was "Cæsar-Augusta." The site was well chosen as convenient for communication between the East and the West, and between the Pyrénées and the Tagus. In the north of Portugal, about twenty-five miles from Oporto, the city of Braga preserves the name of "Bracata-Augusta." A modern traveller speaks of the scenery in the neighborhood as "the most lovely in all Portugal." The Romans gave it the name of the Elysian Fields, and called the Lima River by the name of Lethe or the River of Oblivion. "The banks of the Lima equal any thing Europe contains." Merida is the "Emerita-Augusta" of the emperor. It is still called "the Rome of Spain." The magnificent bridge over the Guadiana, built by Trajan, still stands a noble monument of Roman skill. It is half a mile long, twenty-six feet broad, and thirty-three feet above the bed of the river. It consists of eighty-one arches, constructed of granite. Merida was the capital of the province of Lusitania, the smallest of the three provinces into which Rome divided the peninsula. One of the great reservoirs in the neighborhood of Merida retains the name of the Lake of Proserpine. Nowhere in Europe, indeed, can be found more interesting memorials of Roman engineering than in Spain.

Badajos in the same neighborhood is a corruption from "Pax Augusta." And here also may be found Roman memorials. In the south, Cordova, which the Romans called Corduba, was the capital of the province of Bætica, and so completely was the spirit of insurrection broken that it was not necessary to maintain here any military force. Strabo tells us that in the whole country around the Bætis or Guadalquiver, the natives had so completely adopted the Roman customs that they had even forgotten their own native tongue. Of the three provinces, that of which Tarraco was the head was the largest. In this and in Lusitania, however, a single legion was enough to maintain the authority of Rome. They needed these troops only to protect them against raids from their own mountaineers. Agriculture, trade, and industry flourished through all Spain. Italy needed all the grain which she could furnish, and the supply of the demand gave an ample market to her farmers. In the contest which followed, wars and insurrections died away, and in four centuries, as we have said, Spain disappears from military history. In the fifth century the historian Orosius writing, alas, with too little of the spirit of prophecy, says, "All Spain fell back into eternal peace." Yet Livy writing while Augustus was living, had said that Spain, which was the first province outside of Italy which Rome attempted to subjugate, was the last of all the provinces to be completely subdued.

Such were the triumphs of peace in the exquisite valleys of the south, that, after the Augustan conquest, it was observed that no province in the Roman empire produced so long a list of historians, poets, and philosophers as the schools of Bætica.

Indeed, if we left out the Spaniards, the list of the authors who have distinguished the early days of the empire would seem very meagre. The two Senecas,

—father and son,—and the brother of the younger, known to us best as the Gallio of the Book of Acts, were all born in Cordova. Lucius Seneca, the minister of Nero, who met death at Nero's command, was born in the second or third year of the Christian era, and died in the year 65 A.D. During his lifetime Lucan, the author of the Pharsalia, was born at Aduba in Spain, and not long after, the poet Martial at Bilbilis,—which is in our Arragon. The rhetorician, Quintilian, is another Spaniard. He was born at Callagurris, now Callahorra, in the upper valley of the Ebro. These six distinguished men of letters lived in Rome nearly at the same time. It is also known that the Emperor Vespasian was favorably affected toward Spain, because this was the first province whose troops gave a cordial assent to his appointment as Imperator. It is easy to see that Spain and Spaniards may have been, so to speak, the fashion in Rome in the middle of the first century of our era and at its close.

The three Senecas do not seem to have spent much time in Spain. Lucan died in his twenty-seventh year. Martial returned to Spain at the end of his life. He went there in the third year of Trajan, the year 100 of our era, and married a lady named Marcella, who lived on the banks of the Cello. He speaks warmly of her, as he should have done from mere gratitude; for in her house on her means he lived for the three remaining years of his life.

In a playful little ode to his friend Licianus or Licinianus, Martial amuses himself by bringing in a sheaf of the names of different places in Spain, with some of which apparently Licianus was familiar.

>Come and see our Spaniards, Lician,
>   Other lands shall never shame us;
>Come and see my Bilbilis
>   Both for arms and horses famous.
>Come to craggy Vadavero;
>   Come and and rest you in the groves
>Of my dainty, sweet Botrodes,
>   Which the blithe Pomona loves.
>You shall bathe in warm Congedus
>   Which the water-nymphs environ;
>Or in freezing Salo cool you,
>   Where we cool our blades of iron.
>Beasts and birds shall make your dinner,
>   As you cross Vobisca's meadows,
>Golden Tagus shall refresh you
>   Underneath her leafy shadows.
>
>Are you thirsty? here's Dircenna,
>   And Nemea's melted snows;
>Or, when fierce December rages,
>   And the Gallic north-wind blows,
>We'll go down to Tarragona,
>   To Laletania repair.
>You shall shoot the does with arrows,
>   You shall shoot the wild boar there;
>The keeper shall bring home the stag,
>   And you on horseback course the hare.
>
>Far away be squabbling clients,
>   Far away Liburnus too;
>Not a dun shall break your slumbers,
>   You shall sleep the morning through.
>You shall hear no woman whimper,
>   And no senator debate;
>Other men to bores shall listen,
>   Others hear the fools dilate.

> You know how to taste the pleasure
> When your Sura wins his meed.
> We know how to keep the treasure—
> How to live, and live indeed.

In quite a different strain from that of this playful poem of Martial's is an ode by Prudentius, also a Spaniard, the Christian poet of the fifth century. Probably Prudentius had in mind Martial's catalogue of hard proper names, as he tried his skill in weaving into Sapphic and Adonian verses the names of the Spanish cities. He also was born, like Martial, in the modern Arragon. As it happens, none of his names are the same as those used by Martial, but the reader will be able to place most of them.

The verses come at the beginning of a long poem, called the "Peristephanior," which is an elaborate and somewhat theological tribute to the memory of the martyrs of the Church. It will be seen that he claims credit for his own Saragossa, that she had more than any of such martyrs among the Spanish cities. What is curious is, that he intimates that Rome herself scarcely exceeds her in this regard.

> Dear Saragossa offers, all together,
> Sacred memorials of her eighteen martyrs;
> Well may we hail her "City of Augustus," *
> rich with such Treasure!
>
> Thou who hast been the home of mighty Angels,
> Thou shalt not fear, though worlds shall fall to ruin,
> Thou who canst offer, all at once, so many
> gifts to a Saviour!
>
> When the great God shall scatter far his Lightnings,
> Put forth at last His hand to weigh the Sinner

* "Cæsar-Augusta," whence Saragossa.

ROMAN AQUEDUCT, SEGOVIA.

From the red cloud in which so long He hides it,
    judging the Nations,

Then shall each city, from our many peoples,
Hasten to meet Christ Jesus with their Tributes,
And in rich baskets bear along the priceless
    gifts of their Treasures.

Dear Cyprianus, eloquent and learned,
African Carthage offers Him thy relics;
Cordova brings Acisclus and Zoilus,
    while Tarragona

Weaves in one diadem her triple honors,
And, on the crown which Fructuosus left her,
Fastens twin gems which shine with equal glory,
    blazing with Fire.

Little Gerunda, rich in sacred relics,
Joins with the rest in honor of her Felix;
Our Calagorris* joins the host to carry
    two whom we honor.

Barcelona brings the ashes of Circufas,
Beautiful Narbo bears along her Paulus,
Excellent Aretas never will forget thee,
    holy Genæsis!

Merida, queen of Lusitanian peoples,
Going to meet thy Saviour, thou shalt carry
Her, the brave girl whom thou dost well remember,
    up to the Altar!

Noble Complutum, in the same procession,
Carries together Pastor and his Justus,
Pressing, as brother by the side of brother,
    one bed of Glory.

Tingis among Massilian kings remembers
Cassian the blest, still living in his ashes,

---

* Calagorris was the birthplace of Prudentius.

Who with Christ's yoke—the yoke so light and easy—
    conquered the Nations.

Nay, all the cities, all the little hamlets,
Gladly come forward with such honored tribute;
One, two, or three they offer to the Saviour
    those who confessed Him.

Thou, Saragossa, city of the Cæsars,
Thou shalt record twice nine upon thy banner,
Wearing the olive crown of Peace Eternal
    won in his Service.

Thou, in such graces richer than the richest,
Standest supreme amid thy crowd of martyrs,
Honored beyond all others in the radiance
    of Light Eternal!

Scarcely great Carthage, parent of the nations,
Scarcely great Rome, upon her throne of Empire,
Vying with thee in rivalry of service,
    boasts of such Glory!

If the American reader will remember that the peaceful domination of Spain by Rome lasted four hundred years without a serious ripple, and if he will also remember that this is a longer period than has passed since the discovery of America by Columbus, he will understand, as we are not apt to, how Spain became largely Roman in those centuries. The student of Roman antiquities has therefore, as has been implied, much to learn in travelling in Spain. He may find in an ancient town the same arrangements of the *atrium* and the chambers around it, which have puzzled him as he read the classics. He will find the curtain stretched over the *atrium* to protect it from the sun or a sudden shower. He will find the *implurium* in the middle, the *cubicula* and other rooms arranged substantially as in classical times. He will understand exactly what defence such Roman city as Jaca, which has been spoken of, offered against the attacks of armies which had no cannon. From well-built fortifications like these, round to such details as the bells jingled by a train of mules, the traveller who has even a smattering of classical reading is reminded every time he is in Spain of the Roman origin of manners and customs.

But the most remarkable memorial of Rome in Spain is in the Spanish language. In a later chapter of this book we shall try to show how under the influence of Northern invaders the Latin of Quintilian and Lucan gave way and became eventually the Spanish of to-day. It is enough here to say that the roots of the Spanish language are almost without exception Latin. The traveller meets them in places where he would least expect them. Thus in the days of the early settlement of a wild country, as in the woods of Wisconsin or of Maine to-day, the wayfarer in the wilderness knows that when he comes to a farm he may expect shelter and some form of hospitality. The trace of such a stage of civilization lingers in the Spanish language, where the word *fonda*, derived from the Latin *fundus*, a farm, is now the word for an inn, or what in the East would be called a caravansary. With such roots the Gothic invaders worked strange havoc in forming the grammar of their language, and Spanish may be called a language of Latin radicals with a Teutonic construction.

We have not space here to follow out the curious illustrations of the persistency by which the Roman language has held its own, century after century. But even a novice in the Spanish language will be interested in studying such illustrations, and they force themselves upon the attention of every traveller. It follows, of course, that to natives of the country the classical literature of Rome may become almost as familiar as their own.

PART II.

CHAPTER VI.

ATAULPHUS—EVARIC—400-500 A.D.

THE peaceful condition of affairs which removed Spain from military history for four centuries, came to an end when the Northern invaders from the forests of Germany poured down upon Southern Europe. The southern provinces of France, which were so completely under Roman sway that they are spoken of as *The* Province, and even now known as " Provence," held back the invaders from Spain only so long as their comforts and wealth satisfied the barbarian necessities. From the beginning of the invasion of Western Europe the destinies of Spain, had she known it, were changed. The comparative serenity, which Orosius even then described as eternal peace, was at an end. There have been intervals when, for a generation or two, Spain has known some such tranquillity within her own borders, but it has never happened since that for four centuries together she was " withdrawn from military history."

We are to observe in the story, to which we now introduce the reader, of the Conquest of Spain by the Goths, and the permanent establishment of a Gothic dynasty there, that this dynasty long considered Southern France as its military base, so that in Southern France were its favorite capitals. The elegant Roman civilization of Spain of which we have spoken belonged in the south of Spain. It founded centres in the cities of Cordova, Hispalis, and Cadiz. But between the fertile valley of the Guadalquiver, where were the luxuries of Roman civilization, and the Northern Pyrénées, were hundreds of miles of country but little occupied, and, in some mountain valleys, a sort of Scotch highlands still in the possession of barbarous tribes. In the cities of the northeast and the country behind them, there was the wealth and prosperity which belonged to their commercial position. Such wealth and prosperity attracted the attention of the Gothic settlers in Provence, and as soon as they were strong enough they seized upon them. The advance of their armies pressed before them southward, their vandal precursors, into the valley of the Guadalquiver, and some time elapsed before the Gothic leaders themselves made that region a place of favorite residence. It took its name Andalusia, originally Vandalusia, from its new possessors. Indeed, the history of the conquest of all Spain resembles that of other conquests where a strong military power takes possession of a region of a more refined civilization. Those who are conquered in arms subdue their conquerors in the gradual empire of the arts. And the history which we are to follow, whether of social organization or of religious controversy, is this history of action and reaction. We shall find the strong organization and the vigorous military hand of the Goths steadily taking possession of Spain. On the other hand, we shall find the arts, the accomplishments, or, one may say, the civilities of Southern Spain gradually taking hold of the Goths. At the beginning we shall find the Goths retaining their seats of government at Narbonne, at Toulouse, and at Arles, on the northern side of the Pyrénées. At the end we shall find that their capitals were in Spain, and that their French possessions were regarded more as outlying provinces.

English readers may find a rough parallel with this gradual occupation in the possession of England by the Normans. Just as the Norman dukes gradually found it a greater thing to be kings of England than to be dukes of Normandy, and as finally their Norman possessions fell away or were torn away, so the Gothic conquerors of Spain began by considering Spain the outlying province, but ended in surrendering more or less unwillingly their original possessions on the north of the Pyrénées.

In that remarkable development of civilization which is connected with the name of Provence, to which the world has owed so much and to which, but for the stupidity and cruelty of Dominic, it might have owed so much more, a large part is due to the infusion of Northern blood by the arrival and conquest of the Goths. New vigor came to the highly civilized Roman province from that manliness which is innate in Teutonic institutions. At the beginning of the fifth century the Roman general Stilicho, gathering every man he could command, to keep out the Northern deluge from Italy, stripped Southern Gaul of troops. It was simply a matter of course then that one wave of the deluge flowed west and overran Gaul. They overpowered the garrisons of Franks and Alemans whom Stilicho had left to guard the fords of the upper Rhine; they even took these garrisons into their train, and, on the last day of the year, "like a sullen winter storm," swept into undefended Gaul. They stopped only at the foot of the Pyrenees. The Basques, who were used to the cold of winter and not used to be interfered with by conquerors, arrested their progress. From that moment to this moment descendants of these Northern tribes have lived in what we call Southern France, nor did many years elapse before such conquerors found their way across or around the mountains. The Sueves plundered Galicia, the Alans Lusitania, and the Vandals Bœtica. In such incursions Rome could do nothing to interfere. She was herself besieged by Alaric, was obliged to capitulate and to pay an enormous ransom to her conquerors. This ransom consisted of 5,000 pounds of gold, 30,000 of silver, 4,000 tunics of silk, 3,000 pieces of fine scarlet cloth, and 3,000 pounds of pepper, the pepper being then worth almost as much as gold.

Fortunately for the Roman emperor, Alaric died before the year was ended. The Romans then began to negotiate with Ataulphus,* with whom, as the reader will see, they had one valuable intercessor. As a result of these negotiations all actual conquests were respected. The Goths were in Southern France and

* The Adolphus of Gibbon.

in Spain. It was admitted that they were there. They accepted what they already had as a grant. They did not object to being called nominal subjects of the empire on the single condition of military service. Honorius on this condition gave them what they had already—two thirds of the cultivated lands between the Pyrénées and the Garonne. Toulouse was chosen as the residence of their king. They retained their own laws, customs, and magistrates, while they acknowledged in form the imperial sway.

ATAULPHUS A.D. 411-415.

The wife of Alaric the Goth had a brother named Ataulphus, and he became the second king of the Visigoths. These people, wild, barbarous, and rude at first, were becoming civilized through their intercourse with the Romans, for though they were so strong and bold that they could overcome the Romans in battle, they had much to learn from them in using their minds, and in making life worth something, instead of spending all their time in killing wild beasts for food, and afterward eating them.

Ataulphus was with his brother-in-law, Alaric, in Italy, and helped him in the siege of Rome. There he saw Placidia, the sister of the Roman emperor, Honorius, and later, when he marched away, he carried her off with him as his captive, as these barbarian conquerors often did with the women of their enemies.

But Ataulphus loved Placidia so much that he wished to marry her, and the Roman maiden, who had fallen in love with her brave, strong suitor, with blue eyes and blond hair, consented. Honorius at first thought it best to make friends with so powerful a chieftain, and he yielded to him the fertile provinces of Southern Gaul, and all that part of the Spanish Peninsula which was under Roman rule.

To take possession of his empire, Ataulphus had first to drive out the Sueves and Vandals who were ravaging it, but this he did, and in the town of Narbonne, now a large city in the south of France, he established himself with his Roman bride. He tried to please Honorius by a constant warfare with their mutual enemies the Vandals and Sueves, who laid claim also to lands in Spain, and by showing his reverence to the Roman supremacy.

"It was at first my wish," he said, " to destroy the Roman name, and erect in its place a Gothic empire, taking to myself the place and the powers of Cæsar Augustus. But when experience taught me that the untamable barbarism of the Goths would not suffer them to live beneath the sway of law, and that the abolition of the institutions on which the state rested would involve the ruin of the state itself, I chose the glory of renewing and maintaining by Gothic strength the fame of Rome, desiring to go down to posterity as the restorer of that Roman power, which it was beyond my power to replace. Wherefore I avoid war and strive for peace."

But all the efforts of the barbarian king to keep on good terms with Honorius were of no avail. Another lover of Placidia, who had wished to marry her, a Roman, better suited to her than the Goth by birth and blood, instigated the emperor to make war upon the Goths; so he and his armies were driven out of Gaul, and retreated into their Spanish territories.

They did not give way without a struggle, fierce and sharp, as the battles of the barbarians always were. They burned Bordeaux before they left it, and the Roman arches which stand there now, bear the marks of the Gothic destroyer's hand.

Ataulphus and his court retreated to Barcelona, and there he established himself. Barcelona is a lovely city on the Mediterranean Sea, on the shores of Catalonia, as has been said, one of the seaports early visited by traders from the East, raised to a town by the Carthaginians, and prospering under the Romans, who left behind them columns, altars, and temples, of which the ruins are still standing.

Ataulphus made it the capital of his kingdom which he called Hispana-Gothia, and there he strove to reign peacefully, adopting the manners and civilized habits of the Romans. But this it was not easy to do, for his Goths, by whom he was surrounded, thought he was growing effeminate; they disliked to submit to Roman laws, and they considered the Roman soldiers cowardly and lazy, as no doubt they were, compared with the turbulent, stormy, fight-loving Goths.

Ataulphus, therefore, had a hard time of it between his countrymen who were always grumbling, and his haughty, handsome, dignified Roman wife, Placidia, who probably sometimes found fault with the rough manners of her husband. They were happy together, however. They had six children, who were growing up to inherit the brave characteristics of their warlike father, and the refinement of their mother.

The king thought the best way to manage his soldiers was to keep them fighting, and as this would suit his Roman connections also, he arranged an expedition against the Sueves and Vandals, to drive these tribes out of the Peninsula, and make himself king of the whole of it. But the Goths could not fight cheerfully side by side with the Romans; there was great dissatisfaction in the camp.

One day, in the great court-yard of his palace, at Barcelona, the king in all his state was watching the evolutions of his cavalry, surrounded by his wife and children, who were thinking only of the display of men and horses, when a dwarf employed about the palace stealthily crept up behind Ataulphus, and pierced him with a sword. Instantly all was confusion, but so great was the feeling against the murdered monarch that the poor queen found no one to avenge him. Another Goth, Sigeric, succeeded him, one of those who most hated the Roman influence. The first thing he did was to kill the six children of Ataulphus, and, thinking doubtless to please the people, he compelled Placidia to walk barefoot through the streets of Barcelona. But such barbarous conduct caused a reaction in the minds of the excitable populace. After a few days of triumph he was killed in his turn.

The election of the Goths now fell upon Wallia, who was a chief well worthy of their choice. Their feeling against the Romans was gratified by an expedition against the Roman possessions in Africa, and a fleet started in that direction from Barcelona. But a violent tempest drove them back and scattered the troops, and before they could be collected again, a strong army came from Rome towards the Pyrénées, and Wallia was obliged to gather the remnant of his forces to go against this enemy.

Fortunately for the Gothic king, the general of the Roman forces was Constantius, the Roman lover of Placidia. Now that she was a widow, the Emperor had told him that he might marry her, if he could win her, so he came to love rather than to fight. No sooner were the two armies encamped in sight of each other than Constantius proposed peace, on condition that Wallia should surrender the royal widow.

Wallia was willing enough to do this. It smoothed his way to send Placidia back to Rome, and she was glad enough to go, having by this time come to hold in horror the rude Goths who had killed her husband and her children.

She was transferred to the Roman camp, and to the keeping of her faithful suitor Constantius, and went back with him to Rome, forgetting, perhaps, her troubled life with the Gothic king, and her palace at Barcelona. She became, by Constantius, the mother of the Emperor Valentinian.

Another condition of peace was that Wallia should march against the other nations who held ground in the Peninsula, to secure it for the Romans, and this he was ready and willing to do. But he had the same difficulty that his predecessor had, to reconcile his followers to fighting for the Romans. He showed more tact and judgment than Ataulphus, for before he gave any answer to the Roman general, he laid the subject before his soldiers, in a little speech, in which he said:

"Invincible Goths! with arms in our hands we have opened a path from the North to the far West; nothing has arrested our progress; distance, climate, mountains, rivers, wild beasts, the valor of many enemies, have been opposed to us in vain. Now the Vandals, the Alans, the Sueves dare to assail us behind, while the Romans are in front. It is for you, valiant warriors, to choose which most pleases you; which enemy you will take first.

"Choose as you will, I am confident that your bravery will ensure victory, while, at the head of men to whom fear is unknown, I have no reason for fear myself. If the decision were left to me I should remember only that I am your king; I should listen to courage alone, and select the enemy most worthy to contend with us. As to the Romans, you know them well enough; you know how often their cities have felt the weight of our swords, how the gates of their very capital have opened at our command; why waste any time on such a despicable set of cowards? There is more glory in despising than in subduing them."

He concluded by advising them to deliver up Placidia,—which he had already himself decided upon,—and to march against the fierce northern tribes, who had the boldness to hold a country which of right belonged to the Goths alone.

A shout of approbation followed. Placidia was restored and peace made with the Romans.

Hostilities were now begun in earnest against the

ROMAN TEMPLE AT VIENNE. (SOUTHERN GAUL.)

barbarians. The right which Wallia the Goth asserted over the northern regions of the Peninsula was questionable, for had the children of the earlier inhabitants been consulted, they might have said that Goth and Vandal were alike invaders of their mountain homes; but in those days Might made Right.

At all events the force of the Gothic arms triumphed. The tribe called the Alans was almost entirely destroyed, and their name even disappeared forever from the Peninsula. The Vandals were driven into Gallicia, and the Sueves put themselves under the protection of Rome.

Honorius the emperor was well pleased with these successes. He rewarded the victor, Wallia, with lands in Southern Gaul, from Toulouse to the ocean.

Wallia made Toulouse the seat of his kingdom, and died there after enjoying for two years the fame of his conquests.

Five Visigoth princes reigned there after Wallia, of which the first was Theodoric.

In the second half of the fifth century, the formidable invasion of the Huns happened. These Huns were the terror of all the nations of Western Europe.

They had nothing in common with any of them, neither in their appearance, language, nor their habits of life. The face of the Hun was sharp and angular, the brown skin drawn tight over the bone, with little holes for the eyes, which peered out with a vicious expression,—his nose was flat and broad, his ears enormous and projecting, his beard was scanty. "They are beasts on two legs," says an early writer.

They came across the vast steppes between Asia and Europe in enormous chariots, or mounted upon small but untiring horses; their food on these journeys was meat, which they ate after keeping it long enough between the saddle and the back of the horse, and mare's milk.

This was the people which swept down upon Europe, and destroyed every thing in its path.

Attila their king and leader, " the Scourge of God," compelled every tribe he met with to follow his armies. With an immense force he crossed the Rhine into Gaul. The whole population of the country fled before him, for wherever he passed he left not one stone upon another, destroying city after city, until he came near Orléans, where he made a stand.

Orléans was even then an ancient city, the key to the cities around it. At that time there was living there the bishop St. Aignan, a brave man who kept up the courage of the inhabitants, until a strong force arrived to resist the barbarians, composed of all the armies of all the different nations then in Gaul, combined to further resist the Huns.

Theodoric the Visigoth, was there with an army from Toulouse, successor to Wallia, already a great general, who had made successful war with the Romans, and gained fame in battle.

There was a fierce encounter not far from Orléans at Châlons, or the Catalaunian plains (451), and in the end Attila was conquered.

He shut himself up in a camp composed of all his war chariots ranged around the enclosure in a circle, and there, on the day after the battle, the conquerors could see an immense pyre made of saddles heaped up on one another. Attila himself had mounted to the top of it, and there he stood while all the Huns left after the bloody combat surrounded the pile, with torches in their hands ready to set fire to it as soon as they were attacked.

The allies did not press their advantage, and allowed the vanquished foe to pass free. Perhaps they were filled with a sort of admiration of this lion thus standing at bay before them.

Attila died the next year and his empire perished with him, but not the terrible remembrance of his name and his cruelty.

Theodoric, the Visigoth, was killed upon the field of battle. To him and to the Roman general Ætius, were due the glory of the defeat of the Scourge of God. His son became king after him, but he was put to death by his brothers, one of whom reigned in his stead. He was soon succeeded by the remaining brother, Evaric, who is said, in his turn, to have gained his throne by assassinating the king, his brother, in his capitol at Toulouse, but perhaps he had no immediate hand in the deed. He became a great monarch and extended the kingdom of the Visigoths far to the north and east, while he was master of a great part of Spain. A writer of his time gives a glowing idea of the power of Evaric, and the splendor of the court at Toulouse, to which all nations came as the centre of luxury and pleasure.

"There was the blue-eyed Saxon, accustomed to playing in the surf of the ocean; the old Sicambrian, shaved when he was made a captive, with his hair just coming again on his forehead since peace had restored him to liberty; the Herulean, with his cheeks tattooed with blue, the color of the waves; the tall Burgundian, seven feet high ; the Ostrogoth, proud of the protection of Evaric against the attacks of the Huns ;—and envoys came from the far-off kingdom of Persia."

We can imagine this description to be the work of a reporter, just as if he were writing an account of the collection of people at any modern capital. The writer was a poet of the period, he says: "I have been at court while the moon has twice completed her course, and in all this time have gained but one audience from the king ; the master of these regions has little leisure for such as I ; the whole universe is asking his notice, and awaiting it with submission."

The predecessors of Evaric had not had much to do with Spain, busy with fighting their enemies and keeping up their state in Southern Gaul. He despatched an army into the Peninsula against the Sueves, and afterwards drove out the Roman colonies, so that they renounced all their provinces to him, and thenceforward the Goths regarded Spain as their lawful inheritance.

Evaric, therefore, was the founder of the Gothic kingdom of Spain. He was also the first legislator of the nation. The laws which he collected and committed to writing served as the foundation of the famous Gothic code, known as the Fuero Juzgo, which has had much to do with Spanish jurisprudence ever since.

By this time the Goths had lost their character of barbarians, and were a civilized and enlightened people. The language they found there was that of the Romans, Latin, but corrupted by a mixture of the tongues of the earlier people. The Goths added to the confusion of the mixture their own words, but their books were written in Latin. The Spanish historian Orosius, about this time, wrote a book to combat the notion that all the miseries of mankind had been occasioned by Christianity. It was a history of the World from the creation to the reign of Wallia, relating all the plagues, famines, earthquakes, wars, and all other sorts of calamity that had happened since the world began, in order to prove that things have been no worse since the birth of Christ than they were before. He conceived it to be worth while to write this book, because there was a very general habit among the Pagans to say that all the wickedness then existing was caused by Christianity.

The work was received with great enthusiasm when it appeared in 419; the greater part of it has no title as to historic value, but the portion describing events nearest the time of the writer are still relied on by historians.

In this period of one hundred years the character of the Goths changed from a wild barbaric race to a proud and civilized race, whose king held a court among the most brilliant in the world. The ancestors of Ataulphus had swept down upon the Roman Empire like a whirlwind; it was his descendant Theodoric who, armed for the cause of law and order, and fighting side by side with a bishop of the church, put a stop to the ravages of the fierce barbarian Attila.

Ataulphus, king of the Goths, was despised by the courtly Romans, as scarcely worthy to be the husband of Placidia, the sister of the Emperor, but in less than one hundred years Evaric, king of the Goths, regarded himself, doubtless, as equal, if not superior, to any reigning monarch. The Romans had, by this time, ceased to be the proud and powerful nation they had been, while the arms of the Goth everywhere triumphed.

ROMAN GATEWAY AT TRÈVES.

Thus far the Visigoth monarchs had not held their courts in Spain itself, but made their capitals in Southern Gaul. Evaric, at the time of his death, was at Arles, a town as old as Julius Cæsar, with an amphitheatre of which the ruins are still standing.

To these Gothic kings, accustomed to the luxuries of Provence, Spain appeared a rough territory, to be fought for, to be guarded from invasion, but not to be lived in, as they notably saw but little of the fertile fields of Andalusia.

The government of the Visigoths was, in appearance, an absolute monarchy, but the power of the king was so restrained by the influence of the prelates of the church, that it might be called a theocracy. In the beginning the Gothic kings were controlled by their nobles, they had no royal descent, no hereditary houses, but were elected by their peers, like the emperors of Germany.

Every fierce, proud, and haughty chieftain, therefore, considered himself as good as his king, for he might become one at any moment. As the dignity was originally military, conferred on superior bravery and warlike skill, these qualities might in any case lead to the throne; the early electors were too barbarous to form any notion of other qualifications. It was the sword which had opened them a path from the far North to their fertile abodes in the Southern Peninsula, and by the sword only could they preserve their dominion.

In the times of the first Visigothic kings the whole ceremony of electing a chief consisted in making the successful candidate promise that he would behave valiantly in war, and rule with justice during peace. He was then raised on a buckler above the heads of the surrounding multitudes, who hailed him as their leader. Later, when the elective power had come to rest with the clergy as much as in the warlike chiefs, there was more pomp and circumstance attending the inauguration. Both the secular and spiritual chiefs were assembled for the purpose of nominating the candidate. He swore to observe the laws, to administer justice without partiality, and received oaths of fidelity and obedience from every one asssembled.

CHAPTER VII.

ARIANS.

THE Eternal Peace, of which the fond historian of Spain wrote, was to be broken by a Gothic invasion. The most careful students of the history of the Goths do not affect more than tradition as their authority, in supposing that they had come originally from Scandinavia. History really knows them just near the mouth of the Vistula, in the region now covered mainly by Prussia. The Vandals, who, with a different name, seem to be but another tribe of the same great people, lived west of them. In their original residence in Scandinavia, those Goths who lived at the eastward, had been called Ostro-Goths, and those at the westward, Visi-Goths. But Ostro-Goths and Visi-Goths are the same people, speaking substantially the same language. And in the period of which we are speaking these names are to be taken simply as names, and the reader is not to puzzle himself by expecting to find any geographical relation remaining. Among the Vandals, who were frequently their allies, and who belonged to the same race and shared their characteristics, were tribes which had the names of Lombards and Burgundians, which have since been transferred to parts of Europe very far from the original seats of the conquerors. The Heruli were a third Vandal tribe, once equally distinguished, but their name has disappeared from geography.

Pressed by some wave of eastern invasion, perhaps, or perhaps led by some spirited soldier's ambition, or perhaps directed from their own homes by an oracle, Goths and Vandals swept southward on the Roman Empire. In the third century, their attack pressed most heavily on the line of the Danube. Eventually they crossed that river, and, building ships for themselves on the Black Sea, attacked, with success the coasts of Greece and of Asia Minor. The history of the end of that century, and of the fourth century is the history of Roman wars with Goths and Vandals, and of the truces and treaties by which such wars were, for a time, arrested. In the middle of the fourth century, Ulfilas, as he is called by most modern writers, converted these barbarians to the Christian religion. In the language which he wrote, first of all men, his name is Wulf-i-las—" The little wolf." The piety, the learning, and the energy of this man, and the inestimable results which have followed from his devotion, give him a high place among the founders of modern Europe and the benefactors of mankind. The Gothic language was reduced to writing by him. He used twenty-two of the Roman letters and invented one letter, w, and a letter for th, which has since fallen out from the German alphabet. Ulfilas did this, that he might translate for the use of his converts the Scriptures of the New and Old Testaments. His translation of the New Testament was complete. Of the old Testament, it is specially said, that he omitted the four books of Kings from fear of the effect upon the warlike passions, so difficult at best to control, of his converts. All the stores of German, Dutch, and English literature have their origin in the experiment which " The Little Wolf," thus tried of the capacities of the Gothic language.

His converts seem to have accepted the new faith seriously and with determination, as has been the religious habit of their race from that time down. When Alaric, the great Gothic leader, established his western court at Toulouse, the dignity of its worship and the seriousness of its morals were such as to put to shame the Christian Court of Constantinople at the same time. And those who make the mistake of considering religion a mattter of books, —where the learned have better chances than the ignorant,—must remember that such dignity and seriousness were attained by a nation of new converts, who had no literature but a part of the Bible which a few of them had but just learned to read. As we shall see, the simplicity of their training had much to do with the ecclesiastical quarrels of the next century. The conversion from Pagan worship did not diminish the respect which the Goths were always accustomed to pay to their priests. When they were in the forests of the north, the priests shared with the officers of the army in the government of the people; and we shall see, as we go on, that priests and bishops had no less power in the affairs of the converted nation.

This Gothic nation, having rested itself by taking possession of Southern France, almost without opposition, is the power which in the fifth century broke in upon the dream of peace in Spain. Before this time the Franks had sent invading bodies across or around the Pyrenees. But they had made no permanent establishments. When the Goths and Vandals came to Spain they came to stay.

The reader will observe in following the history of this conquest, and of the contemporaneous movements of Gothic leaders further east, that we have passed the period in their history when they became a Christian people. Indeed, Ulfilas, the father of their faith, died about the year 390. After this time, in the great contests which follow between North and South, we have, for the first time, a conflict of two Christian nations against each other. But the Christianity of the North was as simple and as untheological a form of religion as can be conceived. For its theological basis was what was called Arianism. Little wonder, indeed, that prelates and doctors at the South refused to call it Christianity at all. Suppose a South Sea Islander of to-day, who has just been trained to read the four Gospels in his own language, and from them has his only idea of Saviour, of God, or of heaven, were brought into a meeting of theologians at Rome or at Oxford, or to the discussions of a clerical association in the United States. The amazement which this poor man would feel, and his utter inability to understand even the terms of discussion, show precisely the experience of the intelligent Goths of the first generation of invaders, when they found themselves in presence of the subtleties of the church of the Mediterranean shore. For Italians, Greeks, and Spaniards, Christianity was now a matter of more than three centuries of history, literature, and study. It was as old as Protestantism is to-day. It is safe to say that its dogmas had been refined upon with more intricate discussion than has shown itself even in the discussions of Protestantism. It had been discussed by literary men, trained to rhetoric and logic. It had been discussed by philosophers, trained in Greek philosophy, in Asian extravagances, in Egyptian mysteries, and in African readiness to assent. Thus it had become a complicated theological system, all wrought in with the intricacies of a highly organized social order, through which ran all the electric nerves of the great imperial system, and in which every fashion, every habit of speech, and every mental process, was allied to whatever was the ruling theological dogma of the time. In that social order, bishops and often prelates, were leaders. They were the advisers of monarchs, and sometimes even took their places in council, and in war.

The Gothic leaders and the simple Gothic people found themselves of a sudden in presence of this complicated social order, with which they had scarcely one point in sympathy. That point was, their veneration for Jesus Christ, the Saviour of the world. But they did not know Jesus Christ by any of the epithets which had been developed by the learning

TOLEDO.

of three centuries. They knew him only in the simple phrases which they had spelled out in the simple version of the four Gospels which their beloved apostle had made for them. They knew him as the well-beloved Son of God. They knew him as him whom the Father had sent into the world. In this sense they knew him as Emanuel—God with us. They knew him as the Messiah who claimed to fulfil Jewish prophecy. But when bishops or other teachers spoke to them of a Trinity of three persons and one God, they used words which these Germans had never heard before, and of which they did not know the meaning. They used words which, to this hour, the German languages have never been able to translate, and which they have been obliged to incorporate with their own.

But it was on no theological subtlety such as the world has played over for fourteen centuries since, without any satisfactory solution, that the Gothic Arians of Spain came to battle with the Roman Catholics whom they found there. The real conflict was that of a nation without science and without a literature, meeting another nation with science and with a literature. As it happened, the literature was orthodox in its theology; and the science, such as it was, borrowed the orthodox expressions and belief. But the Goths, whom we are following, had neither literature nor science. When the conflict began, they were perfectly true to the intelligible and simple theology which they brought with them. But as, man by man, they entered into the fascinating arcana of learning and art, by which they were tempted in the older civilization of Spain, they followed almost, of course, in the steps of their teachers. Two or three generations were quite enough to bring the sons and grandsons of Gothic princes to follow very meekly the directions of the learned prelates of their times. Who should understand these mysteries, indeed, if not the learned men who studied them? The contest was a contest between unlearned simplicity and a cultivated and learned theology. So far as there was any tribunal to which both parties could appeal for a decision, such appeals must be rendered to Rome herself. In such a contest there was, from the beginning, no question what the end must be.

It would be foolish, then, to make any attempt to decide which of the two parties in the contest which swept over Spain now for nearly one hundred years had made the nearest approach to absolute truth. The statement of neither party would now be accepted as final by any theologian in the world. The conflict, as has been said, was not really a conflict as to the Divine realities. It was the conflict which must come where a simple people without letters is living in the same streets with a people who are using a literature, complicated and refined, which has stood for hundreds of years.

Civilization will have its way. It will be for the reader to see, in the narrative which follows, which of the parties exhibited more of the true Christian spirit. Nothing need be added here but to say that the learned still find some traces of the Arianism of Spain left in the texts of the Spanish liturgies. Its most valuable gift to Spain was probably that spirit of proud independence which for centuries enabled the Spanish Church to defy the decrees of the Roman Pontificate. It was this same independence which so long preserved separate rituals and administrations in the Spanish churches. To-day, the northern traveller in Toledo, led by his sympathy for freedom in religion, goes to worship in the little chapel of the cathedral, where what is called the Muzarabic ritual is still maintained,—though he and the choir-boys be the only congregation, and the priest who conducts the service himself seems to wonder why they are there. This traveller will remember that this anomaly in the ritual of that church, which would be glad to have one ritual in one language for every country under heaven, is the survival of the simple independence of those unlearned invaders who brought into Spain such Christianity as Ulfilas had taught them from the four Gospels. They were not trained to the Christology or the theology, which could be better studied in the schools of Toledo, of Rome, of Athens, of Antioch, and of Alexandria.

Exactly as in the case of the Roman occupation, the principal memorial which the Goths have left in Spain is the impress of their language. As has been already said, Spanish is a language of Latin roots with a Teutonic grammar. Because this is so, a piece of good Spanish has all the aspects to the English reader, of a piece of bad Latin, as Latin is written by a school-boy in the first months of his training. Without disrespect to a noble language,

Spanish has been compared to the "hog-Latin" of an English school—such as a boy if he meant to write in Latin "I have spoken," would say "Ego, I; habeo, *have;* dictus, *spoken.*" This would be as bad Latin as it could possibly be. Every word would be wrong and one might say that the arrangement would be wrong. Now all the southern and modern languages, which are made on Latin roots, make this boy's curious error of changing a passive perfect participle into an active one. The Roman language had no active perfect participle; Gothic and French speakers of Latin needed one as the school-boy does. They took the passive participle and used it as if it were active. The Frenchman says "j'ai parlé,"—and the Spaniard "yo he hablado." To such rough treatment of Latin,—common to all this group of languages,—Spanish adds peculiarities of its own. The indefinite article, which the German retains as *ein*, is in Spanish *un*, as in French, and its use follows old Gothic analogies. By a habit, difficult to understand, the definite article is used in ways more familiar to Englishmen than to Frenchmen. For instance "l'honneur" and "la Patrie" are forms which would not be found in Spanish.

The reader who takes any interest in the comparison of languages may like to look at the four versions of the beginning of the Sermon on the Mount in Spanish, Italian, French, and English.

"Y viendo *Jesus* las multitudes, subió á un monte; y sentándose él, se llegaron á el sus discipulos. Y abriendo el su boca los enseñaba, diciendo: "

" Ed egli, vedendo le turbe, sali sopra il monte;

e postosi a sedere, i suoi discipoli s'accostaronoa lui. Ed egli, aperta la bocca, gli ammaestrava; dicendo:"

"Voyant la foule, Jésus monta sur la montagne; et après qu'il se fut assis, ses disciples s'approchèrent de lui. Puis, ayant ouvert la bouche, il les enseigna, et dit : "

"And seeing the multitudes, he went up unto the mountain ; and when he had sat down, his disciples came unto him ; and he opened his mouth and taught them, saying : "

It happens, curiously enough, that some gradual changes, such as the philologists would account for by Grimm's Law, have even changed familiar radicals in the same way in which they have been changed in English, where the Norman French introduced Latin roots into a Saxon language. Even the philologist finds it rather hard to account for "mucho" in Spanish and "much" in English,—two words, which, on their way down from the original Sanscrit, have, after an eventful history, come out almost as much alike as twin sisters should.

It is for this reason that English readers, who have any knowledge of the Latin language, find Spanish so easy a language to learn. For reasons understood by the philologists, the combination of Latin roots into Teutonic grammar made by the Franks, does not retain so many German peculiarities. In Italian fewer still are found. Of the three languages, therefore, Spanish is the easiest for an English speaking person, who has any knowledge of Latin, to guess his way through.

The relations of Spain with England and America,

in modern times, have done a good deal to increase the resemblance between the English and Spanish languages. Here, we are not to trace a long descent from an original Sanscrit ancestry, but merely find cases where the word has been bodily transferred, for convenience, from one language to another. It is curious to see that England, since then the mistress of the seas, took many of the words now in familiar use in maritime affairs, from Spanish authorities. Thus our word "mizzen" is from the Spanish "mesana"; our "gaff" is the Spanish "garfio." In military affairs the same transfers took place, probably in the times of wars in the Low Countries. Our " canteen " is the Spanish "cantina," whose root is to be found in the Latin "quantus," whence we get our word "quantity." A traveller in Spain who arrives at an inn asks for "cuartos" for his party—that is for "rooms." The word originated in the division of a house into four rooms, each of which was a fourth part of the whole. When in England or America, a person tells you he is changing his *quarters*, he uses the same phrase, without knowing, perhaps, that he is talking Spanish. In later times the relations both of navies and of armies have been somewhat changed; and in Spain, as in all the rest of the world, the language of steam-engineering takes most of its phrases from the words carried by the countrymen of Watt and Boulton, Stephenson and Fulton.

From point to point, as the Story of Spain goes on, we shall have occasion to show how the remarkable literature developed, by the people who have used this language of great power, has interested all Western Europe, and has won a commanding place in the literature of modern times. The romance authors of Spain led the way in the series of stories long so fashionable, which were the first books Europe had to read after it escaped from merely monkish literature. One may say, in passing, that there is hardly one of the romances which does not show signs of ecclesiastical training in the author. Coming later down, the statesmanship and diplomacy of Spain, in the days of Ferdinand, of Charles V., and his immediate successors, brought the Spanish language to the general attention of civilized Europe. So soon as Cervantes and Lope de Vega wrote, their works were translated into every Western language, and there are high authorities who even insist that we owe "Gil Blas" to a Spanish original, though that original has never been found. For centuries, indeed, the plots of French and English and German plays were borrowed from the Spanish, as certainly and as confidently as the plots of English plays have since been taken from the French, and those of French plays from the German. It has happened in some instances that the translations from language to language have been made by master hands. The "Don Quixote" of Smollett, for instance, might be reckoned almost as an English classic.

To people of this generation, Spain seems set apart from the rest of the world, and men travel there as they might go to the planet Mars or to Japan. In Seville they find what reminds them of Arabian Nights. In the rest of Spain they find traces of the Roman arts, or mingle in customs which carry them back to their recollections of Scott's novels of the Middle Ages. But, in other times, the relations of Spain with the rest of Europe have been very intimate. To these relations we owe the origin of the modern novel—the history of which cannot be traced without going back to Spanish originals. In giving to the world "Amadis," "Esplandian," and the other romances, "Don Quixote," "Gil Blas," and the plays of Cervantes, Calderon, and De Vega, the Peninsula has made a permanent mark on the literature of Europe. For the reasons which have been hinted at, the student of English or American blood comes to the great originals with perfect ease and satisfaction.

CHAPTER VIII.

LEOVIGILD—RECARED.

LEOVIGILD was a great and warlike king (568-601), who was always successful in keeping enemies out of Spain with his army. He would not allow people in the kingdom who acknowledged any one else but himself as their sovereign, and drove out from Granada and other towns the imperialists who considered themselves under the rule of the Roman emperor. He had to put down rebellions which arose in several parts of the country. These were manifestations of the Spaniards, or descendants of the early inhabitants of Spain, who had never become wholly blended with the Goths. Their religion was not the religion of the king, for he was an Arian, and this heresy, as it was called, had no foothold among the fierce inhabitants of the northern mountains, where the Christian religion, taught by zealous priests of the Roman Church, had displaced their earlier barbarous worship. These wild tribes were hard to subdue. For ten years the king was hard at work establishing peace throughout his dominions, from the Bay of Biscay to the Straits of Gibraltar.

Leovigild was twice married. His sons, Erminigild and Recared, were grown up when their father gave them, as step-mother, Goswinda, a princess of great decision of character, who was, like her husband, an Arian.

The young prince and heir to the throne, Erminigild, was at the time married to Ingunda, a princess who came from France, although she was descended on her mother's side from Gothic kings.

Athanagild, king of the Visigoths, had two daughters, both of whom he gave in marriage to French princes, hoping thus to buy the friendship of the Franks. An early historian describes the grief with which the queen-mother parted with her daughter whom she sent to seek an unknown lord in the North. The description shows how much the Goths had advanced in civilization, by their life in Spain, since the mother regarded the journey of her daughter as a return to barbarism. The sequel showed that she was not far wrong.

"When the ambassadors of the Franks, at Toledo, presented themselves to salute the future bride of their king, they found her sobbing in the arms of her mother. Rough as they were, they were touched, and dared not mention the journey for two days, but on the third, they ventured to approach the queen and point out to her that they must hasten their departure, on account of the impatience of Chilpéric, their master, and of the length of the journey. The queen with tears besought them for one more day. 'But one day more,' she said, 'and I will ask nothing further,—yet know you not that where you are carrying my daughter there will be no mother for her!' After every possible excuse for delay, Athanagild imposed his authority as king and father, and in spite of her mother's tears, the princess was consigned to the charge of those who were to conduct her to her future spouse.

"A long train of cavaliers, chariots, and baggage, filed through the narrow streets of Toledo towards the northern gate. The king followed the escort of his daughter as far as the bridge over the Tagus, at some distance from the city, but the queen could not make up her mind then to turn back, and chose to go on further. She left her own carriage and sat in that of the princess close to her daughter, and thus went on day after day for a distance of more than a hundred miles. Every day she said, 'I will just go on to the next stopping-place'; and when they reached that, she still went on. As they approached the mountains, travelling grew difficult, and as the queen's own people and baggage greatly increased and complicated the dangers of the journey, the Gothic lords made up their minds not to let the queen go a step further. They convinced her that she must resign herself to a separation which was inevitable, and the tender scenes of parting were renewed.

"'May you be happy my daughter,' she said, 'but I have grave fears for you; be on your guard, always on your guard.' The princess wept bitterly at these words, for she felt some presentiment of evil.

"'God wills, I must submit,'" she sadly said.

"Then a division was made of the cavaliers and carriages, some going forward with the princess, while the rest turned back towards Toledo. Before

THE WINDING PASS.

mounting the chariot which was to take her home, the Queen of the Goths paused by the way-side, and fixed her eyes upon the departing conveyance of her daughter, which she followed until it vanished at a turn in the winding pass.

"The princess pursued her destination in the North. With her escort, composed of lords and warriors of both nations, Goths and Franks, she crossed the Pyrenees, passed through Narbonne and Carcassonne, which still belonged to her father's kingdom, then, by way of Poitiers and Tours, she came to Rouen where the marriage was to be celebrated. At the gates of every large town the cortège stopped in order to make a grand entrance. The knights laid aside their travelling mantles and appeared in all the splendor of rich dresses; the princess exchanged her heavy travelling carriage for a triumphal car in the form of a tower all covered with plates of silver.

"The wedding was celebrated with great magnificence. The Frank warriors took oaths of fidelity to the foreign princess, and waved their swords in the air pronouncing an old Pagan formula which condemned to the sword him who violated this oath. Then the king solemnly renewed his vows of constancy and conjugal faith, and swore, with his hand upon a casket containing sacred relics, never to repudiate the daughter of the king of the Goths, his lawful and only wife."

This promise was kept for a while. In less than six months, the Gothic princess was strangled in her sleep by the orders of the king, to gratify a rival in his affections.

There were two Gothic princesses who were thus sent to France. This was the fate of one, the other was the famous Brunhilda, whose career and whose crimes have been the subject of many a romance. She lived to a wicked old age, and was finally killed by her enemies who accused her of the death of no less than ten kings.

The daughter of Brunhilda, born in France, came to Spain to marry a Gothic prince, Erminigild, the son of Leovigild. She was warmly received at the Gothic court. Her husband, the heir to the throne, was already associated with his father in the royal dignities, and treated with the greatest liberality and affection.

Unfortunately the princess Ingunda had been brought up in the Catholic faith, while Goswinda, her step-mother, was a violent Arian. The two princesses early declared war against each other. The queen was no longer young, her temper was violent, she brooked no opposition. The French princess was but sixteen when she arrived at court, very beautiful, with the vivacious spirit and love of power of her mother. Such causes were enough to breed jealousy and quarrelling; differences of religious faith were made the grounds for dispute and bitterness, leading to violence which the principles and precepts of neither creed were able to restrain.

Goswinda was determined that her step-daughter should embrace the religion of the Goths; Ingunda was equally resolved that no force at battle should induce her to do so.

Goswinda was of a violent disposition, it is said,

and, when resisted, resembled a fury rather than a woman. She so far forgot all sense of dignity, not merely, but of decency, as to punish the obstinacy of Ingunda with blows. She seized her one day, says Saint Gregory of Tours, by the hair of her head, threw her down and trampled on her, and afterwards forcibly thrust her into the water to be baptized by an Arian priest. Such treatment was not to be borne. Ingunda flew to her husband, and poured out her injuries in a torrent of French invectives. The prince went, of course, to his father, but Leovigild had no influence with his angry and offended wife, who hated her step-daughter the more, the worse she treated her. The repose of the court was broken up by such scandals, divided into two parties, which espoused the two causes of the rival princesses, and, after the manner of good society, reported, surmised, and discussed each scandal as it took place, and invented others which did not occur.

The two husbands, whose mutual affection was in nowise disturbed by the want of harmony between their wives, agreed that such a life was intolerable, and decided to separate. The elder established his court at Toledo, while the younger, with his fair young princess, lived at Seville, in a splendor little inferior to that of Leovigild and Goswinda.

Erminigild had not long been installed in his new palace when he abjured Arianism and embraced the Catholic religion. This was a great triumph for his wife, Ingunda, to whose influence it was chiefly due, as she had by this time acquired great power over her husband. She was aided by the arguments of a bishop they happened to have in the family, St. Le-

PUERTA DEL SOL. TOLEDO.

ander, the brother of Theodosia, the first wife of Leovigild. This lady is celebrated as the sister of three saints—all uncles of Erminigild, and one of them bishop of Seville. Under these circumstances, it was natural enough that the prince should abjure a faith made so unamiable in the person of his violent stepmother, for another made attractive by the charms of his fair young wife, and recommended by all his own mother's relations. The change was most unwelcome at the court at Toledo. Leovigild, though of a soul naturally noble, was violent when roused, like his queen. That the heir to his throne should abandon the ancient faith of his fathers, filled him with indignation. In the first moments of anger, he declared that the crown of the Goths should never adorn the brow of an apostate. Goswinda encouraged this temper in her lord and master, and fostered it with all the bitter arguments she could think of.

Leovigild, however, could not long maintain in his heart hard feelings against a son he so deeply loved. He sent to him requesting an interview, in the hope that he might change the resolve of the young man; perhaps if they could have met, they would have agreed to differ without quarrelling, but the prince refused to meet his father. Probably his advisers thought it dangerous for their new convert to be exposed to the arguments and entreaties of an affectionate parent. For the Catholic bishops it was a great gain to have a prince and heir to the throne converted to orthodoxy. They were even eager to take up arms and dethrone the Arian monarch, in order to place his orthodox son in his stead.

Erminigild opened intercourse with his father's enemies, and took advantage of his own conversion to win for his cause such subjects of Leovigild as professed the orthodox belief. Among them was Mir, the king of the Sueves, in Galicia, where a number of these people still remained, after all the attempts of the Gothic kings to turn them out of the Peninsula. Mir marched to his assistance, but before he reached Seville, he was surrounded by the royal troops, and compelled to swear that he would aid his liege-lord. For Erminigild, the undutiful son and audacious rebel, had to deal with an able opponent in the king, his father, who had already proved his skill as a leader of armies. He besieged Erminigild in Seville. The city was closely invested by a powerful army; yet the prince was so well supported that the place held out for a year. At the end of this time, their provisions were giving out, their patience exhausted. The prince succeeded in effecting his escape before Seville capitulated. He fled to Cordova, but that city was compelled to surrender by the troops of Leovigild, and after several attempts to defend himself, his troops cut to pieces, his fortifications destroyed by fire, he betook himself to sanctuary in a church whence he implored pardon.

The king, justly incensed with the undutiful conduct of his son, which in his eyes could not be excused under the plea of religious fervor, since the father regarded the new professions of his son as extreme errors, nevertheless promised to spare his life if he would leave the sanctuary. Prince Recared, another son of Leovigild, entered the church and persuaded his brother to come forth. Erminigild appeared and threw himself at the feet of his parent, with every sign of grief and repentance. The king raised him with much emotion, kissed him, and wept bitterly. His anger was forgotten, and he felt all his affection returning for his favorite son. But the rebel must be punished; he was despoiled of his ornaments, the signs of royalty, and exiled to Valencia, there to live as a private man.

Erminigild withdrew to Valencia, but it was not likely that he would rest there quietly, nor that Ingunda, the ambitious French princess, would allow herself to be thus extinguished, while her rival, Goswinda, triumphed at Toledo. It was not long before Erminigild had collected an army combined from those of the enemies of his father, and invaded his territory.

The old writer who describes these things, being orthodox, regards the cause of Erminigild as a holy one, undertaken for the true faith, and he relates a miracle which took place in the contest between the rebel forces of Erminigild and the veteran troops of his father, Leovigild, the Arian. He says that Leovigild's soldiers everywhere plundered and burned the churches and monasteries of the orthodox, and massacred the inmates without compunction. On one occasion his army advanced upon a monastery in such force that the monks all fled in terror, leaving their aged abbot alone and unprotected. The old man, in all the splendor of his priestly robes, stood in the gate-way, armed only with his cross. A soldier raised his sword against the holy man, but was instantly struck dead, seeing which his comrades fled with haste. When the king heard of it, he acknowledged the interference of Heaven for that monastery, and forbade it to be plundered.

The cause of the rebel son was hopeless, in spite of the support it received from the orthodox party in Spain, for this was not strong enough to resist the force of well-trained arms, and the power of existing institutions. Ingunda herself saw this, and urged her husband to escape into France, where they might persuade her brother to arm in their cause. Erminigild decided to try this, too late; he was seized by emissaries of his father, and thrown into prison in Tarragona.

Leovigild seems to have shown great patience with his son, for in spite of all he had done he was not executed, as might have been expected from the customs of irritated fathers in those times. Leovigild was convinced that the difficulty was caused by the connection of his son with the Catholics. He hoped, and almost felt sure, that if Erminigild could be separated from their influence, he would return to his old allegiance and affection for his father. The old man underrated the influence of Ingunda on her husband, although he must have known in his own case the force of conjugal counsels.

He despatched confidential messengers to the prince in prison, promising not only pardon, but a full restoration to royal favor, if he would return to the Arian faith. Erminigild remained firm, but his father continued to work upon him, hoping at last to win him back to the creed of his childhood. The prince resisted promises and threats, and after every interview declared his unalterable resolve to live and die in the Catholic communion.

Leovigild's persistence was due in the first place to his own strong conviction that the Arian creed was the only true faith, in which view he was supported by the determined convictions of his wife, who would not have allowed him to think otherwise, and also by his wish to separate his son from the opposite party, and thus ensure his allegiance for the rest of his life, since the strong body of Catholic Christians were the most powerful opponents there were in the country, to the reign of an Arian king.

One night the king sent an Arian bishop to the dungeon where Erminigild lay, to tell him that he need not even admit really the Arian faith, but that if he would but receive the communion from the Arian prelate, so that it could be publicly announced that he had, nothing more should be required of him, and his full pardon should be immediately signed. The king doubtless thought it would be enough to spread the report that the prince had outwardly conformed to Arianism, in order to break the bond between him and the rebels of the Catholic faith.

The bishop entered the cell, and went over all the ground of persuasion, which the prince had heard so often that his mind was weary of giving attention to arguments which did not affect him in the least. His mind was made up. Whether conscience forbade him to receive outwardly a sign which he did not inwardly accept, whether the memory of Ingunda, or the ancient wrongs inflicted on him by his step-mother, prevailed, he grew more and more restless and irritated by the conversation of the bishop, and at last, starting up and longing to get rid of him, he exclaimed: " As the minister of the Devil, thou canst guide only to hell. Begone, wretch! to the punishments prepared for thee!"

This was not a very pleasant answer for the bishop to receive, and he retired in great wrath. It was not a politic one for Erminigild, for when the king heard of it from the lips of the insulted and angry prelate, he broke out into a fit of ungovernable fury, and gave orders for the execution of his son. They were promptly obeyed. His head was cut off without delay, and thus ended the life of this prince of the Goths. It is said that Leovigild bitterly regretted the deed, decreed in a hasty moment, after long years of patient hope for a reconciliation with his son. Yet there is no doubt that the prince deserved the death of a traitor for his rebellion against the crown.

Erminigild was regarded by the orthodox as a martyr, and was canonized as a saint. Ancient chronicles record that the dungeon, on the night of his execution, was illuminated with celestial light, that angels hovered over the corpse, and celebrated his martyrdom with holy songs.

After they received the news of Erminigild's death, the relations of his widow, the Princess Ingunda, armed in the cause of their sister, and marched into Gothic Gaul, but Leovigild sent his remaining son, Recared, to oppose them, and he expelled the invaders.

Leovigild was now a great prince, the undisputed master of the Peninsula. He assumed more splendor than his predecessors, wore the crown in public, erected a magnificent throne in his palace at Toledo, and displayed everywhere his wealth and power. He is the first of the Visigoth kings represented on ancient coins with the royal diadem on his brow. He built cities and introduced improvements into the national legislation. He put an end to the domination of the Sueves, who had for nearly two hundred centuries troubled the country.

He stained the lustre of his reign by a relentless persecution of the orthodox or Catholic party. He bribed, or terrified the prelates into apostasy, or if they withstood him, he punished them with exile, imprisonment, or death. Goswinda, his Arian wife, was now at the summit of her power. Her rival was driven from the court, her religion was in the ascendant, her royal consort firmly seated upon his throne, the splendors of which were furnished by treasures stolen from the orthodox churches and monasteries, which he plundered without hesitation, on the plea of true religion. But her triumphs and his glory did not last long. But a few years after the execution of his rebellious son, Leovigild died, A.D. 587. He had already associated his other son with the royal dignity, and on the death of his father, Recared was unanimously acknowledged sole king of the Goths.

Strangely enough, the subject which had shaken the whole kingdom in the time of Erminigild, creating dissension and civil war, and bringing death to this turbulent prince, was now, by his brother, quietly disposed of, and the very change accomplished which the former wished to see.

Before the death of his father, Recared had been converted from Arianism to orthodoxy, but, more prudent and less impetuous than his brother, he concealed his new sentiments; above all, we may suppose, from his step-mother, Goswinda.

As determined in the new faith as his father had been in the old, Recared conceived the plan of reclaiming his subjects from heresy, which he now considered the faith of the Arians to be. He well knew what difficulties he would encounter, and had seen by experience how unwise the course of his brother had been, in attempting by arms and violence to gain his cause, the same, in pretence at least, as his own. He knew that the Goths were too fierce a race to be compelled to any measure, especially to one against which their inveterate prejudices were allied. Time and patience, with the greatest prudence, were necessary for the success of his project.

He had the happy inspiration to invite the Catholic and Arian prelates to dispute in his presence, and, by assuming the appearance of perfect impartiality between them, he laid the foundations for a change. He professed himself an enemy to all persecution for conscience sake, and exhorted the two parties to peace and harmony, and, by his own moderation, he disposed the minds of both parties to calmness and reflection. Meanwhile, he despatched messengers, who were in his confidence, to teach the same lessons in the same moderate manner throughout the provinces.

His next step was a bolder one. He restored to the Catholic churches the treasures of which they had been deprived by his predecessors, and especially by his own father. The influence of his personal character was so great, that this was accomplished quietly, and without exciting the displeasure of his Arian subjects, while, of course, the Catholic ones were well pleased. He was deservedly popular; for he was liberal to the poor, generous to all, kind and gentle in his manners, but inexorably just when occasion demanded.

When Recared saw his preparations sufficiently advanced, he assembled all his nobles and clergy at Toledo. This was on the 8th of May, 589.

He first prevailed on the assembly to pass three consecutive days in fasting and prayer, and not until these were over did the consultation begin.

He opened the business in a well-considered speech. He represented religion as a concern of the highest moment to man—not only as it involved the happiness or misery of an eternal state, but as affecting human welfare in the present life, since no society could long remain organized without its sanction. He next adverted to the two religions, Catholic and Arian, in a mild tone, but at the same time with great resolution. He appealed to the miracles alleged to have been wrought in behalf of the Catholic faith to prove its divine origin, expressing his firm belief in their reality.

His address was clear, eloquent, and long. He concluded by saying that, as after mature deliberation he himself was convinced of the truth of the Catholic faith, he had already determined to make public profession of it, though he disclaimed all intention of forcing the conscience of any other man. He submitted, however, to the assembly the consideration, that, if unity of religion could be restored to the kingdom, an end would be put to the troubles which had so long agitated it, to the destruction of national prosperity and individual happiness.

Lastly, he caused an instrument to be read, containing his abjuration of Arianism, and the confession of his belief in the co-equality of the Three Persons, and in the authority of the Catholic and Apostolic Church, and entreated all who were present to follow his example.

This discourse of Recared was received not merely with applause, but when he and his queen, who fully shared his convictions, had solemnly signed the act of confession, most of the prelates and nobles in the assembly hastened to do the same. Probably their minds had been prepared beforehand for the scene, so that the abjuration of the king did not burst upon them with the shock of surprise. So much may be effected by judicious management, rather than violence.

The Catholic faith was thus quietly declared the religion of the state. Spaniard, Sueve, and Goth were now joined in one communion, and a canon was drawn up at the suggestion of Leander, with the full concurrence of the several members present, that thenceforth no person should be admitted to the Lord's Supper who should not previously recite the symbol of belief as sanctioned by the Council of Constantinople.

Leander was the uncle of Recared, under whose influence the unfortunate Prince Erminigild had taken up arms for the Catholic Church. His second nephew possessed a balance and judgment, lacking in his brother, which made the same counsels turn to good for the cause they both espoused, rather than evil. Leander was canonized, and is one of the present saints of the Spanish Church.

Goswinda, the queen dowager, did not receive calmly the news of so great a change in the religion of the state. We may be sure she was not invited to the assembly at Toledo, and that as soon as she heard of it, she endeavored to arouse the Arian prelates to resistance.

These denounced the action of the assembly as apostasy, and in public and private inveighed against it. There were plots against the life of Recared in which Goswinda was deeply implicated, but these conspiracies were discovered, and punished, but not with rigor. The old queen, powerful no longer, was left to Heaven and her own conscience.

Recared succeeded in suppressing the French who again attacked his possessions in Southern Gaul. Carcássonne, the stronghold of the Goths, fell into the hands of the enemy, but they could not retain it, and near the same city they were utterly routed. He controlled the antagonistic elements within the kingdom. The rest of his reign was a continual effort to promote the happiness of his people; his administration was prosperous, and he enjoyed their confidence and affection.

It has been said of this king that in all his wars he was victorious, all rebellions he crushed, all conspiracies he discovered.

Recared died in 601.

CHAPTER IX.

TOLEDO—WAMBA.

TOLEDO was the capital of the Visigothic kings, a city old even in time of Leovigild, who removed the court there from Seville. According to tradition it was founded by Jews, six centuries before Christ, and named by them Toledoth, " the mother of people." Before it became the capital, it was chosen by the Spanish Church for the seat of its councils, the first of which was held there in 400 A.D.

It is on the top of a high hill, with almost perpendicular slopes descending to the river Tagus, which surrounds it on three sides. It is now approached by two bridges, on opposite sides of the town; near one of them, the bridge of San Martin, is supposed to have been the palace of the Gothic kings, close to the river and overhanging it. The cathedral, one of the finest in Spain, stands on the site of a very early building, of whose foundation nothing is known. Its stone of consecration is still preserved in the cloister of the present cathedral; it reads that the church Santa Maria was consecrated under King Recared, the Catholic, in the year 587 A.D., and that several councils took place within its walls. Tradition says it was founded by the Apostle Saint James, who is firmly believed by the Spaniards to have visited their country in person. It was dedicated to the Virgin Mary, and legend says that she descended from heaven to visit her church, and to present its bishop, Ildefonso, with a splendid chasuble or cloak. The mark of her footprint upon the stair is still shown in a chapel of the cathedral, and Murillo, the great Spanish painter, made the legend the subject of one of his beautiful pictures.

In this lofty city, protected by its position from the sudden attacks of enemies, the Goths reigned for several centuries. The city became very prosperous and important, and its wealth enormous. There were always many Jews living there, perhaps ever since the founding of the city, a people who have always brought commercial success to the places where they live, but also often dissension, for the intolerance of Christian sovereigns has led them to persecute the Jews. In the sixth Council of Toledo, a canon decreed that all future kings were to swear that they would rigorously enforce the laws against "that accursed people."

In the second half of the seventh century, when the Gothic kingdom in Spain was thus prosperous, the Catholic religion firmly established, her enemies subdued, the alien tribes merged with the older inhabitants, it became necessary to choose a king, and the electors searched about to find one wise and good enough for the office. They chose a man of princely descent, who had filled some honorable posts at court, but, tired of its splendors, he had retired from public life and was living far off from the capital. The legend goes that Leo, a holy man, afterwards Pope, at the earnest request of the electors, prayed that they might be divinely directed in their choice. He was admonished in answer to his prayers, that the man to be sought, who must wear the crown, was a laborer living in the west, and his name was Wamba. Soldiers were despatched in search of him. They travelled towards the west inquiring for him, and at last, when they were nearly out of their own country, on the borders of Portugal, they came to the place where they had been told he was living. They were sent out into the fields, and there, to their surprise no doubt, they found the future candidate to the throne of Spain following the plough and turning up his own furrows. Nevertheless, as the servants of the Gothic electors knew they must obey orders, however singular they were, the messengers bowed before the ploughman, and informed him that he had been selected as king of Spain.

Wamba laughed, and taking the information as an elaborate joke, replied lightly:

"Yes, and I shall be king about the time that my pole puts out leaves." As he spoke he struck the pole into the ground, and suddenly, as they all stood looking at it, it began to bud, and in a few minutes was covered with verdure. After this there was nothing to be said, and Wamba, yielding to the power of the miracle, suffered himself to be carried to Toledo and crowned.

So much for the legend. According to historians, Wamba was visited by the dukes of the land who informed him of the honors intended for him. He urged his advanced age, which made him loath to undertake duties requiring such labor and activity. Prayers and tears were vainly employed to move him. At length one of the dukes of the palace placed a poniard at his breast, probably a Toledo blade, and bade him choose between the sepulchre and a throne. Such a choice was no longer difficult, and Wamba yielded his assent. He begged, however, for delay, thinking that perhaps the electors would change in favor of some other candidate, but they were consistent, and he was crowned in nineteen days after his forcible proclamation.

Though Wamba was so attached to a private life and so unwilling to leave it to become king, he was fully equal to the difficulties of his new situation, although they became many, partly in consequence of his own course. He issued a decree banishing all Jews who refused to be baptized; this was not worthy of his reputation for wisdom, for the exiles all flocked to Nismes, in Gothic Gaul, where there was already a rebellion against the throne, headed by Hilderic the Count of Nismes. The Duke Paul, a Greek, despatched by Wamba to reduce the rebellion, joined it himself, took lead of the malcontents, and even prevailed on the Goths in Gaul to proclaim him king.

Wamba was armed and in camp when he received this intelligence, accompanied by a whimsical letter written by the Duke Paul in a boasting vein, as if his success had already turned his head. Wamba had found himself, at his accession, in control of an admirable army. He marched across the Pyrenees, subduing on the way all the places which had risen against him, and came to Narbonne, the old stronghold of the Goths, where Ataulphus kept his honeymoon with the Roman princess Placidia. Paul had fled to Nismes, leaving Narbonne in the hands of an able general, who, with the citizens, made a vigorous re-resistance, but the city was forced to yield, and the royal army marched against Nismes, where Paul was entrenched with his bravest troops. The assault was made with great fury and as furiously repelled. During a whole day the Goths made no impression on the place, and when the darkness of night stopped the desperate struggle, they were still further depressed by the report that a considerable body of German and French auxiliaries were advancing to the aid of the rebels. This report was a fabrication of the artful Paul; but for a time it answered his purpose. He was soon, however, confounded in his turn by the arrival of ten thousand fresh troops, despatched by Wamba, who was himself now approaching the scene of strife. At the dawn of the following morning Paul beheld, from the top of a tower, the increased force of the enemy drawn up for a new and more vigorous assault. But Paul was no coward; he resolved to withstand the coming onset as befitted one who had staked every thing for a throne. Knowing that something must be done to relieve the sudden despondency of his followers, he hastily assembled them, and harangued them with characteristic volubility. He said: "Old Wamba has triumphed hitherto, but only because he has found little or no resistance. He finds now that he has to do with hard walls and with hearts still harder than walls, and he accordingly begins to display his natural cowardice. He has brought up all his force to resist us; destroy that handful of men in the plain below, and you may march unopposed from the Rhine to the Bætis."

His discourse somewhat relieved his troops, though he could not prevail on them to sally forth and fight on the plain. The contest was for some time vigorously maintained from the fortifications; but the arrows and other missiles of the assailants were so destructive that the ranks of the besieged were fearfully thinned.

"These Goths are no cowards, Paul!" they exclaimed, as they cast reproachful looks on the leader who had sacrificed them to his selfish ambition.

The combat had continued for five hours without intermission, when Wamba's general cried:

"Come, soldiers! bring fire and scaling-ladders! The sun is high, and shameful it will be for us if we do not enter the fortress to-day!"

Instantly the gates were burned, the walls surmounted. The struggle on the summit was terrible, but short. It was renewed in the streets, where the sword of the Goth still pursued its victims. Such of the defenders as could escape fled to the amphitheatre, an immense Roman building like the Coliseum at Rome, built long before for the exhibition of athletic games. Its ruins are still standing in the fine old city of Nismes.

But here the rebels fell in with some of the inhabitants of the city, incensed with them for bringing them into misfortune, who, also with the idea of winning the favor of Wamba, now they knew he was hard by, pursued and massacred the flying crowd. Paul himself every moment expected death, but he was intentionally spared by the indignant populace, while they wreaked their vengeance on his relatives. One of these was pierced before his eyes, another at his side, as he, left unharmed, stood on the steps of the amphitheatre.

As the day began to close, Paul threw off his royal apparel, and with a few of his companions sought refuge in the vaults of the huge building. There he passed a night more bitter than death.

The next morning the inhabitants, resolving to throw themselves on the clemency of their victor, sent their bishop to meet him. The prelate, in his splendid pontifical robes, found the monarch about four miles from the city, and by a touching address obtained a promise that no more blood should be spilt. Wamba now entered triumphant into Nismes, and was received by the pardoned inhabitants with unfeigned gratitude.

Paul, with the other leading rebels, was dragged by the hair of the head from the vaults of the amphitheatre and consigned to a prison to await the doom that was to be awarded him. The conqueror caused the dead to be buried, gave liberty to many captives, and endeavored to repair the evils which the city had sustained, and then he ordered his crestfallen rival to be brought before the tribunal.

The behavior of the duke was now as humble as it had been bold. When he was asked by his sovereign what reason he had to rebel, and whether he had ever received just cause of offence, he admitted that he had received only benefits from the hands of the king, and that it was his ambition alone which had impelled him to ingratitude and treason. He prostrated himself at the feet of the victor, and begged that his life might be spared.

"Thy life," replied King Wamba, "and the lives of thy companions have I promised to spare, though such indulgence is little deserved."

The judges of the tribunal, hastily assembled for the occasion, voted for the death of the most guilty, but the merciful monarch satisfied himself with condemning them to have their crowns shaved and to submit to a religious confinement within the walls of Toledo.

Gothic Gaul was now pacified. Wamba deposed the governors of some places, and put others more trustworthy in their stead. He banished all the Jews, as the moving cause of contention, and then went home to his capital.

The return of the king was met with great rejoicing, and his entry into the capital triumphant. Before him marched the rebels, their heads and chins shaved, their feet bare, and their bodies clothed in camel's hair. Paul was conspicuous among the rest by the crown made of leather which adorned his brow, as an emblem of his futile pretence at sovereignty. The jeers of the populace and confinement for life were, for that time, a mild punishment for the treason he had committed against his sovereign.

After these glorious exploits, Wamba applied himself to the interest of his subjects, and cultivated the arts of peace. He strengthened the walls of Toledo, improved the temporal condition of his people, and stimulated the efforts of the clergy in making them good Christians. He persecuted the Jews who remained with vigor, forcing them to assume the name of Christians and conform to their habits, which seems now unwise and tyrannical.

But the customs of the Jews, as well as their denial of Christ, were detestable and loathesome to the Christians, and all their thrift and wealth, which was generally regarded as ill-gotten, could not recommend them to their neighbors who professed a different faith. So although they built splendid palaces and lived in them, and possessed jewels and precious stones they dared not wear in public, they could associate only with each other, in their own quarter of the city, closely watched by royal authority, and performing the rites of their religion by stealth. From time to time, such oppression resulted in rebellion, then banishment, then matters settled down again, to repeat once more and again the same course. The advantages they found in Spain for their commerce, then very lucrative, induced many Jews to keep on living there, in spite of the severity with which they were treated. Naturally they detested a government with which they were in no sympathy whatever, and were always ready for rebellion.

Wamba's zeal, judgment, and vigilance foresaw the danger of invasion which already threatened his country from the Saracens, as they were called, followers of Mohammed, who lived not far off on the shores of

Africa, masters of all that region from the Nile to the Atlantic ocean. The fleet by which Wamba defended the coast long kept these Mussulmans in awe, and had his successors shown equal prudence and activity, they might have saved Spain from the Saracenic invasion.

In the midst of his wise and active career, a strange thing befell King Wamba, which put a premature end to his reign, though not to his life.

On the 14th of October, 680, the king fell into a state of insensibility, and seemed to be deprived of life. All the servants and members of the court who surrounded him were convinced that he was dying, and as there seemed to be no doubt about it, in conformity with the custom of the time, his head was shaved, and he was transformed from a layman into a member of the monastic profession.

This custom came about from the practice of pious persons who, when they found themselves in danger of death, used to assume the tonsure and the penitential garb, engaging to continue them through the rest of their lives, if God spared them. This penance became so common, that those who did not use it were regarded as wanting in piety, and so, if the sick man were unable to ask himself for the monk's habit, his relations or friends made bold to invest him with it; and in case he recovered, his obligation to a penitential life was just as great as if it had been imposed at his own request, since as he was charitably assumed to be pious, he must wish to become a penitent.

This custom had already given rise to such abuses,

that a late king of the Goths had decreed that such obligation imposed by others should be void unless the penitent shall ratify it when returned to a sound state of mind; but in spite of this innovation, in the time of King Wamba the practice was in full force.

The king recovered his full health and sense in about twenty-four hours, but his doom was sealed. Though his profession of penitence had been entirely involuntary, his head was shaven, he wore the garb of a monk, he was no longer of the world, and must retire from public life.

Thus strangely disqualified from pursuing his accustomed life, and fulfilling all the schemes he had on hand for the benefit of his kingdom, Wamba submitted, without resistance, to the force of circumstance, and passed the remainder of his days in a monastery near Burgos.

No one tells us whether he made a good monk, whether he cheerfully returned to the plough whence he was taken to become king, whether he murmured against the will of Heaven, as he regarded it, or was glad to be relieved from the cares of state.

People wondered, then and afterwards, whether Wamba's brief, but serious, attack of indisposition were a natural or contrived event. Two chroniclers of the ninth century assert that the trance of the king, and his consequent tonsure, were the work of Ervigius, a royal prince who had long aspired to the throne. According to their view, he administered a draught to the monarch which he intended to be powerful enough to destroy reason, if not life itself. The effect, if not that he had anticipated, was just as well suited to his aim ; in the lethargy which followed the dose, the monastic penitence was imposed upon the king, perhaps in good faith, by the piety of his royal attendants.

However this may be, Ervigius became the successor of Wamba upon the throne, in consequence of three authentic instruments which he was able to produce : the first, which was signed by the great officers of the palace, stated the fact of the habit and tonsure being imposed ; the second, signed by Wamba himself, contained his renunciation of the crown in favor of Ervigius ; and the third was a paper, also signed by Wamba, enjoining upon the bishop of Toledo to proceed with the coronation of his successor.

So Wamba passes out of history, into the shadow of a monastery, and Ervigius reigns. But from that time, the power and splendor of the Gothic kings declined towards their fall.

Toledo, as it now stands upon the summit of a barren hill, retains but few traces of the days of its ancient Gothic splendor. Since Leovigild established his court in the city his palace has fallen to pieces, and its site is only guessed at. Another more splendid cathedral has risen upon the ruins of that where Recared abjured Arianism, and other churches, of architecture called Gothic, in a style little dreamed of by the builders of that early time, are also falling into ruin, leaving only the broken fragments of pointed arch and slender spire. The steep streets, winding about the almost perpendicular sides of the hill, and so narrow that you can touch both sides at once, were the work of the Moors who followed the Goths; and so are light and graceful buildings of arabesque tracery and the horse-shoe arch, also falling into ruin. Yet still in many of the low, solid structures of stone, we may imagine we see the work of the real Gothic builder. It must be remembered that the style of architecture called Gothic, came into use many centuries after the kingdom of the Visigoths in Spain was forgotten, so that even in their ancient capital the arches and towers called "Gothic" have nothing whatever to do with the Goth, but are of much later date, erected by Moors or Christians who took pains to destroy whatever was left of the early architecture of the real Goths.

The guide-book leaves little foothold in this present age for the Goth in Toledo, but there are houses still there which one may imagine to have been standing in the time of Wamba. A huge gate-way frowns upon the narrow street, with stone pillars surmounted by balls. Inside the great door is a smaller door, which opens mysteriously in answer to a knock. Within is a court-yard; and a narrow stairway, built into the wall, and lighted by a dim lamp from an alcove, leads to a corridor from which open long, low rooms with heavy beams across the ceiling, and huge mysterious side doors, that may not have been unlocked within the memory of man. These houses may be modern, may be Moorish, but the romantic traveller prefers to fancy that they were in existence before the glory of the Visigothic kings had departed from their ancient capital, and that the ghost of Wamba, after a life so abruptly withdrawn from the cares of the world, or the restless spirit of Roderic might at any moment slowly open that unfrequented door, green with damp and stiff with the rust of ages.

CHAPTER X.

RODERICK, THE LAST OF THE GOTHS.

WHERE a monarchy is elective, we must not expect the same regularity of succession and the same precision of dates as if, at the death of one king, all men had determined that his son should succeed him. It seems probable, indeed, that Witiza and Roderick reigned in different parts of Spain at the same time. It seems probable that Roderick drove Witiza into exile. It is certain that the vices of Witiza and his selfish administration of power enraged his people against him. While Witiza reigned at Toledo, Roderick reigned in the south, in Andalusia. Roderick had been in danger under the cruelty of Witiza, as it is supposed that his father suffered from him. For it is said that the tyrant put out Theodofred's eyes. Roderick was the son of Theodofred. Fearing a like fate or worse, Roderick escaped from Spain, and allied himself with the Greek emperors. They consented to assist him in a struggle against the tyrant. Witiza's fate is uncertain. As we have said, he seems to have been exiled and to have died in exile. What is certain is that Roderick, who had before held control in Andalusia only, assumed the rule of all Spain in the year 709.

But he did not assume this rule without opposition. The sons of Witiza still lived and expected to succeed him. The bishop of Toledo, Oppas, either their uncle or their brother, was at the head of the church. A certain Count Julian, who held an almost independent command in Africa, where the Goths possessed the posts of Ceuta, opposite to Gibraltar, Tangier, and Arsilla, belonged to their party of opposition. It was in the face of as formidable rivals as were thus represented that Roderick assumed the crown. Some form of election probably preceded his coronation, but the history, or rather the legend, is very vague about this, as it is in all the early history of Roderick.

It was now a century since the success of Mohammed had given the signal for that marvellous wave of conquest, in which the Saracen armies swept so soon over Northern Africa and Western Asia. At the point where Africa comes closest to Europe, where they say even that it once touched Europe, the wave of their conquest had been flung back by the stubborn resistance of the three Gothic garrisons which have been named. The Goths, in their prosperity, had taken possession of this part of Mauritania, which we now call Morocco. It should not be forgotten that it is one of the most fertile regions of the world, and were it not for its wretched misgovernment, the wheat harvests of Morocco would supply the food of Europe to-day. Indeed, when Roderick assumed the crown, the only considerable experience which the Goths had in war, was on these African fields. Excepting in the contests by which he had secured his own supremacy, the Goths had known no considerable wars for generations on Spanish soil.

Of the Spanish army in Africa, Count Julian, as has been said, was commander. He had defeated Musa, the Saracen leader. Musa was called El Zahani. He was commissioned as governor of these regions by Miramolin Almanzor, who was the caliph of all Northern Africa at this time. But of a sudden, wholly to Musa's surprise, he received a visit from Count Julian, who offered to surrender to him the strongholds of the Goths, if he would give the assistance of the Saracen army to the party which was opposed to King Roderick. Musa was afraid to meddle with such lofty treason himself, and sent the traitor to Arabia with letters introducing him to Miramolin, the caliph. The caliph received him gladly, approved his plan, and sent him back to Musa with his approval. The treason was so atrocious, that to this hour Count Julian is called "the Traitor" in the legends and histories of Spain, almost as if there were no other traitor. Musa put his sincerity to a test by sending over a hundred Arabs and four hundred Africans, under Tarif, to the northern shore. This chief, almost unknown, has had this curious fortune, that he has given the name to Tarifa, the place where he landed, and thus, because of the duties of goods imposed there, his name lives in the word "tariff," used so largely in the commercial legislation of the civilized world. All passed as Julian had promised. The men of the desert found themselves free to range at their will through exquisite Andalusia. They gave, as well they might, the most tempting accounts of the country which had been betrayed to them. The next spring Musa sent over five thousand soldiers, under the command of Tarik, whose name, also, lives to us in "Gibraltar," where he landed, which was "Gebel-al-Tarik" (the mountain of Tarik).* The reader will remember that Gibraltar and Ceuta were the two pillars of Hercules. The symbols of these pillars still survive in the arms of Spain, on the Spanish coins, and in the familiar mark taken from them to designate a dollar ($), which represents the two pillars of Hercules encircled by the scroll "*Ne plus ultra*" (nothing beyond). It was the destiny of Spain, in opening the western world to Europe, to demonstrate the falsity of her own ancient motto.

Roderick heard of the treason of his officers, and did not flinch in his duty. But, at the best, the contest was not an easy one, and Roderick and his Goths were not at their best. His own right of succession was disputed. Beside this, the Goths had been for generations now at peace. It is at this juncture that we are to place the legend of his visit to the cave of Hercules:

There came to the king the keepers of that house which is in Toledo which they call Pleasure with Pain; and it was called also by another name, The Honor of God. Now this house had been built by Hercules, and Hercules had commanded that neither king nor lord of Spain should seek to know that which was within. And every one instead should put a lock upon the doors of this house, and fasten it with his

* The reader must not confound Tarif and Tarik.

GIBRALTAR.

key. And the King Don Roderick did the same. But remembering this afterward, in an evil moment he insisted on opening all the locks, his knights in vain attempting to dissuade him. They opened all the locks, and the king pushed the door and entered with his chiefs. Here, in a square hall, they found a bed, and in the bed the statue of a man exceeding great, and in the man's hand was a scroll. And on the scroll the king read that the man was Hercules the Strong—" Never could any conquer me, save only Death. Look well to what thou doest, for from this world thou wilt carry with thee nothing but the good which thou hast done."

After Don Roderick had read this he was very sorry he had undertaken this enterprise. But he would not retreat, but pushed on with his chiefs. They came into an apartment of which one part was white as snow, and that over against it more black than pitch. One part was green as emerald, and that which was over against it was redder than fresh blood. There was a door in it, cunningly made, and on the door a legend that Hercules built this house in the 306th year of Adam. And when the king had read these letters, and understood that which they said, he opened the door, and when it was opened they found Hebrew letters which said: " This house is one of the wonders of Hercules." And when they had read these letters they saw a niche made in that pillar, in which was a coffer of silver, right subtly wrought, and after a strange manner, and it was gilded, and covered with many precious stones, and of great price, and it was fastened with a lock of mother-of-pearl. And this was made in such a manner that it was a strange thing, and there were cut upon it Greek letters which said: "It cannot be but that the king, in whose time this coffer shall be opened, shall see wonders before his death: thus said Hercules the Lord of Greece and of Spain, who knew some of those things which are to come." And when the king understood this, he said: "Within this coffer lies that which I seek to know, and which Hercules has so strongly forbidden to be known." And he took the lock and broke it with his hands, for there was no other who durst break it; and when the lock was broken, and the coffer open, they found nothing within except a white cloth folded between two pieces of copper; and he took it and opened it, and found Moors portrayed therein, with turbans and banners in their hands, and with their swords round their necks, and their bows behind them at the saddle-bow; and over these figures were letters which said: "When this cloth shall be opened, and these figures seen, men apparelled like them shall conquer Spain and shall be Lords thereof."

This picturesque fiction, as we need hardly say, is the work of later times. The hard fact is that Theodemir, Roderick's lieutenant in Andalusia, reported to his sovereign the invarion of the Saracens. Their first force of five thousand soldiers was enlarged by reinforcements of seven thousand more. Theodemir wrote to Roderick that a horde of Africans had landed—"So strange is their appearance that we might take them for inhabitants of the sky. Send me more troops without a moment's delay. Collect all who could bear arms." Roderick was, at the moment, attempting to reduce some of the adherents of Witiza's family. But the call was too pressing to be disregarded. The king rallied his utmost forces, and appeared on the scene of action with an army so large that the Moors were dismayed. It is said that he had ninety thousand men in arms. But Tarik had literally burned his ships behind him. His men knew he had. He told them that in victory was their only chance. And the result was the reward of his desperate courage. In the opening skirmishes of the war the Moors held the advantage which they at first won. And in the great conflict, which for its consequences must be counted one of the critical battles of history, they were successful.

The two armies met on the plains of Xeres, about two leagues from Cadiz. It is the Xeres, whose vineyards are so well known to the modern world for their wine. The little stream of the Guadalete, which falls into the bay near Cadiz, divided the two armies. After three days of skirmishing they joined in serious battle. Stories which cannot be fully credited speak of Roderick as going into battle on a car of ivory, drawn by two white mules, in a robe of silk embroidered with gold. And Gibbon well says that Alaric, the great Gothic leader, might well have blushed to see his unworthy successor. But the chariot and the robe, and the diadem of pearls which go with them, are probably the creation of the sneers of conquerors. Roderick does not seem to have misbehaved in the fight itself. The multitude of the

Goths indeed would have secured their success, had they been quite sure of the loyalty of all their forces. As it was, they pressed the Moors severely. Again Tarik had to remind his men that they could only retire to the sea, and ask what they would do there. He led the way in person, in an attack on the enemy. His men followed willingly, fighting for victory or paradise. The Goths were not used to such enemies. They did not yield without a struggle. It is said that sixteen thousand men were killed in the battle. The issue was, that the Gothic army was broken by Tarik's impetuous attack. The divided sections of it retreated, and at last fled in confusion. Roderick himself in the flight was drowned in the Quadalquivir. The Moors took possession of his diadem, his robes, and his horse. And some head, called Roderick's, was sent as far as the palace at Damascus, as a trophy of the battle. But in truth the body of the king had been lost in the river.

The historians of both parties account for this rout by alleging treason in the army of Roderick The two sons of Witiza, and his brother the Bishop of Toledo, held important posts, and their defection at a critical juncture is enough to account for the defeat, without any cowardice on the part of the king. The pursuit continued for three days, and the remnants of the Gothic army were for the moment scattered.

Tarik received from Musa instructions which bade him wait before attempting the subjugation of the Peninsula. But Count Julian, "the Traitor," gave other and wiser advice. He knew the Gothic force, and he knew that they must act promptly, if they were to succeed at all. By a bold push he took the town of Cordova. The garrison retired to the church, and there maintained a siege for three months. Tarik advanced, through La Mancha, to the Tagus, and appeared under the walls of Toledo. The city capitulated on terms which allowed the continuance of religious rites in some churches, and permitted such citizens as wished, to depart with their property. From that time the Moor reigned in Toledo, though Cordova and Granada were more agreeable capitals. And this quaint and curious city still shows memorials of Moorish sway, mixed with the houses of Goths, which still show the escutcheons of the men who fought with Roderick. Tarik rewarded the Jews he found there, by terms of toleration, which repaid in a manner the essential services they had rendered him from the beginning. Tarik did not tarry at Toledo even. He continued his triumphal march to the bay of Biscay, and only returned to Toledo when it was necessary for him to meet the wrath of his master Musa.

Musa had followed his lieutenant with a new army of eighteen thousand men. He marched against Seville and Merida, which were still held by garrisons loyal to Roderick. When he beheld the remains of Roman art, which have been described in another chapter, Musa said: " The human race must have united their art and power to found this city. Happy shall be the man who masters it." After a long siege of the city, the "*Emeriti*," whose ancestors had been so called because the veterans of Augustus, surrendered. Musa was able to go on and meet his disobedient but successful lieutenant.

Tarik met him midway between Merida and Toledo. Musa demanded and received a rigid account of the treasures of Spain. Tarik was suspected and abused; he was imprisoned, reviled, and scourged. Yet, after these insults, Musa appointed him to command in the reduction of the northeast. The Gothic armies were driven, by his success, beyond the Pyrenees. After three hundred years of conquest they had to take refuge in the " Province " of Gaul.

Little more than two years sufficed for the reduction of Spain to a province which rendered allegiance to the caliph at Damascus. In some of the valleys of the mountains were left Christian fugitives who had not surrendered. In most of the conquered cities the Christians were permitted to maintain their rites. For some time Theodemir, the spirited officer, whom we have seen as first meeting the onslaught of the Moors, maintained that sort of war in which Spain delights, and of which her name— " guerrilla," " a little war "—has been adopted by all nations. But Theodemir at last consented to pay tribute, to give up some cities which he held, and not to make any further efforts against the caliph.

It was in the year 411 that Ataulphus had taken possession of Spain, where Vandals, Ulans, and Sueves had led the way, and had established his capital there. Just three centuries after, in the year 711, Roderick lost his kingdom and his life. He is popularly called the last of the Goths, and properly so if we mean the last of the Gothic kings. Theodemir can hardly be called a king, and Pelayo, from whose valor later kings will claim, is only a rebel, in the mountains.

The downfall of Roderick and his people makes a subject too pathetic to have been neglected in literature. Mr. Southey's "Roderick, the Last of the Goths," published in 1814, had in that day a reputation of its own. But it won that reputation rather by the learning with which the author had compiled it, than to any interest which he added to Roderick's mournful story. A very short extract is sufficent to give a notion of its quality. Here is a passage in which the siege of Merida is referred to:

RODERICK, THE LAST OF THE GOTHS.

" They went forth ;
They cross'd the stream ; and when Romano turned
For his last look toward the Castilian towers,
Far off the Moorish standards in the light
Of morn were glittering, where the miscreant host
Toward the Lusitanian capital
To lay their siege advanced ; the eastern breeze
Bore to the fearful travellers far away
The sound of horn and tambour o'er the plain.
All day they hasten'd, and when evening fell,
Sped toward the setting sun, as if its line
Of glory came from heaven to point their course.
But feeble were the feet of that old man
For such a weary length of way ; and now
Being pass'd the danger (for in Merida
Sacaru long in resolute defence
Withstood the tide of war), with easier pace
The wanderers journey'd on ; till having cross'd
Rich Tagus, and the rapid Zezere,

They from Albardos' hoary height beheld
Pine-forest, fruitful vale, and that fair lake
Where Alcoa, mingled there with Baza's stream,
Rests on its passage to the Western Sea—
That sea the aim and boundary of their toil.

MOORISH TOWER. TOLEDO.

PART III.

CHAPTER XI.

THE CALIPHATE OF CORDOVA.

THE people who defeated Roderick the Goth and took possession of his kingdom, were the followers of Islam, or Mohammedans, who were persuaded by their creed that they could conquer the whole world. They were so successful in battle that they overran the whole of Arabia, Egypt, and Northern Africa, and in less than a hundred years from the time when their religion was established they had made for themselves a foothold in Spain.

Mohammed, the founder of their religion was born in Mecca about five centuries after Christ. His followers believe him to be the real Messiah, and date their years from him as we date ours from the birth of Christ. The Koran, which is their book of laws, exacts military service from every one, and assures the joys of heaven to every martyr who falls in battle, so that the armies of their chiefs were large, and the courage of their warriors reliable. Those with whom we have to do are called Moors, because of their residence in Morocco, and in general they bear in the history of that time the name of Saracens, by which name they were called by the Christian writers and crusaders of the middle ages. They were the detestation of the Christian world, because they denied the supreme authority of Jesus Christ, and because they very early took possession of Jerusalem and the Holy Sepulchre, which they have retained, with brief intervals, until this day.

In all the full force and glory of their first triumphs they swept over Northern Africa, and made their way into the heart of Spain, intending to carry the banner of the prophet to the very shores of the Baltic, and, indeed, subjugate all Europe on their way back to Damascus, which was the home of their highest ruler.

Abderahman, their leader, carried the Moslem army into France, destroying every thing before him; but near Tours he was checked in a memorable battle by the famous Charles Martel (A.D. 732). Three hundred thousand Saracens fell under the sword, say the old chroniclers, with their usual exaggeration. It was a great victory, and all Christendom breathed freely when it was over. The fight was long and bloody; when darkness came the ground was strewn with bodies, and Abderahman, the Moslem leader, was among the slain. But the Christians could not be sure that the victory was theirs, and they remained in their tents under arms all night. At break of day they were prepared to renew the struggle; the tents of the Arabs, extending as far as the eye could reach, were still before them, but not a living creature came forth to meet them. The enemy had abandoned their camp, their own wealth, and the immense plunder which they had amassed in their hitherto victorious progress.

Relinquishing all for the sake of safety, they had silently crept away, in this case without folding their tents, after the manner of the typical Arab.

Christendom was saved. Pope and monk, prince and peasant thanked heaven in an ecstasy of devotion for so signal a victory.

After this the Moslems, as the followers of Mohammed were also called, recognizing that they were not invulnerable, moderated their ambition; and those who had established themselves in Spain now turned their attention to prosperous living there.

The country was governed, at first, by viceroys called emirs, sent from the caliphate at Damascus. This lasted about forty years, but they were not years of tranquillity. Twenty different emirs had been either appointed, or had raised themselves to direct the government. Jealousy of one another, revolt, rebellion, disturbed the repose of the country. The caliphs were too remote to remedy such evils.

At this time there reigned at Damascus the house of the Omeyyades, but civil dissensions prevailed there, as in Spain, and in a contest between this family and another called the Abbasides, all the Omeyyades were treacherously massacred by the others, who took the throne for themselves. All but two were killed: one of them fled to a corner of Arabia, where his descendants ruled for a long time; the other became great in Spain.

He was named Abderahman. He effected his escape from Damascus with horses and money, and choosing unfrequented paths, succeeded in joining a band of Bedouins, wandering Arab tribes, who from time immemorial have lived in tents, passing from one place to another, with no continuing city. Their tents were then, doubtless, as they are now, dark brown, with low, shelving sides like the roof of a house. They wear a woollen garment with a belt round it containing their weapons, which are numerous and dangerous; over their head is thrown the picturesque *kufia*, or square handkerchief folded cornerwise. Their hands are against every man, and and so it has been always; but they lead peaceful lives among themselves with their flocks and herds, and practise, after their own fashion, an open hospitality.

They received the prince kindly, and he lived with them some time, accommodating himself to their simple habits, but passing from one tribe to another for fear of being traced and discovered by the enemies of his house. From Arabia he thus wandered into Africa, through Egypt, as far as Barca, where the governor, who was devoted to the Abbasides, heard about him. Learning that a young stranger was within his territory, who might answer to the description of the fugitive prince everywhere sought by the new caliph, this governor sent out agents in all directions to seize the youth.

The tribe of Bedouins with whom he was, became very fond of him, and, besides, they were always ready to do an ill-turn to the agents of civilization. When, therefore, a troop of horsemen, one evening, surrounded their tents, inquiring for a handsome young Syrian, they thought of nothing less than

MOORISH MILLS, CORDOVA.

betraying their guest. They replied that they had seen such a person, and in fact he was at that moment out hunting wild beasts with some of their own young men; that very likely the party might be found passing the night in a valley, at some distance, which they described at length, with a careful description how to get there. The officers of the governor were very much obliged, 'and rode off towards the valley. As soon as they were surely off, the Bedouins ran and woke up their guest, who, all the time, had been comfortably asleep in the best spare tent.

Abderahman was full of gratitude. As it was no longer safe for him to linger there, he fled with some of the bold young men of the tribe into the desert. After some days of fatigue and thirst on friendless plains of sand, he reached a town in Mauritania, of which the sheik was a kinsman of his mother. Here he was well received and protected.

About this time there was a meeting in Cordova of some eighty of the wisest chiefs of the Arabs, to discuss the condition of affairs of state, the confusion around them, and the anarchy at Damascus. Their chiefs were all devoted to the family of the Omeyyades, and they regarded the Abbasides as usurpers.

One of the members of the meeting, a sheik named Wahib, recited the tale of the wandering prince of the royal Omeyyades, and ended by saying:

"Abderahman still remains in Mauritania; let him be our sovereign."

The proposal was received with unanimous applause. Wahib, with a companion, deputed by the assembly to offer an independent crown to the young prince, passed over into Africa, found him, and laid before him his mission. They did not disguise the difficulties to be contended with, but they assured him of their own fidelity, and of the obedience of many tribes. The prince immediately accepted the proposal.

"Noble deputies," said he, "I will unite my destiny with yours. I will go and fight with you. Young as I am, misfortune has already proved me, and has not yet found me wanting."

Abderahman felt bound to consult his relatives, the sheiks, who had so kindly received him, and take their opinion.

"Go, my son," said his kinsman, the oldest of all. "It is the finger of Heaven that beckons you. Your scimitar shall restore the honor of your line."

Every young man in the tribe longed to accompany the prince; he selected from them seven hundred and fifty well-armed horsemen for the expedition.

It was a bold undertaking, to overthrow the agent of a well-established government, and to build up an independent kingdom in a country full of turbulent spirits. The Christians, although conquered, were not subdued, but ready to rise at any moment, while the officers of the ruling caliph, both great and small, were prepared to resist the overthrow of the existing power.

The emir then in control of Spain under the new Abbaside caliph, was named Yussuf. He happened to be returning from Saragossa with a couple of captives laden with chains, when, as he was halting one day in his pavilion, on account of the heat of noon-day, among the mountains, on his way from Toledo to Cordova, he was surprised by the appearance of a messenger, hot and breathless with haste, who presented to him an anonymous note addressed to himself. The letter informed him that his reign was about to expire, that the destroyer of his power was rapidly approaching.

While Yussef was trying to make out what this could mean, another messenger, despatched by his son from Cordova, came up, with the startling intelligence that a prince of the Omeyyades, invited by Arabian, Syrian, and Egyptian sheiks, was already advancing with a body of troops.

In a transport of fury, Yussef ordered the two prisoners he had with him, although they had nothing at all to do with the business, to be cut to pieces, after which, having disposed of them, he hastened towards Cordova, despatching messengers in all directions to raise troops for his defence.

Abderahman landed on the southern coast of Spain in the early part of the year 755. The people received him with open arms, and shouts of welcome. His appearance was greatly in his favor, his bearing majestic, his countenance open and gracious. His march to Seville was one continued triumph, twenty thousand scimitars, it is said, were at his disposal. The towns through which he passed and those in the neighborhood sent deputies with their submission, and the offer of their services.

Yussef and his party offered a stout resistance, but the bravery of Abderahman and the enthusiasm of his followers drove them from their territory, and made the emir negotiate for peace. In the short space of one year the prince had triumphed over all opposition, and established himself as king, independent of control from the Caliph of Damascus, whose sovereignty he did not acknowledge.

Abderahman, now at peace, devoted himself to the improvement of his capital. Under his rule and that of his successors, Cordova came to be a magnificent city. Abderahman, by building embankments, narrowed the bed of the Guadalquivir, and transformed the space rescued from the waters into extensive gardens. He is said to have been the first who transplanted the palm into the Peninsula, where it was not native, although the climate suits it well. He is described by Arabic poets as saying to the tree: "Beautiful palm! thou, like me, art a stranger in the land ; but breezes from our West kiss thy broad leaves, thy roots strike into a fertile soil, thy head rises into a pure heaven. Before I was banished from my home, my tears bedewed thy kindred, upon the banks of the Euphrates, but the palm and the river have forgotten my grief."

For nearly three centuries after this, Spain was governed by the descendants of the house of Omeyyah, of whom the first was the fugitive Prince Abderahman. During this time the sovereign of Damascus was not of this family, because the throne had passed into the hands of their enemies, of the house of Abbas. These caliphs were too much occupied with troubles at home, in securing their own seats, to disturb the new dynasty in Spain, a province too far off in those days to be easily controlled. Yussuf, the deposed emir, and after his death, his sons were always ready to make trouble, and raise sedition; but the party of the king always proved the stronger, and the government, although seldom without discord, became firmly established.

The period during which the family of Omeyyah thus reigned in the Peninsula forms the most brilliant part of the history of the Arabs in Spain. The new government resembled in form that of the Eastern caliphs. The sovereign was called the "Commander of the Faithful," and his supremacy was both spiritual and temporal.

The caliph had the right to select a successor from his own family. The princes of the blood were entrusted to the care of learned men, to be taught the duties befitting their station. In the academies of Cordova, which were celebrated, they mingled in disputation, and often carried off the prizes for poetry and eloquence. Many of them amused their leisure with writing poetry, and wrote elaborate works, which have maintained to this day their reputation with Arabic scholars.

The Omeyyades, in general, ruled their kingdom with an authority founded in the affection of their subjects, as is shown by their long reigns, their peaceful deaths, and the unbroken line of succession in one family for many years. They supported a large military force, often keeping two or three armies in the field at the same time. The flower of these forces was a body-guard of twelve thousand men, some of them Christians, superbly equipped, and with officers belonging to the royal family.

These monarchs displayed their munificence in building palaces, mosques, and hospitals. The Arabs have always shown a love for moving water, and a knowledge of the great importance of irrigation. They constructed aqueducts which rivalled in their porportions those of the Romans, penetrating the sides of mountains, or crossing the valleys upon lofty arches. Fountains sparkled in their gardens, and places now parched and bare, were, in the days of the Spanish Arab, rich and verdant gardens made by the careful irrigation they understood so well.

It was in the reign of another Abderahman of this family, that the splendid palace of Azhara was built, of which now nothing remains but a few fragments of broken pillars. It was a fairy palace. The roof is said to have been supported by more than four thousand pillars of variegated marble. The floors and walls were of the same material; the chief apartments were adorned with fountains. The whole was surrounded with magnificent gardens, in which a pavilion stood, resting on pillars of white marble ornamented with gold, in the centre of which was a fountain of quicksilver which played all the time, reflecting the rays of the sun.

Not a vestige of this splendor remains, but the Mosque of Cordova, although it is denuded of its original decorations, and most of its ornament, is still standing, to give an idea of the scale of magnificence of the Spanish Caliphs. The first impression on entering it is of a maze of pillars. It has often been compared to pine-forest, where vistas of lofty trunks are seen overarched by branches. Of these pillars there were once more than twelve hundred, all different, for they were brought from different countries, France, Carthage, and even Constantinople. They are of marble of different hues and kinds, green and red jasper, deep black, white, red rose, and emerald porphyry.

In the day of its glory, the gates of the Mosque were of embossed bronze; myriads of lamps illumined the lofty roof, which glistened with gilding and vivid colors. Its walls were carved like lacework, and its arches were studded with emeralds and rubies.

The jewels and gold have long been stolen, the rich coloring of the walls is hidden by whitewash; in the very middle of the forest of pillars, a modern chapel was built in the time of Charles V. But in spite of so much ignorance and neglect, enough of the building remains to testify to the magnificence and religious ardor of the dynasty, which could spend vast wealth in its erection.

The Spanish Arabs reached the height of their importance in the reign of Alhakem the Second, a monarch who employed his despotic power for the real happiness and improvement of his subjects. In his refined taste, his desire for knowledge, and his liberal patronage, he may be ranking among the most enlightened rulers. He assembled the eminent scholars of his time, both native and foreigners, at his

MOSQUE AT CORDOVA.

court, and to Cordova. He made his palace the familiar resort of men of letters, and selected suitable persons to write books for him about natural history, or the history of mankind. He was himself a student, and above all intent upon collecting for himself a fine library. He employed agents all over the world, to collect manuscripts for him.

Such a spirit in the sovereign gave a literary impulse to the whole of Spain. Not only men, but women, of the highest rank devoted themselves to letters, and contended for prizes in eloquence and poetry. Cordova was the centre of all this learning. The reputation of its schools attracted scholars from all Christendom. For this period of Saracen literary brilliancy corresponds with a time of deepest barbarism in the rest of Europe, when the only libraries were collections, in monasteries, of three or four hundred volumes. The great library of Cordova is said to have contained six hundred thousand.

Such an elevation of wealth and intellectual development did not last very long. The successes of Alhakem were less distinguished, and the empire was broken up by dissension. The magnificent capital dwindled into a second-rate city.

The son and successor of Alhakem was but eleven years old when he ascended the throne, and Almanzor was made regent, a man of great genius, valor, and activity. He made constant war upon the Christians, who were all this time increasing in power in the northern parts of Spain. Almanzor's hostility was active against the enemies of the Crescent, but the Christians were sometimes ready for him. On one occasion both armies met near the walls of Leon.

When the regent beheld the dense ranks of his opponents, he felt some anxiety for the result. Turning to one of his generals, he asked:

"How many good soldiers dost thou think we may number in our army?"

"Thou shouldst know thyself," replied Mustapha.

"I do not," said Almanzor; "dost thou think there are a thousand?"

"A thousand! nothing like the number."

"Five hundred?"

"No!"

"Fifty?"

"To speak candidly," replied Mustapha, "I would not vouch for more than three." He was, of course, obliged to explain, as the camp was crowded with armed men. It seems that a Christian knight, as was the custom of these times, had just presented himself with a challenge to single combat. Two had accepted, and had been, one after the other, overthrown. No third opponent appeared, and the Christian knight was much elated, crying out with a loud voice, "Why do ye loiter, cowards!" The Christians applauded, the Moslems foamed with wrath, and an Andalusian horseman left the ranks for the encounter, but he too was laid low. The victor mounted a fresh horse, and returned to challenge the whole host of the misbelievers.

Almanzor, summoned by the words of Mustapha, witnessed the last challenge, and turning to him, he said, "You are right. I perceive that I had but three men of valor among my soldiers."

"Wait a moment, sire," said Mustapha. "Dost thou perceive that beautiful tiger-skin which covers his horse? It shall soon be thine!" and mounting his steed he advanced toward the Christian.

The knight keenly eyed his fourth antagonist, and proudly demanded, "Who and what are thou?"

"Here is my nobility," replied Mustapha, shaking his lance; and, plunging at once into combat, the Moslem, after a severe struggle, wounded the Christian, who reeled in his saddle and fell to the ground. Mustapha dismounted, cut off the knight's head, and returned with it to Almanzor. He presented the tiger-skin to his liege lord, who, however, allowed him to keep it, as a reward for his prowess.

Internal dissension, treachery, the murder of kings for the sake of succession, destroyed the noble race of Omeyyah, and the Caliphate of the West ended with Hixem III., who retired, before the mob who demanded his deposition, to private life. From this period (A.D. 1031), Moslem Spain was governed by independent petty kings. The great kingdom of the Omeyyades fell by the turbulence of its own children.

Cordova, their capital, once the centre of European civilization, the successful rival of Bagdad and Damascus, the seat of learning and science, is a small, silent town, a city of the dead. The gardens and orchards are gone, and the valleys are parched and dry, without trees, and bare.

CHAPTER XII.

THE SONG OF ROLAND.

IN the year 777 Charlemagne had convoked at Paderborn in Westphalia, an assembly of the various nations which were subject to his sceptre. Thither came before him as a suppliant, Ibn-el Arabi, the Saracen governor of Saragossa. He came to implore the aid of the great king of the Franks against Abderahman, the Omeyyad usurper, whose genius and daring had made him all but master of Spain.

Charlemagne eagerly grasped at the occasion. Possibly he might win and keep some Spanish cities, possibly alleviate the condition of the Christians. In any case, there were influence and glory to be gained, so he assembled a mighty army, and in the spring of 778 marched towards the Pyrenees. He crossed them, passing through the valley of Roncesvalles, took Pampeluna, and moved straight upon Saragossa. But there his good fortune ended. The presence of the detested unbeliever had united all factions of the Moslems. Saragossa made a desperate defence. The Franks failed to capture it, and a negotiation entered. Charlemagne, according to the chronicles, received large presents of gold with hostages, and promises of fidelity. However this may have been, he certainly raised the siege and marched toward France, levelling to the ground the walls of Pampeluna on his way. But when, with the van of his army, he had passed through the defiles, a new enemy, the Basques, or Gascons of the mountains, assailed his rear.

"While the army, compelled thereto by the nature of the ground and the straitness of the defile, marched in a long and narrow line, the Basques, who lay in ambush on the crests, rushed suddenly from their heights on the men who were stationed in the rear-guard to protect those in front. The Basques cast them down into the valley beneath, and, in the battle that ensued, slew them to the last man. Having pillaged the baggage, they made their escape, and rapidly dispersed under favor of the night, which was now drawing on. The success of the Basques was greatly due to the lightness of their arms and the character of the ground. The Franks, on the other hand, heavily armed, were in every respect an unequal match for their enemies. In this battle perished Aeggihard, provost of the royal table; Anselm, count of the palace; and Hrustlaudus, prefect of the march of Brittany. There was no means of taking vengeance for this blow, for the enemy dispersed so rapidly that no information could be had of the place where they were to be found."

This is the account of the battle of Roncesvalles, given by Eginhard, the secretary of Charlemagne. The event was the subject of many ballads, sung or recited perhaps soon after it happened, and one of them has become very famous—the song of Roland. It belongs almost as much to Spanish story as to France, since the scene of it is on or near Spanish soil. There are many points of divergence between the history and the legend ; for instance, in the latter, Charlemagne is in the extreme of old age, with his white beard flowing down over mail and belt. At the epoch fixed by his historians for the disaster, he was thirty-six years old.

The song relates how our king, the Emperor Charlemagne, hath been for seven full years in Spain. City, keep, and castle alike went down before him, except Saragossa, held by King Marsillius, who seeks not the grace of God, but serves Mohammed, who, however, saved him not from his fate.

King Massillius made his council-seat in Saragossa upon a throne of azure marble. There stood his courtiers around him, and before him twenty thousand men and more, and he sought counsel from his dukes and counts. One of them, a wise heathen, advised him to humble himself before Charlemagne with tribute of seven hundred camels and a thousand hawks, four hundred mules laden with fifty wagon loads of silver and gold, and the offer of hostages. All assented to this, and ten messengers on ten fair mules of snowy white, with olive boughs in their hands, rode to seek the emperor where he sate besieging a city in the Pyrenees. They found him in a jocund mood, for the city had just fallen. He was in an orchard, surrounded by his brave cavaliers, full fifteen thousand, sitting upon white carpets playing games of chess or lightly fencing. Charlemagne himself sat under a pine close beside an eglantine, upon a throne of beaten gold.

The ten messengers alighted before him with all observance and gave their errand, promising the hawks and mules and camels, and also that later on the king would come and be baptized as a Christian.

The Saracens were treated with great hospitality, and the next morning, the emperor held a council of his knights, under a pine-tree. There among the rest were Roland and his faithful Olivier, and there was Ganelon, by whom was the deed of treason done. When the emperor had explained the message of the Saracen king, Roland rose, and said : " Trust him not. He hath ever been a traitor. Lead us on to battle and to Saragossa." But Ganelon advised the opposite cause, and all the knights agreed with him that peace was better. It was questioned now who should be sent to King Marsillius with the reply of the emperor, a dangerous mission, but a glorious one. Roland proposed Ganelon, who, as it happened, was his step-father. Every one thought this a good appointment, but Ganelon burst into rage against Roland, accusing him of wishing to send him on a fatal errand. "Let me go then!" cried Roland. But Charlemagne said no, that Ganelon was the one. Ganelon was thus forced to go, but he went unwillingly home to his hostel, and donned his choicest of arms and harness, mounted his charger Taschebrun, with his good sword Murgleis at his side. His followers stood about him in tears as for one who was going to his death, and they all charged it upon Roland, who had proposed it with a hope for his destruction,

Ganelon passed on his journey, and left their sight, and joining the Saracen envoys, they rode along together, till they drew bridle in Saragossa and alighted beneath a yew-tree.

FUENTARABIA.

They found the monarch of Spain under a pine-tree, upon a throne covered with Alexandrian silk, surrounded by twenty thousand Saracens, from whom came no breath nor sound, so did they strain to hear the tidings of the messengers.

When Ganelon came to the king, he handed him a scroll containing the will of his royal master. If Marsillius should become a Christian, peace should be declared. He should keep half his kingdom of Spain, the other half to be given to Count Roland, the nephew of the king. If he should refuse these conditions, the scroll ran: "You shall be bound in strong fetters, and led to Aix, and there your head shall be struck off." At first the Saracens were in a great rage, but the king concluded to parley with Ganelon, and between them a treacherous thing was planned, out of the fears of the heathen, and the hatred Ganelon had for his kinsman Roland. In this discourse the heathen said:

"I marvel that Charlemagne tires not yet of war, at his age, which is, I believe, two hundred years, and after overrunning so many lands."

"Not while his nephew Roland lives, will he tire," replied Ganelon, "and Olivier besides, and the twelve peers he loves so much, with twenty thousand Franks beside."

Ganelon then urged King Marsillius to send to the emperor gifts and hostages, and let him go back into France. "But the rear," he continued, "will tarry behind, with Roland and Olivier, and you may there bring upon them your army of a hundred thousand heathens. Roland will be slain, and after that, the marvellous hosts of the emperor will melt away and your land will repose in peace."

King Marsillius kissed him in the neck, and Ganelon swore to Roland's fall on the relics in the hilt of his sword Murgleis, while Marsillius swore upon the book containing the laws of Mahmoud and Termagaunt to keep the compact. Ganelon received gifts from the chief heathen, and Braminonde, King Marsillius' queen, sent clasps of gold and jacinth and amethyst to his spouse, which he hid within his boot. So Ganelon returned to Charlemagne. These were his words: "May God you save! I bring the keys of Saragossa, vast treasure, and twenty hostages. For the Saracen king, before a month, he will follow you into France, and bend the knee to our Christian law, and swear homage to you for his Spanish realm."

"Now praise to God," said the emperor, "and thanks to you, my Ganelon."

A thousand clarions then resounded, the sumpter mules were girt, and the Franks made ready to return to France.

Charlemagne had wasted Spain, sacked her cities, seized her castles, and now his great army are encamped, and sleeping on their way home across the Pyrenees. Alas! meanwhile the heathen here were riding on the track of the Christians, all armed in steel, their lances poised, their helmets laced, their falchions glittering, they rode among the steeps, till in a dark forest they rested till the morning light, four hundred thousand couching there.

When the day dawned, the emperor scanned his host, and asked, "To whom shall I trust the rear?" and Ganelon replied: "You have no knight like my step-son Roland, let him keep the rear." The emperor heard him with moody brow, but Roland begged for the post, and the emperor sadly yielded.

Roland asked his uncle to yield him his own bow; the emperor reached it forth and Roland received it. He donned his peerless armor, laced his helmet, and girt on Durindana, his famous sword, and mounting Veillantif, his favorite steed, he grasped his lance, with its white pennon with edges of gold and fringe that fell down to the handle. Twenty thousand Franks followed him, among them the faithful Olivier.

Through Roncesvalles the march began, fearing nothing, for Roland was there to guard the rear. The Franks wound through the mountains dark and steep, and thought gladly of their homes and their wives, as they looked down on the fields of Gascony. But Charlemagne wept for Roland left behind.

Before three suns were set King Marsillius had mustered four hundred thousand Saracens, under his nephew and eleven barons, among them the Miscreant Monarch of Barbary, Turgis, Count of Tortosa, a Mauritanian Almanzor and the rest. One of them said: "Fear nothing, Peter of Rome is no match for Mohammed." They all donned their hauberks of Saracen mould, their helmets made in Saragossa, their swords of steel, their bright lances with pennons of of azure, red, and white. They leaped upon their chargers, and their resplendent arms reflected the bright sunshine. A thousand clarions sounded, so loud that the Franks could hear it.

"Sir comrade," "said Olivier, I trow there is a battle at hand." "God grant it may be so," replied brave Roland.

Sir Olivier climbed a peak from which he could look far upon the Spanish realm. When he came down, he said: "I have seen the Paynim; never such host on earth appeared. My lords of France, be God your stay, that you may not fall before them." Then all the Franks said: "Accursed be they who fly; not one of us shall blench." "My comrade," said Olivier then to Roland, "sound upon your ivory horn, and Charlemagne will return with all the host." "I were mad," said Roland, "to do the deed. My Durindana shall smite the heathen. It shall never be spoken of me in scorn that I blew one blast for heathen felons.

Then daring Roland and wise Olivier awaited the foe. Archbishop Turpin blessed the host, and assailed the Franks as they knelt on the ground, and then turned to face the heathen, with Roland at their head, upon his true charger Veillantif, joyous of visage and exceeding beautiful of frame. From all the Franks resounded their cry "Montjoie!" and with rowels dashed in their coursers' side they proudly rode to meet the foe. Their Paynim foes too were fearless, and thus they closed.

It was a fearful struggle. Each Paynim knight attacked one of the Christian leaders, and all fought with fiercest bravery. Roland used his lance in fifteen encounters, and when it broke, he grasped in hand his Durindana, making fell havoc of the foe till the field flowed with the bright blood shed. Olivier too wielded his blade with fearful effect, and around them the cry "Montjoie!" arose.

Now a wondrous storm passed over France with thunder and whirlwind. There was an earthquake, and at high noon it was dark, save for the lightning flashes in the cloven sky. A mighty fear came on all, and they said, "The end of the world is near." They spake idly, for it was the great lament for Roland's death.

The Franks fought with such prowess that of a hundred thousand Saracens but one escaped. King Margaris fled alone from the field, but in no disgrace, for he was wounded in four places, to tell King Marsillius what had chanced that day. He fell at the feet of the king, and said: "Ride, sire, ride; you will find the Franks in an evil plight, it were easy now to crush them." And with a mighty battalion the king sped through the valley. When the Franks saw them, they cried, "This is the treachery of Ganelon!" Proudly they mounted, and spurred, like chafing lions, to meet the foe anew. Among them came the Saracen Valdabrun, who owned galleys upon the sea, and was lord of all the mariners. He had erst falsely won Jerusalem and profaned the temple of Solomon. He struck and slew Duke Samson, one of Roland's trustiest knights; and when Roland heard this, he raised aloft Durindana, and smote with uncontrolled passion on the heathen's helmet with its jewelled crown, down through head, and cuirass, and body, and down through the saddle embossed with gold, until the steel was buried in the charger's flank. "A fearful stroke!" said the heathen crew.

Archbishop Turpin fought gallantly among the rest; never has priest sung mass, who has done such feats of his body.

So great was the carnage that at length the

heathen turned to fly. The Saracens cried: "May ill betide the hour we came on this fatal track!" But King Marsillius urged them to continue the battle until Roland should be slain. The Saracens lay dead by the hundred, yet the fight kept on till all the cavaliers of the Franks were slain but sixty. God preserved these that ere they should die they might sell their lives at the highest cost.

Then at last Roland consented to sound his ivory horn. He sounded such a mighty strain that the bright blood rushed forth from his mouth and his temples burst. On and onward the blast was borne until far away it was heard by Charlemagne. "It is Roland's horn," said the emperor, "our men have battle on hand." "Battle," said Ganelon, "there is none. Ride onward, Sire, your mighty land is yet far away." A second and a third time Roland sounds his horn in anguish drear, and at last the king commands to sound the alarm. The barons leap on their steeds and speed back through the passes. Ah! what availeth! it is all too late.

In wrath the emperor had Ganelon bound and consigned to Besqua, chief of his kitchen train. Then full a hundred of kitchen valets, the worst and best, pressed round him. Each dealt him four cuffs of the fist, and beat him with rods and staves, then flung a chain about him and led him like a bear.

The emperor and his train rode back to Roland, dark, vast, and high soared the summits, the waters poured down the valleys. The trumpets made answer to Roland's horn; the Franks were full of grief, beseeching God to let them stand beside Roland upon the field. Ah, timeless succor, and all in vain. Too late!

Roland looked upon the lines of his slain warriors and wept, and then pressed again into the fight. The Franks struck like wrathful lions, but Marsillius bore himself bravely, till his good right hand was severed by Durindana; then he turned and fled with a hundred thousand of the heathen train.

But though Marsillius fled, his uncle, the Algalif, was still there, lord of Ethiopia, accursed land. The black battalions he commanded, with large nostrils, and ears flattened, outnumbered fifty thousand spears. When Roland saw this abhorred race, more black than blackest ink, he said, " Now is the hour of our death close at hand; fight, my Franks, to the last."

The Algalif sate on a sorrel horse; he smote Olivier in the back, and pressed his lance through the harness so the steel came out at the baron's breast. Olivier felt the deadly wound, yet he grasped his sword Hauteclere, and smote on the Algalif's crest of gold, cleaving his head to the teeth.

Olivier knew himself hurt to death, yet he shouted " Montjoie!" shrill and clear, and then called to Roland to draw near to him.

Roland looked Olivier in the face. He was ghastly pale and the bright blood flowed forth from the wound. " Oh God!" said Roland, " is this the end of all thy prowess?" At the words he fainted upon his steed. There were Roland swooning upon his charger, and Olivier smitten with his death wound.

Olivier's eyes were dimmed with bleeding, and seeing nothing he smote a fierce blow upon his comrade's helmet which passed no further, not piercing his head. Roland marvelled at the blow, and said softly: " It is I, Roland, who loves thee so dear ; thou hast no quarrel to seek with me?" Olivier answered: " I hear thee speak, but see thee not. God seeth thee. Have I struck thee, my brother ? Oh, forgive it me ! "

" I am not hurt Olivier, and in the sight of God, I forgive thee." And in love like this was their parting made.

Olivier lay upon the ground and cried aloud his *Mea culpa,* prayed God to grant that he might share Paradise, prayed God to bless King Charlemagne and France, and over all others, Roland. Then his heart sank, his head bowed, and stretched at his length upon the earth, Sir Olivier passed away.

Roland was left alone to weep. " Ah friend," he said, "since thou art dead, to live is pain." He swooned again upon his horse Veillantif, but his golden stirrups held him fast in the saddle.

When his senses were restored he saw what ruin lay around him. All his Franks had perished save two, the archbishop, and Walter of Hum, the latter wounded and dying fast. Yet the three surviving Franks fought hotly. Roland left not one of a score alive, Walter slew six, five were slain by the archbishop. The heathen pour down upon them. A thousand Saracens are struck from their steeds, yet forty thousand remain in the saddle.

Walter was slain and the steed of the archbishop dropped dead. Turpin fell to the ground with four lance wounds in him, but he sprang up, and continued to deal about him deadly blows.

Roland fought on, his body burning and bathed in sweat, a mighty pain in his brow, since his temple had burst when he sounded his horn; yet he lifted his horn once more, and blew a faint and feeble note.

The emperor listened and stood still. "That," he said, "is the blast of a dying man. Sound every trump our ranks possess."

Sixty thousand clarions pealed forth, the hills echoed, the vales replied. The heathen cried, "Charlemagne is at hand!" and they gathered themselves once more to slay Roland.

When Roland saw them, he spurred Veillantif towards them, with Archbishop Turpin at his side. "Let us flee!" said the heathen, "those are the trumpets of France we hear." They withdrew to a distance, and held aloof, but thence hurled their missiles, javelin, barb, and arrow. Roland's buckler was torn, his cuirass broken, Veillantif bled from thirty wounds, and fell dead at last. Then the heathen vanished from the field, and left Roland, on foot, alone.

He turned to succor Turpin, who lay stretched on the sward. "*Mea culpa*," he called out, raised his hands to heaven, and died. Roland took the fair white hands, crossed and clasped them upon his breast, and was now alone upon the field.

Roland felt that his death was near, and stretched himself upon the green grass. A Saracen who saw him sought to take away his Durindana, but the hero roused himself and smote him on the crest, shattering bone and skull with his horn. Then, that no other should ever wield his famous sword, he strove to break it by smiting ten grievous blows upon a dark brown rock. The breach in the stone he made is still there, but the steel was not broken, nor the grain notched.

Then Roland felt his hour was at hand. He beat upon his breast and confessed his sins, and raised his glove to heaven in sign of penance. His resting-place was beneath a pine; he had turned his face to the land of Spain. Many a thought rose upon his memory of the lands he had won, the fields he had fought, of his gentle France, his kin and friends, and his beloved and loving king. He raised his right-hand glove, and St. Gabriel took the gift from his hand. Then drooped his head upon his breast, and he slept with clasped hands the sleep of death. God from on high sent down to him one of his angels, Saint Michael, and with him came Gabriel, and they bore his soul with them back to Paradise.

There is another part to tell of the reprisals, but we will leave Roland here. Charlemagne's grief is dwelt upon, and the chastisement he gave to the Saracens, and his return to France, where the betrothed of Roland came to him to demand her love. When she learned that he was dead she too fell at the feet of Charlemagne and died. A terrible punishment was dealt to Ganelon; he was bound to four wild horses and torn asunder.

The Queen of the Saracens, a captive in the train of the emperor was baptized as a Christian. When the emperor had done all he could for justice, his wrath subsided. Then Saint Gabriel came to him to say that he was called by God to bring relief to a Christian king besieged by heathen.

> Fain would Charles such task decline.
> "God ! what a life of toil is mine ! "
> He wept ; his hoary beard he wrung.

So ends the lay.

CHAPTER XIII.

ALMORAVIDES.—ALMOHADES.

AFTER the fall of the Caliphate of Cordova, the local governors of cities took upon themselves an independent power, and often assumed the title of kings, boasting each of a brief authority, and declaring war upon each other upon slight pretence. These numerous small kings agreed on one subject only, that of renouncing all allegiance to the former seat of empire.

This broken state of things among the Moslems gave a fair opportunity to the Christians to regain something of their ancient power in Spain. The descendants of the Goths, of whom we shall hear more by and by, asserted themselves especially in the northern provinces. Among them the king of Leon, Alfonso VI., was now able to besiege Toledo, which after three years of resistance was compelled to capitulate, and Alfonso triumphantly entered the ancient capital of the Goths, which had remained in the power of the Saracens for nearly four centuries.

Alfonso continued his successes by the capture of many other strongholds of the Mohammedans, so that their chiefs, alarmed, assembled together to confer upon the situation.

In this council an appeal was proposed to the celebrated African conqueror, Yussef ben Taxfin, and the proposal was received with general applause, except by the Governor of Malaga, who exclaimed:

"What! Call in the aid of the terrible Almoravides! Do not you know that these fierce inhabitants of the desert are more like their native tigers than men? Suffer them not, I beseech you, to enter the fertile plains of Andalusia and Granada! They might break for us the sceptre of iron which Alfonso holds over us, but we should wear under them the chains of a worse slavery!"

This was the aged Zagat who said this, but he was overruled. "Any thing," they said, "rather than that Andalusia should become the prey of the Christians. We would rather become humble shepherds, or drive the camels of the Yussef, than reign dependent on these dogs of Christians."

"May Allah then protect us!" said the aged Zagat, thus silenced.

Beyond the chains of Mount Atlas, in the deserts of Northern Africa, from time immemorial, had dwelt two tribes of Arabian descent. Their lives were passed in perfect freedom under their tents; their only possessions were their herds and camels.

An Arab of one of these tribes, whose name was Yahia ben Ibrahim, on his return from the pilgrimage to Mecca, met a famous alfaqui, originally of Fez. Being questioned by the alfaqui as to the religion and manners of his countrymen, Yahia replied that they were sunk in ignorance and lost to all knowledge of the world, but that they were strangers also to cruelty, and were amenable to instruction. This alfaqui and his friends became enough interested in this remote tribe to wish to disturb their ignorant bliss, and one of their disciples, one Abdallah ben Yassim, fired with missionary zeal, was induced to go back with Yahia.

Abdallah was one of those ruling minds, which, fortunately for the peace of society, nature seldom produces. His superior knowledge so won the devotion of the tribe to which Yahia brought him, that he soon conceived the idea of making himself king over them, and to enlarge his kingdom he prevailed upon his dutiful disciples to make war upon the neighboring tribe, which also until now had dwelt in happy ignorance. His plea was that of diffusing the true religion and useful knowledge. The tribe, thus attacked in the cause of progress, submitted. Abdallah gave to his new subjects the name of Murabitins, or Almoravides, which means " Religious People," or men consecrated to the service of God.

The whole surrounding country was gradually subdued by this new apostle, and his authority was acknowledged over a region large enough to make a respectable kingdom, but he left the temporal power nominally in the hands of the emir he found exercising it, and allowed it to go to his successor, whose power and fame spread far and wide, thanks to the counsels and teachings of the progressive Abdallah.

This emir, Abu Bekir, exceeded the instructions of his spiritual guide so far as to extend his dominion by conquest and plunder. He spread his territory beyond the chain of mountains, even to the shores of the sea, and even laid the foundations for a great city, his capital, which was Morocco. Whilst in the middle of his work upon the city he had to go back over the mountains to suppress a quarrel between his different tribes; he left the superintendence of his buildings and the command of his army during his absence to his cousin, Yussef ben Taxfin. This cousin, it appears, was the greater man, whose glory, by gradual steps was prepared by the camel driver, the alfaqui, the apostle, and the chief.

Yussef, we are told, was noble of stature, and tall, his countenance prepossessing, his eyes dark and piercing, his beard long, his tone of voice harmonious, his frame strong, robust, and familiar with fatigue. His mind corresponded with his outward appearance, for his generosity, his care of the poor, his sobriety, his justice, his religious zeal, rendered him the admiration of strangers and the love of his own people.

In this catalogue of his virtues, gratitude, honor, and good faith must be omitted, for scarcely had his kinsman left the city than Yussef set himself to winning away from him the affections of his subjects. He began by marrying the beautiful Zainab, sister of Abu Bekir; then, being all in the family, he went on with the magnificent city of Morocco, and there established the seat of his empire. He encouraged people of other nations to settle there, and soon filled it with a prosperous population, out of which he built up an army which reached the number of one hundred thousand men.

All this time poor old Abu Bekir was away on the

other side of the mountains reconciling his hostile tribes. No telegram reported the state of things at home. No chance newspaper came under his eye, nor did the modern interviewer call to inquire his impressions on losing an empire. He went on quietly soothing his tribes, until he had brought them to his mind, and then he returned from the desert and encamped in his old city of Agmat, where he used to live before Morocco was thought of. Here he learned for the first time what had been going on in his absence; to his mortification, his own horsemen, who went on to Morocco to find out all about it, came back loud in the praises of Yussef, whose liberality to his army every one was talking about.

Abu Bekir, at a loss to know what would happen next, invited an interview with his cousin. The two chiefs met about half way between Morocco and Agmat, and after a formal salutation, took their seats on the same carpet. It was an awkward scene for Abu Bekir, but his visitor seemed not to find it so. The grandeur which surrounded Yussef, his formidable guard, and the alacrity with which he was obeyed, prevented the poor emir from even making the remark that he thought it was about time he should take the kingdom back into his own hand. Yussef, on his side, made no such suggestion, but smoked his pipe and sipped his coffee just as if he had nothing upon his mind. So Abu Bekir meekly said that he had long given up the thoughts of empire, and that his only wish was to pass the remainder of his days in the desert, which Yussef cordially approved, accepting without hesitation the continued care of the kingdom. The sheiks and walis were instantly summoned to witness the abdication of the emir. Yussef sent him a magnificent present the next day, and indeed kept up this custom every year till he died; and Abu Bekir returned to his desert sooner than he had expected.

Yussef now assumed the title of Nazaravin, or defender of the faith, and chief of the already large band of the Almoravides. His power was solid, he was in peaceful possession of a large empire, when letters from the Spanish Moslems reached him asking his aid against the Christians. Yussef consented, and, arming a vast body of soldiers, set forth for Spain.

Alfonso was besieging Saragossa when intelligence reached him of Yussef's disembarkation. He advanced towards Andalusia with all the forces he could muster.

Yussef summoned the Christian king by letter either to embrace the faith of the prophet, to consent to pay him annual tribute, or to prepare for immediate battle.

The indignant Alfonso trampled the letter under foot, and at the same time said to the messenger who brought it:

"Tell thy master what thou hast seen! Tell him also not to hide himself during the action; let him meet me face to face."

The two armies engaged on the thirteenth day of the moon Regeb, A. H. 479. This is the same as our October 23, 1086. The Christians fought with desperate valor, but Alfonso was compelled to retreat.

This victory, however, had no especial result, other than to give Yussef a foothold on the Peninsula. His victories over the Christians did not gain much for the Mohammedan princes of Spain, but, in fulfilment of the fears of the wisest among them, Yussef, one by one, subdued all the princes of Andalusia. Among them was Mohammed, from whom came the original proposal to invite the African chieftain into Spain. Mohammed and his family were thrown into prison until a ship was prepared to carry them in exile into Africa. Surrounded by the best beloved of his wives, his daughters, and his four surviving sons, his hands loaded with chains, he wept as the ship that bore them moved away from the shores of Spain. "It is the will of Allah," said this true Moslem; "my children, let us learn to support our lot with resignation."

The royal party were confined in a fortress at Agmat. We are told that a compassionate poet presented the fallen king with a copy of verses deploring his misfortunes, and that he rewarded the author with thirty-six pieces of gold, which was the only money he had left.

His future life was passed in penury—his daughters earned his living and their own by the labor of their hands.

Thus ended the petty kingdoms of Andalusia, after a stormy existence of less than a century, and now began the dynasty of the ALMORAVIDES or RELIGIOUS PEOPLE.

Yussef was more interested in his great capital, Morocco, than in his new possessions in the Penin-

sula, but he came to Cordova, which he wished to
honor as their chief city, as the Omeyyas had done,
and there he convoked the sheiks and walis, and
caused his son Ali to be proclaimed heir to his vast
empire. The instructions which he gave the young
prince were full of wisdom : to preserve his frontier
fortresses well guarded; to employ the Andalusians
chiefly against the Christians, because they understood, better than the Africans, the enemy's method
of warfare ; to pay his troops punctually, to honor all
Moslems, and to exercise clemency, were among the
admonitions which the prince received from his
father.

Yussef soon afterwards returned to Morocco,
where he died on the third day of the moon Muhar-
ram, A. H. 500, having lived one hundred Arabian
or lunar years, or about ninety-seven of the Christian
or solar calendar.

The empire of the Almoravides had but a brief
duration in Spain. It was never agreeable to the
Spanish Arabs, whose manners, from their contact
with the Christians were refined and superior to
those of the Africans, while the savages from the
desert looked with contempt upon the effeminate
citizens of the Peninsula. The excesses of Ali's
barbarian guard, which consisted in laying waste
the gardens, forcibly entering the houses, and seizing
the property of the people of Cordova, were unre-
strained by the local authorities, and an open revolt
was the consequence. Ali was obliged to listen to
their demands, and to restrain the insubordination
of his guards, but ill feeling continued to prevail.

The Christians were always in arms, and increasing in power, for Saragossa had by this time fallen into their hands, and the north of Spain was already free from Moslem domination.

The cause, however, which was destined to overthrow the dynasty of the Almoravides, at the same time that it changed the whole face of Western Africa and Southern Spain, originated, like the power of Yussef ben Taxfin, in the deserts bordering on Mount Atlas.

Mohammed ben Abdallah (another Mohammed!) was the son of a lamp-lighter in the Mosque of Cordova. He had great curiosity, and an insatiable thirst for knowledge. After studying for some years in the schools of his native city, he persuaded the lamp-lighter to let him journey to Bagdad, where he continued his studies under the celebrated doctors of that capital of the Moslem world.

Of these doctors, none was more famous than Abu Hamid Algazali, and none more free in the expression of his sentiments, which were bold and radical, and, in the opinion of conservatives, dangerous to the faith of Islam. He had written a book on the resurrection of science and natural law, which the Cadi of Cordova had been the first to condemn. Ali himself approved the condemnation, all the copies of the book which could be found were seized and burnt in the public square.

When Mohammed ben Abdallah had reached Bagdad, and taken his seat in the school of Algazali, the first question asked him, very naturally, was not exactly,

"What on earth tempted you to come here?" but "Had you heard of my writings in your native city?" And when he said he had done so, still more naturally he was asked how they were received there, and he was obliged to confess that they had been all burned in the public square by the orders of the cadi, and the approval of the king.

Algazali turned pale, not perceiving that this was as good a form of advertising as he could have desired for his work. He demanded the vengeance of Heaven upon his impious judges, and on the monarch who had sanctioned the deed.

"Pray Allah, also," said Mohammed, the son of the lamp-lighter, "that I may be the instrument of thy vengeance." Algazali added this prayer to the other.

Mohammed acquired, with ardor and diligence, all the views of his master Algazali, and after he had fully learned them wandered from place to place zealously preaching these doctrines. He fell in with a youth named Abdelmumen, who decided to share his fortunes, and together they arrived in Morocco.

One day they entered the grand mosque, and Mohammed immediately possessed himself of the most prominent place. He was informed that those seats were reserved for the Prince of the Faithful. "The temples of Allah belong to Allah, and to Allah alone!" was the reply of the bold intruder, who then, to the surprise of the audience, repeated the whole chapter of the Koran, of which this is the opening sentence.

A few minutes after, Ali himself entered, and all

as usual rose to salute him, but Mohammed did not deign even to cast a glance on this dreaded chief of a great empire. When the service was over he approached the sovereign and said in a loud voice:

"Provide a remedy for the afflictions of thy people! One day Allah will require of thee an account!"

The prince, who regarded him as a *santon* or religiously inspired person, a class much indulged in Moslem states, and privileged to utter disagreeable truths, instead of ordering his head off at once, merely asked what he could do for him.

"Nothing which this world can give," he gravely replied; "my mission is to preach reformation and to correct abuses."

Ali was struck by these words, and allowed him to follow his vocation, not expecting any serious reresults, and trusting in the good sense of the people. But his fanatic discourses so much excited the populace, that he was ordered to leave Morocco, and, building a hut for himself among the graves just outside the city, he preached vehemently to crowds who came out to listen to him, denouncing the impiety of the Almoravides, and the coming of the great *Mahdi*, who shall teach all men the right way and cause virtue and happiness to reign over the whole earth. At first he carefully refrained from acknowledging himself to be this mighty prophet, but afterwards accepted it, assumed the high title of MAHDI, and proclaimed himself the founder of a new people. Followers flocked to his standard, and Ali was forced to march against the prophet, who entrenched himself with a powerful army among the strongholds of the Atlas mountains. The followers of Mohammed called themselves Almohades—that is to say, followers of one God. They were, in fact Unitarians; for their principal pretence was to extirpate alike idolaters who recognized several gods and those Christians who worship Three Persons in one God.

Mohammed entrenched himself in a stronghold among the mountains, where his people maintained themselves by plundering the neighborhood. The suffering people complained to Ali, who intercepted as well as he could by troops, the inroads of these holy banditti, but he had to sustain a siege in Morocco, which was soon invested with vigor by the Almohades.

The affairs of the Almoravides were meantime growing daily worse in Spain, where the Christians openly defied their force, so that, overcome by grief and anxiety, Ali died at Morocco, leaving his son, Taxfin ben Ali, to fight it out with all his enemies.

Meanwhile the great Mahdi died, too, in the midst of his successes, before the walls of Morocco. He conferred all his powers upon his faithful Abdelmumen, and, as a last gift, presented him with the book containing the tenets of his faith, a volume which he had received from Algazali.

Abdelmumen, who now combined the offices of general of the troops and Grand Mahdi, made a vigorous attack upon the new emperor. Taxfin saw that his only hope of safety lay in escaping to Spain. One night he resolved to make a desperate effort to gain the port where his vessels were riding at anchor. Unfortunately he missed his way. The mule, on which he was riding, terrified by the sound of the waves, plunged headlong over a precipice, where, the next morning, the mangled corpse of the emperor was found upon the beach.

Morocco still remained in the power of the Almoravides, though the siege was prosecuted with vigor. It was now under the command of Ibrahim, the young son of the late emperor, who assumed the title. The city had to surrender, and Abdelmumen when he saw the youth of the captured monarch, showed signs of pity for him as he knelt and begged for his life.

"Wretch!" cried one of the captured sheiks of the Almoravides to the boy, "why add shame to misfortune? Art thou kneeling, as if to a father, before a wild beast, who lives only on blood!"

This irritated the prophet, and, at the same time, one of his own generals exclaimed:

"Wilt thou spare the cub of the lion, who one day may devour us all?"

Ibrahim's fate was sealed. Not only was he executed, but a general massacre of all the inhabitants of Morocco was ordered. The few who remained were sold as slaves, the mosques were destroyed, and the tribes of the desert were called to repeople the solitary streets of the splendid capital of the Almoravides.

The Almohades, now victorious in Africa, proclaimed their emperor Abdelmumen as sovereign of all Mohammedan Spain, which they retained with various fortunes in their wars against the Christians under several successive emperors, until the beginning of the thirteenth century, when they in turn suffered a defeat at the great battle of Navas de Tolosa, which gave a permanent ascendancy to the Christian arms.

The reigning emperor had collected for a whole year such an immense army that two months were necessary to convey it across the straits from Africa into Spain. All Christian Europe was filled with alarm. The Pope proclaimed a crusade to Spain. The different kings of Christian Spain, Arragon, Castile, and Navarre, united to repel the common danger, and great numbers of volunteers from Portugal and Southern France hastened to Toledo, where was held a fast, with prayers and processions, to avert from Christendom the greatest danger that had threatened it since the famous victory of Charles Martel on the plains of Poictiers.

On July 12, 1212, the crusaders reached the mountain chain which divides New Castile from Andalusia. Their king was Alfonso IX. of Castile, who commanded the immense Christian army in person. They found the passes and summits of the mountains occupied by the Almohades, and were at a loss how to proceed. Just then a shepherd entered the camp of Alfonso, and proposed to conduct the army, by a path unknown and invisible to the outposts of the enemy, to the summit of the chain. They silently ascended, and entrenched themselves on a level plain large enough to contain all the troops. Below them was stretched the army of the Moslems, whose surprise was great to perceive the heights above them occupied by the crusaders.

On the third day the Christians descended to the plains of Tolosa. The struggle was terrific, but the Moslems at last fled.

Seeing the total destruction or flight of his vast host, Mohammed, the African emperor, sorrowfully exclaimed:

"Allah alone is just and powerful; the devil is false and wicked!"

Just then came up to him Alarab, leading by the head a strong but nimble mule.

" Prince of the Faithful," said the African, " how long wilt thou remain here? Dost thou not perceive that thy Moslems flee? The will of Allah be done. Mount this mule, which is fleeter than the wind of heaven, or even the arrow which strikes it; never yet did she fail her rider. Away! away! for on thy safety depends that of us all!"

Mohammed mounted the beast, and soon outstripped not only the pursuers but the fugitives.

Alfonso's report of this battle was that one hundred and eighty-five thousand infidels perished, and only five-and-twenty Spaniards. Without literally accepting this, it may be admitted as a glorious victory for the Christian arms.

This was the last attempt of any magnitude which the Moslems made to preserve Andalusia. The Christians all over Spain were growing more and more powerful as they united their several small kingdoms, and combined on the common ground of ejecting the misbelievers from the Peninsula. Help from Africa could no longer be expected, even were it to be desired, for the empire of the Almohades was at its last gasp.

In this deplorable situation the followers of the prophet turned to Mohammed ben Alhamar, who, of all the aspirants to power, had shown himself the most able to rule. He fixed his court in Granada, and there established the only state which survived the wreck of the African empire. Here, for more than two centuries and a half, the Moslems withstood the hostile attacks of their Christian neighbors.

CHAPTER XIV.

THE STORY OF THE ABENCERRAGES.

THE Moors, though as a whole making a nation, preserved the patriarchal customs of their ancestors, the Arabs. Each family formed a large tribe, not confounded with any other, more or less powerful in numbers, wealth, and possession of slaves, within which the united members regarded each other as brothers, marched together to battle, taking always the same side in combat, mutually supporting each other, and never separating their fortunes, their interests, or their prejudices, whether for love or hate.

Among these tribes, the most celebrated in tradition and romance was the family of the Abencerrages, descended from ancient kings in Arabia. The very existence of this tribe is now doubted by historians, and the legends concerning their prowess are set down as idle tales, but they form so important, and, at least, so picturesque, a part of the story, of Granada, that they cannot well be left out here. Some foundation must have existed for the legends of their splendor and daring which remain floating about the ruins of the Alhambra.

The qualities of the princes of the Abencerrages

were of the highest sort. Invincible in battle, they were mild and merciful after victory, while their graces and gifts made them the ornament of the Moorish court. They were respected by the Spaniards, whose esteem they won by the kindness they showed to the Christian captives. Their immense wealth was used for the benefit of the poor and suffering. In the tournaments of the Moorish court, in games of skill and chance, the prizes fell to the chiefs of the Abencerrages. It was the boast of the race that it had never been disgraced by a coward, a faithless friend, an inconstant husband, or a perfidious lover.

The rivals of this glorious family were the Zegris, descendants of the kings of Fez. They also were of great distinction. Their valor had time and again carried fire and the sword into the dominions of Castile, hundreds of times their victorious hands had decorated the mosques with banners snatched from the enemy. But these heroic exploits were dishonored by the prevailing trait of the Zegris, a savage thirst for blood. A Zegri was never known to make a captive; every victim perished on the spot by sabre; neither friendship nor love softened their ferocity. They regarded all sensibility as weakness, and looked with contempt on the graces of the court, exchanges of civility, or encounters of repartee. They were fierce and proud, and loved only the field of battle; all they knew was how to fight and conquer, and they despised all other arts.

An intense jealousy existed through generations between the rival Zegris and Abencerrages, and towards the end of the Moorish kingdom of Granada this had increased so much that only the personal authority of the sovereign could restrain an outburst. The principal families of Granada joined either the

THE GATE OF JUSTICE. ALHAMBRA.

one side or the other; and other tribes, more obscure, had followed this example, so that the whole country was divided into two opposing parties.

The last king of Granada, according to the legend,

inclined towards the noble Abencerrages, with whose fine qualities he was able to sympathize; but in order to appease the discontent of the Zegris, he had married a maiden of their tribe. This was Aixa, a princess beautiful, but hardened by the want of sensibility and the inexorable pride of her race. So little did her society satisfy the mind and heart of the king, that he fell in love with a Spanish captive; and the tenets of his religion did not prevent him from making her also his wife.

This caused intense jealousy at the court. The Zegri swore upon the side of the princess who belonged to their tribe; and her son, the young prince, and heir to the throne, espoused their cause in their quarrels with the Abencerrages, while this large family ranged themselves on the side of the Spanish princess.

To divert the minds of his people from this dissension and bitterness, the king encouraged the games and exhibitions of skill, for which the Moors, in all time, had been distinguished.

A romance writer has given a fanciful description of the celebration of a wedding in the Moorish court:

"All the warriors, of whatever tribe, prepared themselves for the occasion by lavishing their treasure on the richness of their armor and the magnificence of their coursers. The beauties of the court sent ribbons, scarfs, devices to their lovers to stimulate them to exertion, and decked themselves in their fairest costumes and richest jewels.

"As soon as the sun had gilded the summit of the palace of Granada, all the people began to gather in the great plaza of the city, the Vivarambla, which was provided with rows of seats like an amphitheatre, to contain the vast assemblage.

"In the middle of the great enclosure, which could easily contain twenty thousand warriors in battle array, was a palm-tree, whose trunk was of bronze, and whose leaves were all of gold. Upon one of the long palm leaves a silver dove was suspended, which pulled down the branch by its weight. This dove held in its beak a ring, which was the object of the contest; and the bird was so constructed by the skill of the Moorish workman, that as soon as a ring was won by the prowess of a knight, another ring immediately came out of the beak of the dove to take its place.

"Below the palm-tree was an enclosure reserved for the judges, and there were also placed musical instruments to announce victory.

"Balconies, covered with precious stuffs, and in the middle a magnificent daïs, were destined for the king, with his family and the court; while every window of the immense square, ornamented with garlands, was crowded with the fairest of Moorish maidens.

"When the judges were all in their places, the king arrived in all pomp and splendor, leading the bride, in whose honor the occasion was made, resplendent in diamonds. The court followed and surrounded him, and filled the balconies; trumpets sounded from the four barriers to announce the combatants.

"First entered the Abencerrages, dressed in blue

tunics embroidered with silver and pearls, mounted on white coursers, whose harness was covered with sapphires. Blue was the favorite color of the Abencerrages, and in their turbans they wore aigrettes of that color. Upon their shields was a lion led by a shepherdess, with an Arabic motto, the celebrated device of their tribe, which means 'Gentleness and Force.' All these warriors were in their first bloom of youth, handsome, brilliant, radiant with hope. They advanced proudly, but with gracious mien, to take their places in their quadrille.

"Next came the Zegris. These wore green tunics embroidered with gold. Their turbans were decked with aigrettes of black, the color of their family. Their horses were almost covered with broad trappings studded with emeralds. They followed, with haughty glances and heads thrown back, their redoubtable leader Ali, who bore upon his shield, as did they all, the device of a scimetar dripping with blood, and the motto 'This is my Law.'

"The two other quadrilles were occupied by two important tribes. One of them, the Alabez, dressed in red, embroidered with silver, and mounted upon *Isabelle*-colored horses, wore in their turbans the blue aigrette of the Abencerrages. The Goméles, allies of the Zegris, wore their black aigrette in the turban. Their dress was a tunic of purple and gold. These four troops, one after the other, came first to salute the king, and then took their respective places.

"Each one of these quadrilles could choose twelve cavaliers to ride for the ring. One failure alone took away the right to try again. A serpent aigrette of diamonds was destined for the conqueror. Other gifts, less magnificent, were prepared to comfort the vanquished.

"The signal given, the first rider to advance was from the blue ranks of the Abencerrages; he sprang forward like an arrow from a bow, and caught upon the point of his lance the first ring and bore it back in triumph. Next came one of the Zegris, who, blinded by his rage against his skilful rival, missed the ring. He snapped his lance in two in his anger, and hid himself behind the cavaliers. Another Zegri wins the second ring; for several courses success alternates between the two tribes. The place resounds with applause. Once, as a knight, by striking the silver dove, made the ring fly up in the air, another one, his rival, caught it before it reached the ground, upon the point of his lance. In the end, a young prince of the Abencerrages had won twenty rings, while no other single combatant had more than five.

"After this came the game of wands. All the cavaliers, armed with light reeds instead of lances, rode against each other, breaking their fragile weapons against the shields, throwing them lightly in the air and catching them with wonderful skill, while their swift coursers turned, attacked, returned, with wonderful evolutions, under the control of their skilful riders.

"The spectators watched the performance with keen enjoyment; but the Zegris had planned a treachery. Under their glittering dress they wore coats of mail, and in the midst of the sport several of them exchanged their light reeds for lances of iron. Several Abencerrages were wounded, a melée ensued. The place ran with blood, and the frightened witnesses fled."

According to the same romance, Abenhamet, the flower of the youths of the Abencerrages, loved the fair Zoraïde, who returned his love. But the prince royal saw her, admired her, and chose her for his own, and she was compelled to marry him, by threats against the life of her lover, if she refused. Abenhamet was driven from the court. Disguised as a slave, with an Asiatic turban round his head, he returned to see, if possible, his beloved Zoraïde.

He arrives in Granada, climbs the steep ascent of the Alhambra, and wanders through the vast courts of the palace.

Night had begun to cast its shadows on the earth. Zoraïde, alone in the garden appropriated to her, was weeping for her love under a rose-tree. She knew nothing of his fate. She had not pronounced his name since her fatal marriage with the prince, but every evening she went to sit under this rose-tree, where, in happier times, she had passed many delightful moments with Abenhamet.

Suddenly, in the midst of her weeping, the queen saw a slave approaching. Looking closely at him she recognized the Abencerrage; she was about to scream, but the danger which threatened them both gave her prudence.

The interview was brief and painful. Abenhamet seized the hand of the princess, then dropped it; she cried: 'Fly, fly, do not stay here to risk your life in this terrible place; go, yet remember that every evening Zoraïde weeps beneath this rose-tree.

Even as she said these words, she thought she heard a noise behind the bush. She started up, forced Abenhamet to leave her, and herself hastened to her apartment, and stepped out upon the balcony overlooking the deep ravines of the Darro. There, in the pale moonlight, she listened, trembling. Silence reigned in the gardens, and she became calm.

But the noise she had heard was no creation of her frightened fancy. Four Zegris had passed behind the rose-tree, and had seen and recognized the form of Abenhamet. Instantly they reported to the prince their discovery. In his rage, he was easily led by the perfidious Zegris to plan a terrible revenge upon all the family of the Abencerrages.

Guards were sent everywhere throughout the Alhambra to search for Abenhamet, and messengers of the king carried to every Abencerrage an order to come at once to the palace.

One by one as they arrived, they were introduced into the Court of Lions; as soon as they appeared they were seized, dragged to the alabaster basin of the fountain, and their heads cut off. Abenhamet was the first. He fell by the sword of the prince himself.

Thirty-six young heroes were thus sacrificed, the whole of the noble family which had lavished its blood to protect the kingdom, and save its capital from the attacks of the Christians. One child alone who had accompanied its guardian to the Court of Lions, fled and reported the carnage to a troop of

Abencerrages who were coming to obey the order of the king. The alarm spread. The retainers of the tribe hastened, armed, to the palace. A fierce encounter ensued. The Zegris, supported by the royal guard, overwhelmed the smaller number of their foes; in spite of their reckless courage, these were forced, after a long contest, to retire. The small remnant who were not slain were driven out of the city, and these few, embittered against the ungrateful country which could thus abuse its defenders, withdrew from Granada, under oaths never to return to it.

Such is one version of the destruction the Abencerrages. The legend has so much credence that every visitor of the Alhambra is shown, in the lovely Court of Lions, the stains of the blood of the Abencerrages upon the edge of the alabaster basin. Yet the guide-book warns us that these marks are not those of blood, but ferruginous veins in the marble, and at the same time asserts that no Abencerrages ever existed.

In the historical account of the fall of Granada it is evident that internal dissension among the Moorish families made it easy for their enemies to effect their destruction, and the story of the Abencerrages illustrates these quarrels by its grains of truth mixed up with fable.

CHAPTER XV.

THE FALL OF GRANADA.

MOHAMMED BEN ALHAMAR became the founder of a celebrated kingdom. His qualities were of a high order, he was intrepid in war, but more inclined to peace, vigorous in pursuing justice, but mild and conciliating, possessing foresight and prudence, yet magnificent in his habits, fond of power, still more fond of popularity. These were all qualities likely to please the Andalusians; they enabled him to piece together the fragments of the several shattered "kingdoms" of the Arabs there, and to make his own firm enough to last.

The Moorish territory of Granada contained within its circuit, narrowed though it were from the broad extent once held by the powerful Arabs, all the physical resources of a great empire. Fertile valleys were intersected by mountains rich in minerals. Its fields, well watered, afforded pasturage to countless cattle, and its coasts commanded the commerce of the world.

The beautiful city of Granada, its capital, overlooked the country from its lofty situation, upon four hills rising from a broad plain. In the days of the Moors it was surrounded by a wall flanked by a thousand towers, and held a vast population. At the summit of the loftiest hill was erected the royal fortress of the Alhambra, including the palace of the Caliphs, begun by Mohammed, who determined that it should surpass in magnificence all the royal palaces that had ever existed. It still stands, the delight and admiration of travellers; its graceful porticos and colonnades, its walls and ceilings worked in delicate arabesque, and glowing with soft tints and rich gold, make us think well of the taste and refinement of the king who designed such a beautiful place to live in. Its airy halls were built around gardens, full of roses, pomegranate, and jasmine, and courts, with fountains playing, and broad pools of water, in which were reflected the deep blue and floating clouds of the southern heaven.

King Mohammed ben Alhamar saw that the best foundation for thrones is the prosperity of the people. He applied himself to building hospitals for the sick, houses of entertainment for travellers, and of refuge for the poor: schools for children, and colleges for youth, not only in his capital but in many other towns throughout his kingdom; he had aqueducts laid for supplying the towns with plenty of water, always a matter of highest importance to the Moors, canals, baths, fountains were built in profusion. He fortified the kingdom with strongholds, both on the frontier and the interior, and although this was done by imposing heavy burdens on the people, in taxation, they did not complain, as they saw the national resources laid out for the good of the community. For the Moors were, as always, an industrious and sober people, devoted to agriculture, which they pursued with an intelligence which produced the best results. From the *vega*, or broad plain which stretches far away in sight of the seat of the capitol, the Arabs obtained a constant succession of fruits and crops throughout the year, by covering it with a network of channels through which flowed water to keep the soil constantly irrigated. They led happy, industrious lives, applying the wealth they so honestly gained, with an Oriental sense of beauty and color, to the adornment and luxury of living.

When the Christians and Moors were not actually at war, there was unhampered intercourse between them; they exchanged visits, formed acquaintances and friendships. The Spanish knight fell in love with the dark-eyed Zegri maiden, and in her honor contended for the prize of valor. The Moslem was not regarded as the "accursed misbeliever," to be shunned and maltreated as the Jews had always been, but as the brave and courtly knight with the same accomplishments and manners as the Christian gentleman.

This state of things might have remained, with continued improvement in the progress of time, each race learning something of the other,—the Moors learning from the Christians the elements of their purer faith, while the Christians would acquire much from them in the way of industry and thrift,—had it not been for the internal dissensions which broke up the empire of Granada, and the desire of the Christian kings to root out the Moslem belief. As the

Moors became more and more divided by petty quarrels, the Christians were becoming more closely united, and were ready to take advantage of every crack thus disclosed in the armor of their antagonists. Still, there were twenty-three kings of Granada who managed to reign in succession, and to conduct their affairs in a certain prosperity, interrupted at times by contests with their Christian neighbors, or jealous rivalries among themselves.

Most of these monarchs, or more than half of them, were named Mohammed. The fifth of the name had virtues, it is said, worthy of any throne, but, like the rest, he was not exempted from the curse of rebellion. He had a brother Ismail, of whom he was so fond, that he presented to him, for his own, a magnificent palace. But the mother of Ismail, who was not the mother of the king, was ambitious for her son and had long planned making him king. Such was one great source of the quarrels among the Moslems. Their laws allowed them at least three wives, so it often happened that the royal princes had different mothers, and each mother desired that her own son should reign, without regarding the question whether he were the eldest, or the most deserving. The mother of Ismail formed a party favorable to her son's interests, and they waited for some opportune chance to depose the king, and put the prince, his half-brother, on the throne.

At last, on the 28th day of the moon, Ramadan, one hundred of the most resolute of them scaled, by night, the palace of Mohammed, descended through the roof and lay hid till midnight. Then, at a given signal, they rushed down the staircase, and along the passages of the beautiful Alhambra, a sword in one hand, a torch in the other, raising loud cries, and putting everybody they met to death. At the same moment, a more numerous body of them overwhelmed and massacred the guard from the outside, and then rushing into the palace, laid hand on every thing they could carry away. These conspirators were so delighted with the riches and treasures they found lying about them, that they forgot the original purpose of the expedition, while they were filling their pockets, and this gave to Mohammed the opportunity of escape. He was clothed by his mother's women in the disguise of a female slave, and succeeded in escaping through the gardens to the open country. Ismail was put upon the throne, to the joy of his manœuvring mother, but her pleasure was of short duration, for the very chief she had employed to elevate her son to the throne, having learned the art of dethroning kings, persuaded the public to proclaim himself as monarch. The head of the unlucky Ismail was cut off and dragged through the mire, to the applause of the people. The conspiring usurper afterwards fell into the hands of the Christians, and was condemned to death for dethroning his lawful sovereign. Mohammed the Fifth, then returned to his throne.

Such instances of the sympathy of the Christains for the Moors were not uncommon. We may repeat the pretty story of a governor of Antiqueia, a frontier town constantly in warfare with the Moors in the neighborhood.

On the eve of an expedition, Narvaez, the governor, despatched some horsemen to reconnoitre the county. The men, perceiving no enemy, were returning, when they suddenly fell in with a Moorish horseman, and made him prisoner. He was a young man, about twenty-three years of age, handsome and attractive, and richly clothed. His arms were of exquisite workmanship, and he rode a splendid horse. Evidently he belonged to the very first families.

He was brought before the governor, who asked who he was, and whither he was going. The youth replied that he was the son of the Alcalde of Reuda; as he endeavored to go on he showed much emotion, in fact his voice was nearly choked with tears.

"What!" exclaimed the governor, "the son of the Alcalde! I know him well to be a brave warrior, but you are nothing better than a woman, for you weep like one. Are you such a coward as to fret for your capture, which is nothing but the fortune of war?"

"It is not the loss of my liberty that I lament, but a misfortune far greater," replied the Moor.

"Ah!" replied the kind-hearted governor, "let us hear your case, perhaps we can relieve it."

"I have long loved," the youth replied, "the daughter of an alcalde in our neighborhood. She loves me, and this very night is the one of our wedding. All is ready, she is awaiting me, and your soldiers have detained me! What will she think? She will doubtless die of anxiety and despair!"

"Noble cavalier!" replied the compassionate governor, "go and see your mistress; I will trust your return."

So the Moor departed, and in spite of the long distance and so much delay he reached the dwelling of his mistress before daylight. He relieved her fears of his constancy, but had to tell her he had come only to say farewell, as he was pledged to return to his captors.

"Generous man!" she said, "My fate must be united with yours; free or slave, you shall find me always at your side. Besides, in this casket are jewels enough to pay your ransom."

The two lovers set forth together, and toward evening they arrived at Antiqueia. They were nobly received by Narvaez, who heaped praises on the fidelity of the cavalier, and the devotion of the maiden. The contents of the casket he refused to touch, and dismissed them loaded with presents, and accompanied by an escort to conduct them safely to Reuda. The news spread through the kingdom of Granada, and became the subject of many a romance.

And now the end was approaching of what may be called the most romantic and picturesque period of modern history. For years two races of different religions had been living close to each other, in the loveliest climate in the world, in the midst of resources which gave them every opportunity for wealth and luxurious living. The age bent itself to romance. People were just wise enough to use their brains to write ballads and dream dreams, not so deeply intellectual as to pierce every mystery with the sword of science. The quarrel between the two kingdoms was an abstract one, based upon their different religious beliefs. Though they might call each other "misbeliever," and "Christian dog," there was no bitter underlying cause to prevent the young people from falling in love with each other. In fact, to judge from the ballads, we may fancy that their business was love-making, and their pastime going to war. Making all allowance for the glamor thrown by distance and poetry over the period, it was still a wonderful time of chivalric splendor and sentimental heroism.

But Ferdinand of Arragon had married Isabella of Castile, and the royal pair, calling themselves the Catholic kings of all Spain, were inspired with a fervid determination to root out of the country the enemies of the Christian religion. The queen herself was especially ardent, assembling troops, consecrating banners, and inspiring her favored knights. All the chivalry of Spain was enlisted in the cause, and the country rang with the promise of victory.

The time was favorable, for Granada was even more divided than usual into quarrelling factions. Muley Ali Abul Hassan was upon the throne, and he perhaps might have been able to keep his political enemies at a distance, but discord at home was too much for him. One of his wives, it is said, was a Spanish lady, whom he greatly loved, as well as her two sons, princes whom he favored with much of his time and affection. This made Zoraya, also his wife, and the mother of his oldest son, very jealous, and much afraid that her darling would be set aside in the succession. Abu Abdalla was the name of this prince; romantic history has given the abbreviated name of Boabdil.

THE FALL OF GRANADA. 221

The beautiful enclosure of the Alhambra was at that time the scene of many stormy interviews and many secret consultations.

It stood, and its ruins stand, on the top of a steep, cone-shaped hill, approached by a long drive-way, from the lower town of Granada. This avenue was irrigated by trickling water flowing down the hill,

VIEW OF THE ALHAMBRA.

and shaded by lofty trees and the thickest verdure. There roses blossomed, and jasmine and all "sweet things"; the nightingale's voice was ever sounding its strange, sad note; and fountains flashed a pleasant welcome to those who, winding up the steep, approached the lofty gates of the citadel.

The enclosure was fortified by a strong wall running round it with towers at intervals, some of which were for its defence, others for the pleasure of the fair ladies who lived there. These little palaces were adorned with all the rich taste of the Oriental monarchs. Within the walls was space enough for something like a small town, its occupants subservient to the needs of the monarchs. It contained streets, gardens, plazas, while the Alcazaba, or fortress, occupied one end, looking down a precipice to the town. Two rivers in the valley flowed about the eminence on which the Alhambra was built, and on one side the walls of the palace itself rose in perpendicular continuation of the steep ascent, so that the windows on that side overlooked the tops of tall trees reaching up from the valley far below. The material of which the Alhambra is built is of a rich yellow-red color, given it by the nature of the soil of which it is made. This gives the name of Torres Bamejas [Vermillion Tower] to an ancient castle without the enclosure; the term would answer as well to almost all the other buildings on the spot.

The palace itself of the Alhambra occupies a large part of the fortified enclosure, one side of it incorporated on the outer wall. The Arabs did not waste much time or money in outside ornamentation, and besides, a great deal of the original palace has been destroyed. The entrance is through a plain, low gateway, but once within, all the beauty of Arabic architecture shows itself.

There was room within the ample confines of the palace for half-a-dozen rival sultanas to keep their court, without interfering with each other. They had baths, and courts, and gardens, and miradors, and tocadors innumerable, all adorned with the graceful ornament of Moorish architecture, and filled with every luxury. Those halls were already rich with legends of departed sultanas, immured captive maidens; the floors of the courtyards were already stained with the blood of treacherous assassinations, and the subterranean depths of the mountain may bave even then contained the hidden treasures of vanished kings.

The Moors had taken Zahara, a stronghold of the Christians, and Muley Ali Abul Hassan returned to Grenada full of rejoicing, which was of short duration, for there he soon learned that the Christians in revenge had seized upon Alhama, one of the bulwarks of his capital, and not far from it.

When the news was brought to the king, the ballad says he would not believe it, but

> —— threw the lines in the fire
> And slew the messenger.

He summoned his army, and hastened to recover this important post ; but was recalled on account of domestic troubles in the Alhambra.

Zoraya, the mother of Boabdil, had thought this a good opportunity to incite the inhabitants of Granada to rebellion, from which she hoped to obtain advantages for her son.

The king, by this time, was well acquainted with the uncomfortable temper of his early wife. He was not surprised to find that she was the prime mover of the rebellion, and thought that he could put an end to it by confining her and her son in one of the strong places which abound in the Alhambra. Then he went away again.

Zoraya worked upon the feelings of her keepers and persuaded them to let her women come to her. The tower where they were confined was one of these overlooking the steep precipice. The women among them, by tying all their ample mantles together, made a rope long enough and strong enough to lower the young prince in a basket to the foot of the hill, where trusty horsemen were ready to receive him.

The prince was free. The anxious mother, from the battlement saw him off and away, and not long after, from the watch-tower of the turret where she was confined, there came up to her from the city, not far distant, shouts and cries which she knew must be:

"Long live the king, Abu Abdalla!"

A struggle followed between the adherents of father and son, in which the latter triumphed. Aided by his mother within the palace, the prince seized upon the Alhambra, and was recognized by the whole population of the foolish capital as their sovereign. Muley retired to Malaga, which adhered to him, and other towns declared in his favor.

Thus the time, blood, energy, and money which should have been all concentrated upon the expulsion of the Christian host which had sate down before the city, was wasted in internal discord. The short-sighted mother of Boabdil was so eager to place her son upon the throne, that she failed to see there soon would be no throne to place him upon.

In the spring of 1491, Ferdinand and Isabella invested the city of Granada, by establishing their camp upon the Vega, close under its walls. The queen herself was greatly interested in the city of Santa Fé, which was built just then for the comfort of the army and court.

The space between the camp and the city walls became the scene of a desperate struggle, which brought out the bravery and daring of the flower of both armies. Many a single combat took place between Moslem and Christian knight, each splendidly armed, and riding on steeds richly caparisoned. Moorish maiden and Spanish lady alike watched the combatants, and encouraged them by their applause, rewarding the victor with a ribbon or a smile.

But while the defence was maintained with so much bravery, the young monarch, Abdalla, *el re chico*, the little king, as he is called in the ballads, was in great secrecy negotiating a surrender with the Christian monarchs.

It was indeed impossible for the Moslems to hold out, and however the proud Zoraya, in one sense the cause of the ruin, might resist, the hour for her fall was come. Gonzaloo de Cordova, a Spaniard who was to become a great general, negotiated the terms of capitulation in the greatest secrecy with the Arab chiefs. A day was appointed for the surrender, but as the news of the agreement spread abroad, the agitation was so great in the city that the time was hastened, and on the 2d day of January, 1492, the last act in the drama was performed.

In spite of the prayers and tears of Zoraya,

Boabdil prepared himself to relinquish the crown he had so foolishly snatched from the head of his father Perhaps the two princes, his half-brothers, with their Spanish mother, silently exulted at the downfall of their rival, while they themselves were joined in the ruin.

The prince left the fortress accompanied by fifty of his chosen cavaliers, and sadly descended the hill from the Alhambra to the plain, and rode up to the position occupied by the Christian monarch, who was surrounded by his court, all splendidly dressed, with banners fluttering, and arms sparkling in the sun. As the Moor approached the Spaniard, he meant to throw himself from his horse and kneel upon the ground in token of homage; but Ferdinand would not allow this; on the contrary, he embraced him with every sign of kindness and compassion.

Boabdil held the great keys of the Alhambra in his hand. He extended them to the conqueror, saying:

"These keys are thine, O king, since Allah has decreed it; use thy success with clemency and moderation."

The Moorish monarch had still to signify his abdication to the Queen Isabella, who with all her retinue was stationed at some distance.

Then leaving the Christian sovereigns and their retinue to enter his city and celebrate their triumph with the solemn ceremonies of their religion and all the signs of exultant rejoicing, the Moorish king turned away, and joining his mother, the ambitious princess Zoraya, withdrew to the Alpuxarias, where he was allowed a barren retreat.

When the little party reached a rocky point among the hills which commanded a last view of Granada, Boabdil checked his horse, and burst into tears as he looked back upon the home of his childhood, the proud citadel and fortress of the Alhambra, over which already waved the Christian standard. His mother bitterly remarked, it is said:

"You do well to weep like a woman for what you could not defend like a man!"

Her son might have retorted: "Because you, like a woman, have deprived me of a kingdom which, not being a man, you could not defend!"

The spot is still pointed out where the Moorish king paused to look back upon his lost kingdom. It is called "El ultimo sospiro del moro."

Abu Abdalla, or Boabdil, did not long remain in Spain. He sold the little dominion which had been allowed him to Ferdinand, and then passed over to Fez with his family, where his kinsmen were princes. It was not long before he died there, slain in battle, defending the throne of the king of Fez.

Thus ended the war of Granada, and with the surrender of its capital the Arabian Empire in the Peninsula was terminated, after seven hundred and forty-one years from the date of the original conquest. Some Moors yet remained in Spain as late as the time of Philip III., but they had no further existence as a nation, and from this time dates the final extinction of a race which had made high advances in civilization, and brought the country they adopted to a state of cultivation and prosperity which it has not since surpassed. Their towns are in ruins, their palaces are deserted. The schemes for irrigation, by which they made the plains fertile and productive, have fallen away by neglect, and in consequence these fields often lie barren.

It is said that in Morocco there still exist those who regard themselves as the descendants of the Moors of Spain. It is a sort of proverb, when such a one sighs in his sleep, to say, "See! he is dreaming of Granada!"

FOUNTAIN OF THE LIONS.

PART IV.

CHAPTER XVI.

PELAYO.

WE must now go back to see what became of the small remnant of the Goths after they were conquered by the Moorish invasion, when Roderick was defeated. For it is evident that in the course of the centuries which followed, while the courts of Cordova and Granada flourished, the Christians must have been recovering their elasticity and strength, to be able at last to overthrow their enemies, and to drive out the invaders from their ancient soil.

The accounts are but shadowy of the early deeds of the Christians, after the defeat of Roderick. Some of the historians are Arabic, some Spanish, and they frequently contradict each other. The legends and ballads are more entertaining, and if not so accurate, still reliable enough to give an impression of the tendency of the times.

The Goths were not all dead upon the field of that fatal battle on the banks of the Gaudalquivir; they fled this way and that, seeking safety where best they could find it, and being driven into the northwest corner of Spain, they gradually found a sufficient body assembled to form a sort of colony, and later on a kingdom. They found there people that in the days of their greatness the Goths had endeavored to subdue, but now, before the terror of the Moslem horde which was sweeping all before it, old quarrels were forgotten and the various races united in a common cause. Thus, the modern Spaniard has in him something of the early inhabitants of those mountain fastnesses,—something, perhaps, of the Roman combined with the Goth in his blood. The discipline of endurance and privation which these refugees had to endure was good for them. The fierce old nature of the Visigoths had been weakened and lowered by years of luxury and success; it had now again to submit to hard work and rough living.

Among the refugees were some of the prelates who, it is said, had carefully carried the sacred relics to the mountains with them, so that they kept up the ceremonies of the Church, though far away from their grand cathedrals. Many of the Goths were of the noblest blood and of great bravery. Among these was PELAYO, descended, perhaps from the royal house of Chindaswind. Perhaps he was a nephew of King Roderick. His origin is wrapped in much obscurity. Let us believe him to be of the bluest blood.

The exiles chose him for their leader and crowned him king with such ceremonies as they could lay their hands upon. The new monarch soon had a chance to prove his kingship in an encounter with the Arabs, who had penetrated to their hiding-place. Pelayo concealed a small but resolute band of his troops in a cavern on the steep, rocky side of some mountain heights. The Arabs, knowing nothing of the cave, came plunging up the ascent to reach their enemy and were much surprised to find great stones and bits of rock tumbling down among them, knocking them over, and sweeping back their dense ranks into the valley below. Thousands were crushed by the great fragments, and so would all the rest have been, except that they ran away in great confusion. The small band of Christians came out of their hiding-place and pursued them, and the Arabs were so terrified by the proceeding, that they stayed away and molested the Christians no longer.

This and other successes fixed the little kingdom upon a firm foundation. The Asturias were left in the undisturbed possession of the new king. The crown, if there was a crown, at all events, the regal office, descended to the son of Pelayo, and afterwards remained in the family. Leon was captured from the Infidel, and gave its name to the kingdom, which steadily increased in numbers and power, for, towards the end of the eighth century, Alfonso II. was able to establish himself in Oviedo with all the ceremonies of a court. He made it the capital of his kingdom, and erected churches, founded public schools and hospitals, built baths, and decorated his palace with silver and gold vases and richly ornamented furniture. All this had come to pass in less than a hundred years from the time when Pelayo is supposed to have been living in a cave. Alfonso had become strong enough to make war upon the Arabs, in which he was often successful.

To his time belong the famous exploits of Bernardo del Carpio. He, the historians cruelly tell us, with his parents, are only creations of the imagination. But this is the story:

Alfonso el Casto, as he was called, was never married, and had no children. Apparently he wished no one else to marry, for he strongly opposed the marriage of his sister, the fair infanta Ximena. But she was beloved by the Count of Saldaña, and, as she loved him in return, they were secretly married and lived happily together, without letting any one know of their marriage, least of all the king. When he found it out, which he did in a year or two, he was terribly angry; he seized his sister and shut her up in a convent; he put her husband in prison for life, and sent their little son, who had been born in the meantime, into the Asturias.

People there imagined him to be the son of the king, and everybody treated him as if he were. He was brought up among the mountains to lead a healthy, out-door life, and became strong and brave, and handsome as the day. As soon as he was old enough he put on armor, and became a knight of the greatest prowess, the terror alike of Frank and Moor—all the time supposing he was the son of King Alfonso, although the king never said so, or treated him as such, except to furnish him with armor and all the accoutrements required for a knight of noble birth.

Now, the unfortunate Count Sancho Diaz was all this time in prison, where accounts were brought him, by his keepers, of the wonderful exploits of the young prince Bernardo del Carpio, as he was called. Sancho knew very well that this was his son—his only son. Some accounts say that the cruel king had caused Sancho's eyes to be put out. Blind and in prison he complained bitterly of the ingratitude of a child who could leave his father languishing in chains, while he rode about joyously on a fine horse, fighting in battle, and winning victory and praise wherever he went. But Bernardo knew nothing about it.

This was the time, according to the Spanish chronicles, when Charlemagne invaded Spain; and some of them say that it was by the invitation of Alfonso, who proposed to him to come and destroy the Moors, promising him in reward the inheritance of his own throne of the Asturias. There is nothing of this in history, nor, as we have seen, in the Song of Roland.

Bernardo del Carpio and all the other nobles of King Alfonso's court resented the plan of giving up the ancient kingdom of the Goths to a stranger, and Alfonso himself repented of his promise, so that when Charlemagne arrived, he found the king who had invited him allied with the infidels against him. According to this account, it was the troops of Alfonso who attacked the rear of the Franks in the pass of Rencesvalles; it was they who gained the victory in the fearful attack when Roland was slain, and their success was ascribed to the prowess of Bernardo del Carpio:

As through the glen his spears did gleam, the soldiers from the
    hills,

> They swelled his host, as mountain-stream receives the roaring rills;
> They round his banner flocked in scorn of haughty Charlemagne,
> And thus upon their swords are sworn the faithful sons of Spain.

When he was returning from this stupendous triumph, in the greatest state, with everybody at his feet, Bernardo learned—some say from the lips of his old nurse, who had kept the story to herself till then—the true story of his birth: how the king was his uncle; how his mother, whom, as a little boy, he dimly remembered, a fair and gentle lady who stroked his long curls, the king's sister, who was shut up in a cloister, not dead as he supposed; and how his father, blind and in chains, was languishing in a dungeon.

Full of wrath, and relying on his recent services to receive whatever he asked, he demanded of the king the release of his father. It was denied. Then Bernardo refused to come to the rejoicings which followed the victory. He shut himself up in his castle and remained there, still pressing the king with importunities for his father's release.

"Sir King and Uncle," said he, "is it fitting that I should be abroad and fighting thy battles, when my father is in fetters? Release him, and I shall think myself well rewarded."

As the king did nothing of the kind, Bernardo went over to the side of his enemies, the Moors. He fortified his castle, and made continual incursions into the king's country, pillaging and plundering wherever he came, and encouraging the inroads of the king's enemies.

At last the counsellors of the king urged him to offer Bernardo immediate possession of his father's person if he would surrender his castle. Bernardo accepted without hesitation. He gave up the keys. joined the king, and with him rode out to meet his long lost parent.

When he saw him coming, clothed in splendid attire, and mounted on horseback, Bernardo exclaimed: "O God! is that indeed the Count of Saldaña?" "Look where he is," replied the king, "and go and greet him whom you so long have desired to see."

Bernardo advanced and took his father's hand to kiss it. The body fell forward heavily; it was only a corpse. The king had caused him to be slain. Bernardo del Carpio swore a fearful vengeance upon the king, and from that moment his sword was lost to the Christians. But we are left entirely in the dark as to the rest of his story.

The historians say that no such person ever existed as Bernardo del Carpio, as they assert that the whole story of Roland and his wonderful horn is a pure fiction. Bernardo's name, they say, was never mentioned until five hundred years afterwards. This is sad, but we may comfort ourselves with thinking that the ballads would never have been sung, the stories told from mouth to mouth, had there not been some foundation for them. The spirit of high renown and bravery was in existence which prompted heroic deeds. The tender friendship between Roland and Olivier was real, or it would not have been made the subject of a song. The deeds themselves and the motives which prompted them, and, besides, the manners and customs of the time in which they are described as happening, are what we care to know about, and these we gather from ballad and tale, and only wish there were more of the same sort to light up the solemnity of historical records.

The early Catholics believed faithfully in their saints, and the best saint for them of all was James the Elder, the brother of John the Evangelist.

James was stoned to death in Jerusalem, but the Spaniards firmly believe that his body was transferred to their country, where the Bishop Theodemir, in 835, found it in Galicia, being led to the place by a star which pointed it out to him, where it lay in a forest. A chapel was erected on the spot, but the body was moved a short distance later to the place now called Santiago or Saint Jago de Campostella, on account of the star having led to the discovery. A cathedral was erected there, and under it, in a subterranean chapel, was placed the tomb of the saint. Pilgrims flocked to Campostella to worship the shrine, which became one of the most famous in the world; and Santiago, from his choice of Spain as a final resting-place, became the patron of the land.

Ramiro, the successor of Alfonso el Casto, had reason to worship the saint. It was not very long after his body had been discovered in the neighborhood, that he showed his watchfulness over the Spanish arms. The occasion was a battle with the Saracens at Clavigo. It had already waged through the whole of one day, and the fortune of war had been against the Christians.   An old writer describes it:

Night arrived, and brought safety to ours, since there is nothing, however small, in war, which may not be turned to good account.

Ramiro drew his troops, alike diminished in number and weakened by fear, to a neighboring hill; there he confessed himself vanquished. The place was fortified, the wounded attended ; yet such were the despair and lamentation that all were engaged in prayer or drowned in tears.

As the king was thus oppressed by grief, and anxious for the result, sleep fell upon him. As he slept, the apparition of Santiago, more majestic than any human figure, bade him be of good courage, since, with the aid of heaven, he might indulge assured hope of victory on the following day.

Cheered by these words of the apostle, and delighted with the tidings, he arose from his couch, commanding his prelates and chiefs to be summoned before him, and then addressed them at length, urging them to battle, and filling them with joy by acquainting them with the celestial vision and promise of victory.

Having thus spoken, he commanded the lines to be drawn out, and the trumpets to sound. With great eagerness ours rushed on the enemy, calling loudly on the name of Saint James, which from this time forward became the common invocation of the Spanish soldiers. The barbarians, astonished at the boldness of ours, whom they considered vanquished beyond redemption, and overcome with fear from heaven, could not bear the onset.

Santiago, as he had promised the king, was seen on a white horse, bearing aloft a white standard, on which was inscribed in red the form of a cross. The courage of ours was increased, that of the barbarian vanished at the sight. The flight was dishonorable, not less the destruction; sixty thousand Moors were slain.

"At this day," says the old writer, "the bones and arms which are dug up sufficiently show us Clavigo where the battle was fought."

The victorious army, in gratitude for divine aid, bowed to the saint under whose guidance the battle had been won, that all Spain should thenceforth be tributary to the church of Campostella, and that every acre of ploughed and vine land should pay every year a bushel of corn or wine to that church.

That Santiago did assist Ramiro is proved by a perpetual miracle. In all the vicinity of Clavigo, where the battle was fought, scallop-shells are found in the stones, so exact and perfect that art could not form a more accurate resemblance. Some say they have been there since the apostle preached there in his lifetime, others refer them to the time of this battle.

The scallop was the mark of a pilgrim to Campostella, as the palm was of those who had visited the Holy Land. The words palmer and pilgrim are therefore not exactly the same.

Perhaps it was this king, perhaps another, who can tell, who had promised to furnish every year, as tribute to Abderahman, one hundred beautiful damsels. He failed this time to keep his promise, and hence the battle. It is hinted that his failure was because so many beautiful women could not be found in the Asturias; the ballad gives a better reason. It tells how a maiden sought audience of King Ramiro, and set before him the folly of sending women to the enemy's camp, as well as the want of gallantry of it. She even threatened him with the displeasure of her sex.

> I pray you, sire, take warning,—You 'll have as good a fight
> If e'er the Spanish damsels arise themselves to right.

Then uprose King Ramiro, and his nobles every one, and went forth to battle, swearing to put an end to the maiden tribute.

> A cry went through the mountains, when the proud Moor came near,
>   And trooping to Ramiro came every Christian spear ;
> The blesséd Santiago, they called upon his name—
>   That day began our freedom, and wiped away our shame.

Legends of the apparition of Saint Jago on the battle-field are many. He is sometimes accompanied by another ghostly warrior and saint.

FROM THE VIDA DE SAN MILAN.
BY GONSALO DE BERCEO.

> And when the kings were in the field, their squadrons in array,
> With lance in rest they onward pressed to mingle in the fray ;
> But soon upon the Christians fell a terror of their foes,—
> These were a numerous army, a little handful those.
>
> And while the Christian people stood in this uncertainty,
> Upward toward heaven they turned their eyes and fixed their
>   thoughts on high,
> And there two persons they beheld, all beautiful and bright,
> Even than the pure new-fallen snow their garments were more white.

They rode upon two horses more white than crystal sheen,
And arms they bore such as before no mortal man had seen ;
The one he held a crosier, a pontiffs mitre wore ;
The other held a crucifix,—such man ne'er saw before.

Their faces were angelical, celestial forms had they,—
And downward through the fields of air they urged their rapid way ;
They looked upon the Moorish host with fierce and angry look
And in their hands, with dire portent, their naked sabres shook.

The Christian host, beholding this straightway take heart again,
They fall upon their bended knees, all resting on the plain,
And each one with his clenchéd fist to smite his breast begins,
And promises to God on high he will forsake his sins.

And when the heavenly knights drew near unto the battle ground ;
They dashed among the Moors and delt unerring blows around.
Such deadly havoc there they made the foremost ranks along,
A panic terror spread into the hindmost of the throng.

Together with these two good knights, the champions of the sky,
The Christians rallied and began to smite full sore and high :
The Moors raised up their voices, and by the Koran swore
That in their lives such deadly fray they ne'er had seen before.

Down went the misbelievers : fast sped the bloody fight,
Some ghastly and dismembered lay, and some half dead with fright :
Full sorely they repented that to the field they came,
For they saw that from that battle they should retreat with shame.

Another thing befell them,—they dreamed not of such woes,—
The very arrow that the Moors shot from their twanging bows
Turned back against them in their flight and wounded them full sore,
And every blow they dealt the foe was paid in drops of gore.

Now he that bore the crosier, and the papal crown had on
Was the glorified Apostle, the brother of Saint John ;
And he that held the crucifix, and wore the monkish hood,
Was the holy San Milano of Cogalla's neighborhood.

There is a story of one of these kings about this time, named Sancho the Fat. He was so very fat that he could not get about comfortably, and as no Christian leech could prescribe for the difficulty, he wrote to the Moorish king, Abderahman III., and asked permission to visit the capital, in order to see what the Arabic physicians of Cordova could do for him, as they were very famous. A cordial invitation was the response of the Caliph.

The king went as a guest to the palace at Cordova, and was received and entertained with magnificence, while the royal physicians were put at his disposition. They brought him a herb which took away all his fatness, and reduced him to his pristine light weight. Moreover, he became so friendly with the Moslems, that they agreed to lend a hand in restoring him to his throne which had been taken from him. The light and agile king, to the amazement of his enemies, returned from Andalusia with an army, drove the intruder from his throne, and prepared to reign comfortably himself. Unluckily he was poisoned not long afterward by one of his Christian allies.

Little states were springing up everywhere, and claiming to be great ones. Navarre, close by the Asturias was a kingdom by this time. Its earlier history is obscure. Wedged in between France and Spain, it has always been a sort of fighting ground for both countries. Pampeluna, its chief city, was the one laid waste by Charlemagne according to the Song of Roland; and its rulers were sometimes of French descent, and, later on, Navarre furnished to France one of the greatest of her kings.

In the early times, the connection was close, often by blood, with the kings of Asturia and Leon, sometimes it was peaceful, sometimes warlike. In fact, it was a question of who was the stronger and who could get and hold the upper hand. No broad underlying rule of policy could be expected of the early kings of the Spanish states. To keep the Moslem from the door was their chief aim, and, in times of great danger, they united upon this. A powerful king, with a talent for ruling, could compel the adherence of those around him, and make himself the leader of them, to invade the region of the Arabs, or to protect his own from them. At his death, his kingdom fell off again, broken up into little states. Yet with all this the Christian territory was spreading over more and more of Spain, while, as we have seen, the Moslems were forced to recede into ever narrower limits.

The courts of Castile, up to this time, had been regarded as dependent upon the kings of Asturia, or Leon. One of them, Fernan Gonzalez, has a story so romantic that the historians can hardly bear to believe that he was a real character. But there is ample proof that he was really alive, somewhere near the middle of the tenth century, in the reign of King Ramiro II., of Leon. Fernan Gonzalez with another Count of Castile, revolted against their sovereign, alleging as a reason that they did not want to fight any more just then against the Arabs. He was on his way to Navarre, to marry Sancha, a princess of that court, when he was seized and thrown into prison by the King of Leon. The ballads say that he was thus imprisoned to please the Queen of Leon, who was also a princess of Navarre, and an enemy of Fernan. The ballads tell, that while he was in prison, a Norman pilgrim, on his way back from Campostella, where he had been to visit the tomb of Saint James, heard something of his story, as he passed near the place where Count Fernan was confined. As this Norman was in no great hurry, he bribed the alcalde of the place, to let him see the illustrious captive.

> The alcalde was so joyful,—he took the gold full soon,
> He brought him to the dungeon, ere the rising of the moon.

They had a long talk, and Fernan told him the story, and how he was pining for love of the Princess Sancha, whom now he might never see.

The Norman passing through Navarre, hastened to the palace, sought an interview with the princess, and told her his tale.

"May God and St. Mary forgive you, infanta!" said the stranger. "You are causing the death of the best man alive. Count Fernan Gonzalez, the hero of Castile, is dying for love of you, but he lies in a dungeon. Unless you help him, you will be the scorn of the world; but if you will aid him to escape, you will be Queen of Castile!"

Sancha hastened to the prison, bringing her jewels to bribe the alcalde. Again he must have thought he was in luck. He allowed her to carry off his prisoner, and they hastened off together through the forest.

Towards evening they were alarmed by the appearance of a troop of horsemen. The infanta ran to conceal herself behind some bushes, when she was recalled by the voice of her lover, who had recognized among the approaching band the pennon of Castile. They were his own vassals, who had left Burgos, his native place, in a body, swearing a great oath never to return without their beloved chief.

There was great rejoicing, and Fernan and the princess were married at the first opportunity.

The count was fond of hunting, and once, although on the eve of a battle with the Moors, he pursued a wild boar into the mountains. He was eagerly following the animal, when suddenly it disappeared in a mysterious manner, and the count, to his surprise, found himself in a grotto converted into an oratory, with an humble altar in it, dedicated to Saint Peter. Moved with reverence at so unexpected a sight, the huntsman fell upon his knees and began his devotions. A hermit then appeared, who, it seems, abode in that place for the sake of a holy life. He received the count with great courtesy, kept him over night as his guest, and when he left him in the morning, gave him the assurance that he would triumph over the misbelievers. The event justified the prediction, and Gonzalez was convinced that the boar had led him by a miracle to the holy grotto.

Later on, during an irruption of the fierce Almanzor into Castile, Count Fernan on the eve of battle sought again the cell of his friend, the hermit, hoping for his prayers and perhaps a sign concerning the fate of battle. The holy man was there no longer; dead, perhaps. But while the count slept again in the cell, now solitary, he saw Pelayo, the hermit, in his dreams, who again promised victory. And next day, in the midst of the battle, Santiago, the martial patron of Spain, was once more seen upon his white horse, with cross and banner unfurled. The grateful count founded a monastery on the site of the grotto dedicated to Saint Peter.

Burgos, the native town of this hero of romance, as well as of the Cid, even more celebrated, has a statue of Fernan Gonzalez, and an arch erected to his memory by Philip II.

History admits that Fernan Gonzalez not only lived, but died (in 970), and that he was the founder of the sovereignty of Castile, of which he made a kingdom. Not long after Castile, as well as Leon, came into the hands of a king of Navarre, for there was much intermarrying between the royal houses of these small states. After this, for two centuries they were sometimes divided, sometimes united,—sometimes one king bore the titles of the three provinces. When this was the case, the successes of the Christians over the Moslems extended their domain more and more toward the south. In 1085 Alfonso VI. regained Toledo from the Moslems, after it had remained in their power for more than three centuries.

CHAPTER XVII.

THE CID.

THE Moorish dominion over southern Spain lasted for seven centuries. At the beginning there was perpetual war on the frontier which parted Mussulmans and Christians. Of this daily fighting there is, fortunately, and, of course, no record. Ballads and legends preserve the memory of this and that incident, which has a special interest for romance; but it would be hard to make out even a dry calendar of the names of the different princes who wore the different Spanish crowns, such as they were. The peaceful habits of the Goths, as we describe them in the period before Roderick's fall, were wholly forgotten. "It was in war that the chiefs found their sport and their spoil: that the king at once employed and gratified a turbulent nobility; that the people indulged their worst passions, and believed that they were at the same time atoning for their sins. And what a warfare! It was to burn the standing corn, to root up the vine and the olive, to hang the heads of their enemies from the saddle-bow, and to drive mothers and children before them with the lance, to massacre the men of a town in the fury of assault, to select the chiefs that they might be murdered in cold blood, to reserve the women and the children for slavery; and this warfare lasted year after year till they rested from mere exhaustion. At one time knights, nobles, and kings never slept unless the war-horse were standing ready saddled in the bedchamber." This is Mr. Southey's description of the generations into which Rodrigo del Bivar, better known as the Cid or Campeador, was born. Cid or Sid is an Arabic word, signifying chief. Campeador has a derivation similar to our word champion, and has a similar meaning.

Among the many sceptics of the nineteenth century, there have risen critics who coolly doubt the very existence of the Cid. They set him on one side coolly, as a being as imaginary as Lancelot or as Amadis. What is to be remarked especially is the curious fact that the poem which bears his name is much more to be relied upon,—or, on its face, appears more probable than what is called the "chronicle." For once poetry indicates a claim to be closer to the fact than prose.

The question regarding the credence to be given to the legends is, as the reader knows, not a peculiar one in the case of the Cid. It is almost exactly like the question regarding the myths of our own King Arthur. Was there, or was there not, a real Arthur, around whom clustered the stories of the Round Table. The reader of "The Story of Spain" has already had a like question in regard to Roland and Olivier,—and the extraordinary "Song of Roland," and his defeat in Roncesvalles.

The politics or intrigues in the midst of which the

Cid fought his first battles and won his first victories, can be written out in detail more than sufficient. More than sufficient, for no reader would remember them for an hour after he had read them, nor would it profit him to remember them a minute after. It is quite enough to say that Don Sancho, the king of Navarre and Leon and Castile, died, leaving three sons, and to each son, as if it were a fairy tale, he left one of these kingdoms, so called. As he might have foreseen, or as even the least experienced reader of fairy tales could have taught him, these sons fell to fighting with each other. " For it was by no means in wars against the Saracen alone that the blood of Christian men was spent."

This is the language of the poet Southey, in the introduction to his translation in the chronicle of the Cid. For our purpose the absolute veracity of the chronicle is not important. We do not read it for the stubborn facts, which are not, after all, of so much importance, as the light which it throws on the manner and customs of the time, on its sentiment and on its faith. The Cid may be roughly remembered as being about the contemporary of William the Conqueror, and his sons. The chronicle of the Cid was written, rather more than a century after, a little later than the time of Richard Cœur-de-Lion. This is to say that it is written in the time when romances began to take the form which they held until the time when Cervantes laughed them out of existence, and, as has been said, the Cid and his affairs belong almost precisely to that mythic or mysterious period to which Amadis of Gaul, Palmerin, and Esplandian, were made to belong by their authors. These are entirely creatures of the imagination, while, as we suppose, Rodrigo del Bivar and his exploits, were as real as Arthur and the Emperor Justinian. After-ages of Spanish chivalry read all the stories with equal confidence. To Cortes and his companions the prowess of Amadis was something as certain as that of the Cid, and when he came to give a name to the peninsula of California, he took it from the romance of Esplandian, where it is given to the farthest island of the east, the island of a Amazon queen or califa, whose home was rich in diamonds and gold.

It will be better for the reader that we shall copy a single story of the life of the Cid, than that we shall attempt to condense the narrative of his various exploits in my abridgement. Enough that he served Fernando, the king of Castile, and considered himself always bound to sustain the honor of Castile. In such duty he fought now against Arragon, now against Leon, now against Navarre, now against Valencia. Sometimes he was against the Moors, sometimes he fought with them. King Alfonso banished him once and again. But the Cid was more than a match for King Alfonso. The Cid's daughters, according to the romance, married the Counts of Carrion, but the Cid and his sons-in-law did not fare well together, and the last years of his life were made wretched by these worse than Paynim hounds.

Here is Mr. Southey's rendering of the scene where the Cid proclaims his unwillingness to serve any king as a vassal.

"My Cid and his company alighted at the gate of the palaces of Galiana, and he and his people went in gravely, he in the midst and his hundred knights round about him. When he who was born in happy hour entered, the good king, Don Alfonso, rose up, and the counts, Don Aurrich and Don Remond, did the like, and so did all the others, save the curly-headed one of Granon, and they who were on the side of the Infantes of Carrion. All the others received him with great honor, and he said unto the king: 'Sir, where do you bid me sit with these my kinsmen and friends who are come with me?' And the king made answer: 'Cid, you are such a one, and have passed your time so well to this day, that if you would listen to me and be commanded by me, I should hold it good that you took your seat with me; for he who hath conquered kings, ought to be seated with kings.' But the Cid answered: 'That, Sir, would not please God, but I will be at your feet; for by the favor of the king, your father, Don Fernando, was I made his creature and the creature of your brother, King Don Sancho, am I, and it behooveth not that he who receiveth bounty should sit with him who dispenseth it.' And the king answered: 'Since you will not sit with me, sit on your ivory seat, for you won it like a good man; and from this day I order that none except king or prelate sit with you, for you have conquered so many high-born men, and so many kings, both Christians and Moors, that for this reason there is none who is your peer, or ought to be seated with you. Sit, therefore, like a king and lord upon your ivory seat.' Then the

PUERTA DI SANTA MARIA, BURGOS.

Cid kissed the king's hand, and thanked him for what he had said, and for the honor which he had done him; and he took his seat, and his hundred knights seated themselves round about him. All who were in the Cortes sat looking at my Cid and at his long beard which he had bound with a cord; but the Infantes of Carrion could not look upon him for shame."

Like most knights of chivalry or of romance who were confident in their own lances and their own valor, " our Cid " was very indifferent to the orders of the king in whose dominions he happened to live. In a fashion he was respectful to him, as has been seen, but absolute obedience was quite another affair. At one time when he had made a raid into the dominions of the Moorish king of Toledo, Alfonso, his own sovereign, who was bound by a treaty with that prince, remonstrated. In the end the Cid was banished from Leon and Castile. His followers, however, refused to leave him.

As he was about to depart, he looked back upon his own home. And, when he saw his hall deserted, the household chests unfastened, the doors open, no cloaks hanging up, no seats in the porch, no hawks upon the perches, the tears came into his eyes, and he said: 'My enemies have done this. God be praised for all things.' So he and his cavalcade came to Burgos. But the people would not receive him there, and he had to take up his lodging on the sands near the town. He escaped from immediate need by pawning to two Jews two chests of treasure, which he told them were full of gold. The Jews ad-

STREET IN VALENCIA.

vanced him six hundred marks on security so good. But alas, when he failed to pay, as he did, it proved that the chests were filled with sand. Such a story as that is told as if it were a good joke, so completely does hatred of the Jews overshadow any gleams of the moral sense in their chivalrous chronicles.

At last, King Alfonso attacks Toledo and takes it from the Moors. As always in the chronicle, the Cid leads the way. His was the first banner to enter, and he is made the first Alcalde of the place. But this does not mean that he accepts permanent service under Alfonso. He always appears as a free lance, serving as he will against some chosen enemy of the hour.

In the course of such fighting, he becomes governor of Valencia and commander, of course, of its garrison. But such a command was challenged by the Moors, of whom thirty thousand, as we are told, invested the city. The Cid never counted the enemy. He sallied forth, and beat them in the field, drove them to the river Xucat, and killed fifteen thousand as he did so.

" Be it known." says the chronicle, " that this was a profitable day's work. Every foot-soldier shared a hundred marks of silver that day; and the Cid returned full honorably to Valencia. Great was the joy of the Christians in the Cid Ruy Dias, who was born in a happy hour. His beard was grown, and continued to grow, a great length. My Cid said of his chin: 'For the love of King Don Alfonso, who hath banished me from his land, no scissors shall come upon it, nor shall a hair be cut away, and

Moors and Christians shall talk of it.'" And this one he kept until he died. He made a count of his own followers. "There are found one thousand knights of lineage, and five hundred and fifty other horsemen. There were four thousand foot-soldiers, besides boys and others. Thus many were the people of my Cid, him of Bivar. And his heart rejoiced, and he smiled, and said: 'Thanks be to God, and to Holy Mother Mary. We had a smaller company when he left the house of Bivar.'"

In the next year King Yussef * invested Valencia again. And this time the Saracens had fifty thousand men. The Cid went out to meet them with four thousand. His bishop, Hieronymo, "a full learned man and wise, and one who was mighty on horseback and on foot," absolved the little company. "He who shall die," said he, "fighting full forward, I will take his sins and God shall have his soul." Then said he: "A boon, Cid don Rodrigo; I have sung mass to you this morning. Let me have the giving of the first wounds in this battle." And the Cid gave him leave in the name of God. And indeed the bishop had fighting enough that day. He fought with both hands, and no man knew how many he slew. Of course, as a sceptic historian writes, the horde of Yussef was destroyed—only fifteen thousand of the misbelievers escaped. The Cid secured the famous sword Tizona, which belonged to Yussef, and he scarcely escaped, sorely wounded.

* Of these invasions of Yussef the reader has seen the calmer account, in history, in a previous chapter.

Bucar, Yussef's brother, comes to avenge him. The Cid arrays his army with the bishop on the right wing. "The bishop pricked forward. Two Moors he slew with the two first thrusts of his lance, the haft broke, and he laid hold on his sword. God! how well the bishop fought. He slew two with the lance and five with the sword. The Moors fled. The Cid pursued Bucar," and made at him to strike him with his sword. And the Moorish king knew him. "Turn this way, Bucar," cried the Cid—"you who came from behind sea to see the Cid with the long beard. We must greet each other and cut out a friendship." "God confound such friendships," cried King Bucar, and turned his bridle and began to fly toward the sea, and the Cid after him, having great desire to reach him. But King Bucar had a good horse and a fresh, while the Cid went spurring Buvieca, who had had hard work that day, and he came near his back. And when they were nigh to the ships the Cid saw that he could not reach him, and he darted his sword at him and struck him between the shoulders; and King Bucar, being badly wounded, rode into the sea and got into a boat, and the Cid alighted and picked up his sword. And his people came up, hewing down the Moors before them, and the Moors in their fear of death ran into the sea, so that twice as many died in the water as in the battle; nevertheless, so many were they that were slain in the battle that they were thought to be seventeen thousand persons, and upward. And so many were they who were taken prisoners that it was a wonder; and of the twenty-nine kings who came with Bucar seventeen were slain.

The reader now has reason for understanding why the narration of the chronicle is dismissed from the domain of stern history. A passage from the poem which has been called the noblest poem in Spanish literature, will give him an idea of the Cid's courage before lions.

" Peter Bermuez arose ; somewhat he had to say ;
   The words were strangled in his throat, they could not find their way ;
   Till forth they came at once, without a stop or stay ;
   'Cid, I'll tell you what, this always is your way ;
   You have always served me thus ; whenever we have come
   To meet here in the Cortes, you call me Peter the Dumb.
   I cannot help my nature ; I never talk nor rail ;
   But when a thing is to be done, you know I never fail.
   Fernando, you have lied, you have lied in every word ;
   You have been honored by the Cid, and favored and preferred.
   I know of all your tricks, and can tell them to your face :
   Do you remember in Valencia the skirmish and the chase ?
   You asked leave of the Cid to make the first attack ;
   You went to meet a Moor, but you soon came running back.
   I met the Moor and killed him, or he would have killed you ;
   I gave you up his arms, and all that was my due.
   Up to this very hour, I never said a word ;
   You praised yourself before the Cid, and I stood by and heard
   How you had killed the Moor, and done a valiant act ;
   And they believed you all, but they never knew the fact.
   You are tall enough and handsome, but cowardly and weak,
   Thou tongue without a hand, how can you dare to speak ?
   There's the story of the lions should never be forgot ;
   Now let us hear, Fernando, what answer have you got ?
   The Cid was sleeping in his chair, with all his knights around ;
   The cry went forth along the hall, that the lion was unbound.
   What did you do, Fernando ? like a coward as you were,
   You slunk behind the Cid, and crouched beneath his chair.
   We pressed around the throne, to shield our loved from harm,
   Till the good Cid awoke ; he rose without alarm ;
   He went to meet the lion with his mantle on his arm ;

> The lion was abashed the noble Cid to meet;
> He bound his mane to the earth, his muzzle at his feet
> The Cid by the neck and mane drew him to his den,
> He thrust him in at the hatch, and came to the hall again;
> He found his knights, his vassals, and all his valiant men;
> He asked for his sons-in-law, they were neither of them there.
> I defy you for a coward and a traitor as you are.'"

Such victories cannot last forever, even under the pen of a romancer of the twelfth century. At last the Cid comes to his death.

He took to his bed. Saint Lazarus had told him forty years before, that in his bed he should die. And for seven nights he saw visions. He saw his father, Diego Laynez, and Diego Rodriguez, his son. And every time they said to him: "You have tarried long here, let us go now among the people who endure forever." And after the seven nights, Saint Peter appeared to him in the night when he was awake and not sleeping, and told him that when thirty days were over he should pass away from this world. And so it was. When the thirtieth day came he bade the bishop, Don Hieronymo, give him the body of our Lord and Saviour Jesus Christ. And he received it with great devotion. And he called upon God and St. Peter, and prayed, and said: "I beseech thee pardon me my sins and let my soul enter into the light which hath no end." And so this noble baron yielded up his soul, which was pure and without spot, to God.

Whether there have been many other such heroes as the Cid, it would be hard to say. What is certain is that there have been few heroes who have been so fortunate in their biography. The poem of the Cid, as has been said, may be more relied upon than the chronicle for historical accuracy. The chronicle is one of the most charming of the romances, having that flavor which no imagination can rival, which greets us where the foundation is true. English readers have the pleasure of reading the chronicle in a translation by Robert Southey, and the poem, as it has been rendered by Hookham Frere and by Mr. Ormsby.

Torre del Oro - Seville.
Saml Colman

CHAPTER XVIII.

ALFONSO X.

Quien no ha visto Sevilla
No ha visto maravilla.

SEVILLE was a prosperous port under the Phœnicians; and was singularly favored by the Scipios. In 45 B.C., Julius Cæsar entered the city; he enlarged it, strengthened and fortified it, and thus made it a favorite residence with the patricians of Rome, several of whom came to live there; no wonder, with its perfect climate and brilliant skies. It was then called Hispalis.

There are still vestiges of its magnificence during Roman rule,—an amphitheatre and an aqueduct,—and Roman coins are still found by those who dig beneath the soil.

The Vandals, driven from Septimania and the north of Spain, made their court in Seville. Andalusia, we saw, means Vandalicia. They remained there until they passed off into Africa to the number of eighty thousand, leaving nothing more than a name behind them.

The Goths held Seville for their capital until Leovigild established his court at Toledo, and left Seville to his rebel son.

GALLERY OF PEDRO I., SEVILLE

A year after the defeat of Roderick it resisted for a month the attacks of the Moors, under whom, in time, it became most prosperous. The capital of the Omeyyades was Cordova, but Seville grew in wealth and splendor until it became the second city of all the brilliant Caliphate. Thousands of industrious Moslems were engaged in manufacturing silks and other fabrics; its schools and universities rivalled those of Cordova.

This city shared the fate of the rest of Moorish Spain, and surrendered to the Christians on the 22d of December, 1248.

This was the achievement of King Ferdinand III., under whom the Crowns of Castile and Leon had become united. His territory extended from the Bay of Biscay to the Guadalquivir, and from the borders of Portugal as far as Arragon and Valencia. His glory was great in the estimation of his countrymen for his conquests over the Moors, and four centuries afterwards he was canonized by the Pope, and is now knows as Saint Ferdinand. He was just and pious, an able ruler, and a valiant soldier. He persecuted heretics with vigor, and was incessant in prayers, fasting, and frequent use of the discipline, for which virtues he was found worthy of canonization.

Ferdinand converted the mosque he found in Seville into a cathedral, of which, however, little now remains of his time. The beautiful Giralda, a belltower of the present cathedral, is Moorish, and is said to have been devised by an Arabic architect named Geber, of whom many tales are told. One of the portals of the cathedral has on it a great stuffed crocodile, said to have been sent to Saint Ferdinand by the Sultan of Egypt, alive, as a present.

In the royal chapel of the present cathedral is a silver urn with glass sides, which contains the body of the saint, carefully preserved. The king is draped in his royal robes, with the crown on his head; his hands are crossed upon his breast. On his right lies the *baston de mando*, his sceptre; on the left, his sword. The precious stones, which once adorned the handle of the sword, were picked out and taken away by order of one of Ferdinand's successors, lest, as he said, they might be carried off by somebody else.

The sepulchre of the saint bears inscriptions in Latin, Hebrew, and Arabic, written by the learned son of the saint. The body is displayed on certain days with a mass and other ceremonies.

Ferdinand lived at the same time with another king who was also canonized—Louis IX. of France, who became Saint Louis. He was the true hero of his time, a prince as pious as brave, who deserved, if ever did earthly sovereign, to be called a saint. The two kings, in fact, were cousins, and the grandmother of both of them was Eleanor, daughter of Henry II. of England.

Spain was now taking such an important place among the kingdoms of the civilized world, that her princes and princesses often made marriages with the other royal houses. It may be that the solid qualities of the Anglo-Saxon race gave vigor to the Southern stock on which these were grafted, to produce the admirable combination which afterwards, in its most brilliant period, distinguished the true Spaniard.

The son of Saint Ferdinand was Alfonso X., called *El Sabio*, the learned, and not, as it is sometimes translated, "the wise." He certainly was not very wise, for he did an immense number of foolish things; but he was such a strange man, that it would be interesting to know more about him than it is easy to do.

It was a period when not only commerce and industry but literature and art were taking a new start in Europe—the time of Roger Bacon and Dante. Alfonso loved his books, and dabbled in science, and was really one of the learned men of his time. It was a pity that he was born to be a king, and had to pass his life amid the cares of state, for he made constant and singular mistakes of policy in his government, while he had to give up to it most of his time, which, if he had been a private individual, he could have spent in intellectual pursuits more to his taste. He laid the foundation of Spanish prose by causing a translation of the Bible to be made in that language, and by writing excellent Spanish himself. His prose is said to be admirable, and his verses to have considerable merit, for a king's. He drew up a Code of Laws which is celebrated for its wisdom and its literary merit; and wrote a Chronicle of Spain, beginning with the creation of the world and coming down to the death of Saint Ferdinand, his father. It gives many of the romantic traditions of his country in a simple and poetic manner. Alfonso was learned in mathematics and astronomy. His "astronomical tables," for a long time celebrated, were probably constructed for him by Moorish astronomers whom he invited to his court.

DIE GIRALDA.

All these things give a delightful idea of Alfonso "the Wise," but, unfortunately, he managed the affairs of his kingdom so unwisely as to irritate his subjects at the time and bring trouble upon his descendants.

His mind was very naturally disturbed by a glimpse he had of being emperor of Germany, a position which had been the most glorious one to be attained in Europe. The dignity was elective, and at that time the electors, for reasons they considered good, had resolved to make choice of a foreign prince. The mother of Alfonso was the daughter of a German emperor; this led some of the electors to turn their thoughts upon Alfonso as a candidate. He aspired to the dignity, and was willing to lavish wealth upon obtaining it. He was, indeed, chosen by one party, but another, and more powerful one, preferred to name Richard, the brother of the English King Henry III. The contest lasted a long time until another emperor was elected, when, having wasted much time and money, having tired out everybody with his persistence, and after the Pope, losing all patience, had excommunicated his few adherents, King Alfonso returned to his books.

Ferdinand de la Cerda, the son and heir of Alfonso, died during the lifetime of his father, and a difficulty arose about the succession which extended over a long time. A Cortes was assembled to decide the question, and it was agreed that Sancho, brother to Ferdinand de la Cerda should be heir to the crown, to the exclusion of the children of Ferdinand, grandchildren of Alfonso. This decision displeased the king of France, for the mother of these children thus left out of the succession was his sister Blanche, a French princess, and he considered that one of them, his eldest nephew, ought to have the crown. Alfonso, who had written a book full of laws, ought to have known the rights of the question. He declared in favor of his son Sancho, and came near having a war with France in consequence. Alfonso, whose only wish seemed to be to please everybody, now proposed to divide his kingdom in favor of the young princes; he made himself also very unpopular by debasing the coin of the realm, and Sancho was persuaded to rebel against his father. The king in vain tried to pacify the rebels by promising to satisfy all his demands; then he applied for aid and sympathy to all the kings in the neighborhood, in vain, for they had agreed to remain neutral, except the king of Morocco, who was willing to be on his side.

At last the goaded king assembled his few remaining adherents in Seville, and, in a solemn act, not only disinherited his rebel son Sancho, but called down maledictions on his head. In the same act he instituted his grandsons, the infantes de la Cerda, as his heirs, and after them, in default of issue, the kings of France.

Luckily the Pope now interfered on the side of the king, although he must have been worn out with the trouble he had with him, first and last. He threatened to excommunicate Sancho and all the rebels if they did not return to their duty. This put matters on a better footing; even Sancho was in the way of asking for a reconciliation, when he fell ill, which moved his old father so much that he forgot all about his displeasure and his malediction, and could do nothing but weep and lament over the sad state of his son. He was, in fact, so much affected that his anxiety threw him into a worse state than that of the rebellious prince. Sancho recovered and was soon as well as ever; but the king grew worse, and soon died, full of grief and affection for his son. He had not, however, revoked his will.

Nobody minded the will, and Sancho was proclaimed king. He reigned, and his son and grandson reigned after him. In the next generation it happened that the succession to the crown came back to the descendants of the La Cerdas, about whom so much trouble had been made.

A saying has been quoted against King Alfonso that "if he had been consulted at the creation of the world, he could have advised some things for the better." If this saying were really uttered, which there are strong reasons to doubt, it is probable that the king had no blasphemous intention in view, but that he was merely ridiculing the system, then received, of Ptolemy.

Alfonso reigned from 1252 to 1284.

The picture of the dreaming king, so absorbed in his books, so pleased with the society of his Arabic astronomers, that he let his kingdom slip through his hands, is pleasanter than that furnished a century later by another king of Castile, Pedro the Cruel, as he was very justly called, unless he has been greatly misrepresented.

The beautiful Alcazar at Seville was his favorite

palace. It is Moorish, and ornamented with the graceful horseshoe arch and lace-like arabesque work the Moors employed. Saint Ferdinand found it a pleasant place to establish himself in when he captured the city, and there his son Alfonso may have studied the stars in the large gardens which surrounded the palace, or pacing the arched gallery running along the enclosure.

Don Pedro enlarged the alcazar, rebuilt and embellished it, but he left the records of a crime in almost every room in the palace.

He came to the throne when he was but sixteen years old, on the death of his father, who left behind him, besides the prince Pedro, his rightful heir, a whole family of children, both sons and daughters, who were half-brothers and sisters of Pedro. For the Christian kings, as well as the Moslem ones, often made the question of succession a cause of quarrelling by having two or more families of children whose mothers were different. The Moslem law allows two wives at least; the Christian furnishes no such excuse.

In this case there was no love lost between the half-brothers, children of Alfonso XI. Pedro hated Fadrique and Enrique, or Henry, as it is easier to call him, and they, it may be supposed, returned the hatred with the added bitterness of those who are oppressed. But Pedro seems to have had a passion for killing and murdering, even when he had no excuse, if there ever is any.

The catalogue of those who died by his orders is too long and dreary to repeat.

Pedro loved, in his violent and cruel way, a very beautiful lady of the court, named Maria de Padilla; but in compliance with the request of his Cortes, he agreed that an embassy should be sent to the French king asking for his wife a princess of his royal house

DOOR IN THE ALCAZAR.

This alliance, to confirm harmonious relations between the two countries, was approved of by the French, and Blanche of Bourbon was sent to Spain, poor thing. Her father was Peter of Bourbon, and from that house afterwards sprang the royal line of the French Bourbons.

The ceremony of marriage took place with due splendor, but only two days afterwards, Don Pedro, the king, left his youthful bride, nor did she see much of her husband ever afterwards.

According to the legends of the time Pedro conceived a hatred for his French bride, which was brought about by enchantment, attributed to Maria de Padilla, who was afraid of losing her influence on the king, if his young wife should prove attractive.

" The young queen had given to her new spouse the most beautiful girdle of gold, ornamented with many gems and precious stones, and this girdle Pedro was pleased to wear out of his new love for Blanche, the giver. But Maria, jealous of the queen, managed to put the girdle into the hands of a Jew, who was a magician, and he so affected it for the worse that on a certain feast day, when the king went to put it on, in the sight of every one present, instead of a belt he was girded about by a horrible serpent. From that moment Pedro held the queen in abhorrence."

However this may be, the unfortunate Queen Blanche was shut up in prison, where no one was allowed to see her, and afterwards taken to Toledo, where, also, she was kept in strict confinement. Her guards there allowed her to go to service in the cathedral, where her appearance so interested the congregation in her favor that they all resolved to protect her at the risk of their lives and fortunes, and she was at once rescued from her keepers. Pedro marched on Toledo as soon as he heard the news, to seize the princess but she was no longer a prisoner; the whole city had taken her part, and placed her under a strong guard in the palace of their kings.

The half-brothers of the king, and the defenders of Blanche, formed so strong a league against the king, that Pedro had to pretend that he had softened towards his wife and meant to live with her, but he had not the faintest intention of so doing. The unfortunate Blanche was transferred, not to his palace to be queen, but to a strong fortress, where she long remained a prisoner, and in 1361, was there killed by the order of her husband, whether by poison or steel is still unknown.

Pedro caused his half-brother, Fadrique, to be killed in the very palace of the alcazar, in a patio where still are shown the marks of his blood, upon the pavement, if marks of blood they may be.

The ballad that describes the death of Fadrique is one of the best in Lockhart's rather poor collection. It begins as if told by the murdered man himself:

> I sat alone in Corinbra, the town myself had ta'en,
> When came into my chamber, a messenger from Spain;
> There was no treason in his look, an honest look he wore;
> I from his hand the letter took; my brother's seal it bore.

Then it tells how the letter was a friendly invitation for him to come to the tournament at Seville, and how Fadrique, with joyful heart, started to accept the invitation, not heeding "a man of God," who stood in the gateway at Seville to warn him not to enter; how he came to the palace, and greeted his brother, who spurned him from him; and then,—

AVIGORNAGNA, BILBAO.

the story as told by Fadrique himself suddenly stops short; and another voice, as it were, relates how the head of the master was brought before the eyes of Maria de Padilla, who had demanded it of the king.

To complete the occasion, the tyrant sent orders for the execution of several knights in various cities of the kingdom, and, it is said, insisted that day in dining in the very room in which lay the bleeding corpse of his murdered brother.

Such deeds roused the hostility of the French. Arragon also, now a powerful state, was already in arms against him; and Pedro in defence sought the alliance of the English king, Edward III., and the Black Prince, who were his relatives; for the sister of Alfonso X. married Edward I. of England.

Edward III., as every English or American boy should know, had large possessions in France. He had even the French king shut up in a prison in London; but besides that, much territory, the best half of France in fact, belonged to him, either by inheritance or the triumph of his arms. He owed these triumphs in a great measure to his noble son, the Black Prince, so called on account of the color of his favorite armor, who fought with such prowess at the battle of Poictiers and afterwards, that he was the hero of the day.

The Black Prince spent most of his time in his French possessions, where he had a large army to guard them. He was, in fact, born in Bordeaux, and this was his favorite city. He maintaind his court there with all the splendor of a monarch. Scattered about in the Pyrenees, there are still standing castles built by the English at that time, and inhabited by the followers of the Black Prince.

This redoubtable hero accepted the cause of his distant cousin, Pedro; on the other hand, Charles V., of France, took sides against the tyrant, with Henry, his half-brother, called Henry of Trastamara. Charles had just come to the throne, through the death of his father in London, and longed to avenge the death of the French Princess in Spain. The famous Bertrand du Guesclin was on this side of the contest, and also the king of Navarre.

Henry was joyfully received at Seville, and acknowledged as king by the whole of Andalusia. His direct claim to the throne was but feeble, for Pedro was the undoubted heir to their father's kingdom, but he had married a granddaughter of one of the Infantes de la Cerda, whose fate had made so much discussion in their day. This recommended him to the favor of the French court.

With treasure found in Seville, from which Pedro had fled, and with powerful allies, the cause of Henry seemed to prosper, but nothing could resist the mighty prowess of the Black Prince. Pedro, for whom he was arming, went about stabbing and poisoning as usual, without looking deep into his affairs, but early in the spring of 1367, Prince Edward crossed the Pyrenees, at Roncesvalles, with an army of Normans and Gascons, and some of the flower of English chivalry.

The great battle of Navarrete was fought on the 3d of April, 1367. The struggle was desperate; the war-cry of "Guienne and St. George!" on the one side, and on the other that of "Castile and Santiago!" were drowned by the clash of arms, the shouts of the victors, and the groans of the dying.

Both the brothers fought bravely; Henry was dauntless, and Pedro was as daring as he was cruel. The victory was with the cause of the rightful sovereign of Castile.

Such a splendid success has not often been found in history; it restored Pedro at one to the Castilian throne; and this he owed to the assistance of the English prince. But this victorious ally met with little gratitude; it was with great difficulty that he induced Pedro to pay any of the money due to the troops. The humane English prince, moreover, was disgusted at the desire the restored king showed to shed the blood of their prisoners.

He refused to do so, and reproached the tyrant for the wish.

"What was the use of your helping me, then?" asked Pedro, with apparent simplicity. "If I do not kill these rebels, they will go back to Henry, and it will be all to do over again."

Edward did not stay long with this bloodthirsty cousin-Spanish. He made peace between the kings of Castile and Arragon, admonished Pedro to obtain the love of his people, and went back to his life in Guienne.

Pedro proceeded to Toledo, where he put to death obnoxious individuals, and far from following the advice of Edward, made himself more and more unpopular. The Black Prince, ever after, let him alone, and the arms of Henry were everywhere successful.

It was by treachery, however, that the king fell into the hands of the enemy. Pedro was persuaded to come into the tent of du Guesclin, who was fighting for Henry, and there the half-brothers met.

It is said that when Henry entered, he did not at first recognize his brother, so much had he altered in a few years.

"There is your enemy," said an attendant.

"I am! I am!" cried Pedro, seeing that he was betrayed. The brothers grappled like lions, and Pedro was slain.

> "Henry and King Pedro clasping
>   Hold in straining arms each other ;
> Tugging hard, and closely grasping,
>   Brother proves his strength with brother,
>
> * * * * * *
>
> "Thus with mortal gasp and quiver,
>   While the blood in bubbles welled,
> Fled the fiercest soul that ever
>   In a Christian bosom dwelled."

This was the end of the bloody reign of Don Pedro the Cruel. If he was not the violent and savage character generally represented, he has been much maligned by his chroniclers.

Henry of Trastamara now reigned. In this house a century later, the crown of Arragon became united with that of Castile, making the whole of Spain, with the exception of Granada, into one kingdom. To tell why Portugal, occupying the rest of the Peninsula, has always been a separate country, with a different language, belongs to some other story.

A daughter of Pedro the Cruel, named Constance, married John of Gaunt, the Duke of Lancaster, a brother of the Black Prince. This duke assumed, after the death of Henry of Trastamara, the title of king of Castile, and prepared to invade the kingdom. In 1386, the duke actually left England with about fifteen hundred knights, accompanied by his wife, the Princess Constance of Castile, as a visible witness to his claim to the crown. He was solemnly proclaimed king of Castile and Leon at Santiago.

The progress of his arms met with little success, and was stayed by the plague, which made ravages in their ranks. The duke became discouraged and retired. The matter was compounded by agreements of marriage, by which Catharine, the little daughter of the Plantagenet, and granddaughter of Pedro the Cruel, was united to the son of the king of Castile.

CHAPTER XIX.

ARRAGON.

WITHOUT going into detail as to the precise boundaries of the petty Spanish kingdoms at different periods, it will be enough if the reader will remember that, roughly speaking, the kingdom of Castile, at the beginning of the fifteenth century, embraced the northwestern part of Spain, including the long coast which borders on the Bay of Biscay, and bordering on the kingdom of Portugal. The kingdom of Arragon, in the same way, had absorbed into itself all the petty states of the northeast of Spain, with the exception of Navarre. That little kingdom, brave to audacity, quite self-sufficient, but none the less aggressive, made itself an uncomfortable neighbor to the French upon the north, and to the province of what we may call Spaniards proper, on the south. The ports of Arragon were those of the Mediterranean, by which, as we saw, Spain had made her early acquaintance with the civilization of Rome, Greece, and the further East. From the seaports of Catalonia and Valencia, there sailed a race of brave seamen, not over scrupulous perhaps, who traded with all the ports of the Mediterranean, and even pushed their conquests, as enterprising merchants will, wherever adventure or profit required. By the achievements of such navigators, the monarchs of Arragon became the lords of Majorca, Minorca, and Ivica, which are still dependencies of the Spanish crown. They also acquired a sovereignty over Sardinia and Sicily, islands which, in the decay of Spain's power, have fallen from her wasted hand. In the farther East, some of the achievements of the Catalonian fleets were to the last degree daring and chivalrous. Roger de Flor, in the year 1303, in a well-equipped fleet of twenty-two vessels, came to the relief of the hard-pressed Greek emperor in Constantinople. The grateful emperor gave him his niece in marriage, and made him admiral of Roumania. He led his Catalans across the Propontis into Asia; they slew thirty thousand Moslems in two battles. He raised the siege of Philadelphia, and was called the deliverer of Asia. In a series of intrigues which followed, in which the Catalans assumed every thing, Roger received the title of Cæsar, the highest title under the emperors. But he now had awakened such terror that the Imperial guard revenged themselves by his assassination. By a similar dash, an army of Catalans, amounting to eight thousand men, took possession of Athens, and till the close of the fourteenth century, Athens was an appanage of the kings of Sicily.

But, as often happens in greater and in less concerns than these, the ruler whose sway was so grand at a distance, found himself strictly hampered at home. An old writer said of Arragon, at that time, that there were as many kings there as there were rich men. There was no moment in all this history the gentry or nobility of Arragon did not maintain their haughty independence, and the twelve peers of Arragon call themselves " great men, or rich men, by nature," implying that they did not receive their nobility from any sovereign.

In 1410, the throne of Arragon became vacant by the death of King Martin, without direct heirs. The nation referred the question of succession to a committee of judges, and they gave it to Ferdinand of Castile, not as king, but as regent for his little nephew.

This brought the sceptre of Arragon, which, for more than two centuries had descended in the family of Barcelona, into the same Trastamara family which was ruling over the Castilian monarchy.

The son of this Ferdinand was Alfonso V., who was very little at home in his kingdom of Arragon, because he had acquired for himself another kingdom, that of Naples. He went there at the request of Joanna, then Queen of Naples, to defend her from her enemies. She adopted him, and bequeathed to him her kingdom, which he kept, although she afterwards changed her mind about the succession. These matters entirely absorbed King Alfonso, who, like many another, was carried away by the lovely climate of Naples, and the intellectual cultivation which prevailed at that court. He left the affairs of Arragon in the hands of his brother, John, with whom we have now to do. It is confusing that his name should be John, for the little king at Castile was also John, having, indeed, been named for him.

John of Arragon was married to Blanche, a princess of Navarre, by whom he had three children, destined to cause much trouble to their father, themselves, and the world in general.

Carlos, the son, by right inherited the crown of Navarre from his mother, the princess Blanche. It was a little kingdom, as we have seen, a bone of contention for the greater powers which surrounded it. France at the north and the united provinces of Spain on the other side of it could never let it alone. Its princes were sometimes most closely connected with the one kingdom, sometimes with the other, without the possibility of any thing like independence. Nevertheless, the kings of Navarre held on to their possessions with as much tenacity as if they had been larger; and Carlos, as was natural, enjoyed to the full his titles and lands. This was all very well, until John, the father, married a second time, thus introducing a step-mother into the family. His new wife was Joan Henriques, of the blood royal of Castile, a woman much younger than himself, of high spirit and unprincipled ambition. She soon obtained great influence over her husband, and when, in due time, on the 10th of March, 1452, her son Ferdinand was born, the interests of the other children were worse than neglected, for they were encroached upon. This infant was to grow to be Ferdinand, the husband of Isabella. He was born in the little town of Sos. One of the flatterers of the next generation says that "the sun, which had been obscured with clouds during the whole day, suddenly broke forth with unwonted splendor. A crown was also beheld in the sky, composed of various brilliant colors, like those of a rainbow." Yet, at his birth, as a younger brother of the heir, there was no visible crown waiting for his head.

Not long after, Joan, the step-mother, went to Navarre to set things to rights there, as she regarded them. She made herself very disagreeable to the young king, as step-mothers do in story books, and irritated or aggravated him to such an extent, that she left the palace of her step-children, and retired to another.

Navarre, at that time, was divided by two powerful families, who were always at discord—the Beaumonts and the Agramonts. The Beaumonts were the partisans of the Prince of Viana, for this was the title of Carlos, the young king of Navarre. They worked upon his naturally gentle temper, and urged him to assume the sovereignty which was his by right. The Agramonts, partly, doubtless, in order to disagree with the Beaumonts, vehemently espoused the cause of the queen. Thus, the two factions, in the enjoyment of their own time-honored quarrel, fostered and encouraged the differences in the royal family.

Carlos had two young sisters, Blanche and Eleanor, who shared his resentment at the intrusion of Joanna, and who made things as unpleasant as two young ladies can under such circumstances.

Carlos even besieged his step-mother in the castle of Estella, to which she had withdrawn. His father was forced to send a small body of troops to suppress the revolt. The two angry factions of Navarre joined the opposing sides, according to their prejudices; the young prince found himself a prisoner, after a well-contested action.

Carlos was released after many months of captivity, and after a little while decided to seek an asylum with his uncle, Alfonso the V., at Naples, in order to refer to him his difficulties with his father.

On his passage through France, and the various courts of Italy, the Prince of Viana was received with the greatest attention, which was due to his rank, and which his attractive personal appearance, his youth, and his misfortune ensured to him. His uncle in Naples received him warmly, and showed him all the sympathy and affection which he had anticipated. As Alfonso was really king of Arragon, and had a right to say how the affairs of that kingdom should be conducted, his influence with his brother would be great in reference to Navarre, therefore his protection might reasonably encourage Carlos to hope for the best issue to his anxieties about his crown. Just then, unfortunately, Alfonso died, of a fever, in Naples, destroying the hopes of the young prince. The dying Alfonso bequeathed his dominions in Spain to his brother John, who had so long been ruling there in his stead. Naples he left to his son Ferdinand.

This prince was of a dark, gloomy character, in contrast to the frank and courteous bearing of Carlos, who in his short stay at Naples had so won the affections of the nobles there, that a large party of them eagerly pressed the latter to assert his title to the vacant throne. Carlos had the good sense to resist this proposal. He passed over into Sicily, where his welcome was of the warmest, for his mother Blanche had once lived there, as queen, and the recollection of her kindly rule was still fresh in the memory of the people. He was, it is said, urged to assume the sovereignty of that island, but Carlos rejected this temptation; passing his time in the society of learned men, with the facilities of an extensive library, belonging to a convent near Messina, forgetting the cares and annoyances of his late years in the study of philosophy and history.

In the meantime, John and Joanna had full control in Arragon and Navarre, but reports of the popularity of Carlos in Sicily came to them in due time, and they began to be alarmed lest he should accept the offers of sovereignty which had been made to him there. They wrote him, therefore, urging him to return, with promise of full reconciliation. Carlos decided to return, contrary to the advice of his wisest counsellors in Sicily.

Barcelona, which had been very indignant at the persecution of a prince whom every one loved, made the most brilliant preparations for his reception, but the prince, fearing that such an ovation would irritate his father, avoided going there until after his first interview with the king and queen, in which he conducted himself with unfeigned humility and penitence. They, on their part, received him with a cordiality which, if not genuine, was the result of consummate dissimulation.

It was now confidently expected by every one that John would hasten to acknowledge his son's title as heir-apparent to the crown of Arragon. But nothing was further from the monarch's intention. He indeed summoned the Cortes for the purpose of receiving their homage himself, but he expressly refused their request to perform the same ceremony to the Prince of Viana, or to allow him to be addressed as successor to the crown.

Such conduct on the part of John was evidently due to the counsels of Queen Joanna. Not only had Carlos deeply offended her, but she regarded him with hatred as the insuperable obstacle to the advancement of her own child Ferdinand. As her influence over her husband was unbounded, she had succeeded in alienating him entirely from all the children of his first marriage. His affections were now all centred upon the little Ferdinand, and he was willing to believe all the artful suggestions of the queen likely to shut his heart wholly against his oldest son.

Convinced at length that there was no use in expecting consideration from his father, Carlos looked about for aid in other quarters, to restore him to his rights in Navarre, at least, without present consideration of the succession to the throne of Arragon. He was offered the hand of Isabella, the sister of Henry of Castile, an alliance in every respect most desirable for him, as it would ensure him the protection of this house. But this scheme suited not at all his parents, for they wanted Isabella for their darling Ferdinand. Their plan was more suitable as to the age of the young people, and it had long been the object of their policy. That Carlos should thus cross their wishes was a new offence. He was arrested and placed in strict confinement, with no explanation whatever.

All classes received this intelligence with surprise and consternation. Deputations were sent to the king requesting to know the nature of the crimes imputed to his son. The answers of John were

SARAGOSSA.

vague, darkly hinting a suspicion of conspiracy by his son against his life.

The whole kingdom was thrown into a ferment. The Catalans rose almost to a man, and marched so promptly on Frega, where John and his queen had taken refuge, that they had barely time to make their escape. The insurrection spread over the country. The king of Castile, aided by the Beaumonts, supported the cause of Carlos in Navarre.

John, alarmed at the tempest, saw the necessity

of releasing Carlos from the inaccessible fortress in which he was secured, and he affected to do this at the urgent request of the queen, hoping thus to lessen her unpopularity. She therefore accompanied the prince on his way from his prison to Barcelona. He was everywhere greeted with enthusiasm by the people of the villages thronging out to meet him. He entered the capital with a welcome such as might be given to a conqueror; but the queen, having been informed that her presence in the city would not be tolerated, thought it more prudent for her to remain at a distance.

The Catalans insisted that Carlos should be publicly acknowledged as the heir and successor to the crown, and John accepted these conditions with apparent cheerfulness. Carlos, happy in the enthusiastic attachment of a brave and powerful people, seemed now to have reached the end of his troubles.

At this very close of his trials, he fell ill of a fever, and soon died, on the 23d of September, 1461, in the forty-first year of his age. So opportune a death, for the wishes of Joanna, led to plentiful suspicions of poisoning, but there is no sort of proof of it.

Carlos, in his will, bequeathed the crown of Navarre, in conformity with the original marriage contract of his parents, to his sister Blanche and her posterity.

Thus, in the prime of life, died the Prince of Viana, just at the moment when the tide of his fortunes seemed to have turned in his favor. His early act of rebellion had been requited by the misfortunes which followed it, and the harsh conduct of his father gave him the sympathy of all.

He is described as "somewhat above the middle stature, having a thin visage, with a serene and modest expression of countenance, and withal somewhat inclined to melancholy." Another description says: "Such were his temperance and moderation, such the excellence of his breeding, and such the sweetness of his demeanor, that no one thing seemed to be wanting in him which belongs to a true and perfect prince." He was fairly skilful in music and painting, wrote poetry, and was the friend of some of the eminent bards of his time.

Carlos dead, Joanna the step-mother transferred her ill-will to Blanche, who, as heiress to the crown of Navarre, became the object of her jealousy. Blanche had been long married to Henry IV. of Castile, but was separated from him, and lived by herself in Navarre. Her father, instigated by his wife, thought to get rid of Blanche by taking her into France, on the pretext of making a new marriage for her. Blanche feared to be taken away from her friends, and besought the king not to deliver her into the hands of her enemies, but in vain; she was forcibly conveyed across the mountains. At a little town on the French side of the Pyrenees, being convinced that she had nothing further to hope from human aid, she formally renounced her rights to Navarre in favor of her former husband, Henry of Castile, also her cousin. She wrote him a touching letter, reminding him of their mutual happiness in earlier days, and of her subsequent misfortunes, and then, predicting the gloomy destiny which awaited her, she settled on him her inheritance of Navarre.

The reason she feared so much was that she was on her way to the keeping of the Count of Foix, up among the mountains. The Countess of Foix was Eleanor, her only sister, and the last remaining member of her mother's family; but Eleanor was her enemy, for if Blanche was out of the way she herself expected to be the queen of Navarre, having received the promise of it from her father, John of Arragon. Blanche feared, with too good reason, to be delivered into the power of her heartless sister, for on the very day she wrote the sad little letter to her former husband, she was taken to the gloomy chateau of Orthez, in Béarn, on a plateau above deep ravines, surrounded by a triple wall.

Here the counts of Foix used to live in great splendor, as Froissart says, "getting up at noon, and supping at midnight; when the count left his chamber to go to table, before him were twelve lighted torches borne by twelve varlets, and these twelve torches were held by the varlets before his table, which gave a great light to the hall, which was full of knights and squires, and the tables were always dressed with supper for whoever wished to sup."

Poor Blanche saw nothing of such revelry, being immured in a dungeon, where she languished for two years, poisoned in the end by the command of her sister.

This cruel Countess of Foix reigned in Navarre, after the death of her father. She had her wish, but she died herself after three weeks of royalty, and the crown was taken from her family by Ferdinand, for whose sake his father sacrificed so much, and stained his own memory with so many crimes.

CHATEAU DE BELLEGARDE.

In the end, however, we come to pity the King of Arragon, whose unkindness to his children, after all, was his chief fault, and this was caused by the malign influence of Joanna, and his exceeding love for her son Ferdinand.

His Catalans turned against him and found powerful support among outside allies, to one and another of whom they offered the crown of Arragon, among others to René the Good, of Anjou. This king is best known to modern readers, perhaps, from Scott's amusing picture of him in Anne of Geierstein. René intrusted his claims to his son, the Duke of Lorraine, who, with a spirited army, crossed the Pyrenees and pushed King John hard in Arragon. In two campaigns the French duke held his own.

The exchequer of King John ran low. The King of France who had promised to be on his side, was Louis XI., a monarch by no means sure to be as good as his word. John found himself unable to raise money for his troops. His daughter Eleanor, the Countess of Foix, now demanded the crown of Navarre, which he had promised her only at his death; and worst of all, since it is personal suffering which makes it hard to bear the misfortunes of our state, his eyesight, long impaired by exposure, now failed him altogether. He was no longer young; he had lived an emotional, adventurous life, and now when he would have liked repose, repose was far from him, for on every hand there was difficulty to encounter.

It might be that in those hours of darkness he should sigh for the gentle presence of Carlos, always as a little boy, sweet and amiable, and recall the prattle of Blanche and Eleanor, children at his knee. All gone—all dead before him, and not by the natural course of events, but through the violence of his will.

His intrepid wife in this extremity put herself at the head of their armies to check the operations of the enemy, and his only remaining son Ferdinand fought bravely against the insurgents. His ardor nearly proved fatal to the young prince, for he was once almost in the hands of the enemy, but he was saved by the devotion of his own officers who threw themselves between him and the pursuing party, so that he escaped at the sacrifice of their liberty.

In the winter of 1468° the queen, Joanna Henriques, died by a painful disorder from which she had suffered for years. In many respects she was the most remarkable woman of her time. She took an active part in the politics of her husband, and, indeed, directed them. She conducted some important diplomatic negotiations to a happy issue, and displayed even capacity for military affairs. Her persecution of her step-son Carlos is the worst stain resting upon her memory. It was, indeed, the cause of all her husband's subsequent misfortunes.

Still, her great spirit and the resources of her genius supplied him with courage and means of surmounting the difficulties in which she had involved him, so that her loss at this crisis left him at once without solace or support.

A physician of the Hebrew race persuaded the king to submit to the then universal operation of couching, and succeeded in restoring sight to one of his eyes. The Jew, who like the Arabs, was a firm believer in astrology, refused to operate upon the other eye, because, he said, the planets wore a malignant aspect. But John, who was above the superstitions of his age, compelled the physician to repeat his experiment, which proved completely successful. Thus, although now nearly eighty years old, the brave king regained his energy and good spirits, and resumed operations against the enemy with his ancient vigor.

The Duke of Lorraine, John of Calabria, died of a fell disease while at the head of his troops. The old king, René, wore garlands and wrote poetry, while his daughter, the unfortunate Margaret of Anjou, followed the falling fortunes of the Red Rose of Lancaster.

By extraordinary efforts John assembled a competent force, and besides other vigorous measures, he instituted a close blockade of Barcelona, by sea and land.

The inhabitants made one desperate effort in a sally against the royal forces, but the civic militia were soon broken, and the loss of four thousand men, killed and prisoners, warned the insurgents to desist.

At length, reduced to the last extremity, they consented to enter into negotiations, which were concluded by a treaty equally honorable to both parties. A general amnesty was granted for all offences. Those citizens who should refuse to renew their allegiance to their ancient sovereign within a year, might have the liberty of removing with their effects wherever they pleased. It was agreed, in spite of all that had passed, that the king should cause the inhabitants of Barcelona to be proclaimed throughout all his dominions, good, faithful, and loyal subjects, which was accordingly done.

The king, after these preliminaries had been adjusted to general satisfaction, declining the triumphal car which had been prepared for him, made his entrance into the city by the gate of St. Anthony, mounted upon a white charger. As he rode along the principal streets, the sight of so many pallid countenances and wasted figures, bespeaking the extremity of famine, "smote his heart with sorrow," says a contemporary. He then proceeded to the hall of the great palace, and solemnly swore there to respect the constitution and laws of Catalonia.

Thus ended this long disastrous civil war, which nearly cost the King of Arragon the fairest portion of his dominions. Its result in the end was to establish the succession of Ferdinand over the whole of the realms of his ancestors; thus, by his marriage with Isabella of Castile, bringing the whole of Christian Spain under one sceptre.

CHAPTER XX.

FERDINAND AND ISABELLA.

IN the union of the two crowns of Castile and Arragon by the marriage of Ferdinand and Isabella, and in the extinction of the old rivalries and civil wars for the moment, it was for the first time for generations possible for the nation to make any head against the Moors. The result, in the famous reign of Ferdinand and Isabella, gave to the nation the most brilliant period of its history. The marriage had been proposed when the Prince of Arragon and the Princess of Castile were both very young. But many an intrigue and misadventure had made it improbable after it was proposed, and it was not until the year 1469, when Ferdinand was seventeen years old, and Isabella a year older, that they were married.

As we have seen, Ferdinand of Arragon was regarded from his birth as a very important personage, and his father and mother sacrificed every thing to his future greatness. Isabella of Castile, on the other hand, began life with no pretensions to royalty. On the death of her father her brother Henry came to the throne, and Isabella retired with her mother into seclusion, where she was carefully instructed in those lessons of practical piety and in the deep reverence for "religion" which distinguished her maturer years.

Many offers of marriage were made for her; she

ISABELLA.

was betrothed to Carlos, the Prince of Viana, when she was but a child; when she was only thirteen, her brother, the king, promised her to the old king of Portugal, but Isabella absolutely refused the marriage.

A brother of the English king, a brother of the French king, and other suitors were proposed to the young princess, after it was pretty clear that she would inherit the throne from her brother, on account of his having no legitimate heir. The person among all these aspirants on whom she turned a favorable eye, was her kinsman, Ferdinand of Arragon. Every argument of policy was in favor of a union between two houses so near each other, speaking the same language, of the same religion, and the same ambitions and objects. Arguments of a more tender nature influenced Isabella. Ferdinand was then in the bloom of life, and distinguished for his good looks. From his boyhood he had displayed a chivalrous valor, combined with a maturity of judgment beyond his years. He had been trained in hardships and in war. He delighted in physical exercises, was fond of field sports, excelled in horsemanship, was temperate and active in his habits of life. Isabella was called by one of her household, "the handsomest lady whom I ever beheld." Her portraits show a symmetry of feature which has been supposed to indicate that harmony of qualities which distinguished her.

But Henry IV. although he had consented to acknowledge his sister as his successor, objected to her marriage with Ferdinand of Arragon, and a large party openly opposed it. Spies were set upon her actions, and every measure taken to hinder the progress of her marriage negotiations. Her enemies even formed a scheme of seeking her person, and many of her friends betrayed and deserted her, but Isabella with great courage sent envoys to her affianced, Ferdinand, to tell him, in effect, that it was best they should be married at once.

The old king, John of Arragon, was then in his worst extremity, sore pressed by insurgent Catalans; but Ferdinand resolved to hasten to his bride, without delay.

He received the message at Saragossa; the distance is not great to Valladolid, where he would find Isabella was, but the country was full of watchful enemies. Ferdinand, accompanied by half a dozen attendants, disguised as merchants, journeyed chiefly in the night. Ferdinand himself pretended to be a servant, took care of the mules when they halted upon the road, and waited upon the others at table. They made the journey all one day with no disaster except that they forgot the purse which contained all the money they had, and left it at the inn where they spent the night. Late on the second night, they arrived at a little place occupied by a body of Isabella's partisans.

As they knocked at the gate, they were saluted by a large stone shoved off the battlements by a sentinel, which came dangerously near the head of the prince.

"What are you about?" he shouted, with a voice as vigorous as he could make it, cold and tired as he was, after travelling two days with but little rest at night.

His voice was recognized, and he was received with great joy and festivity by those within. They escorted him, well-armed through the rest of his journey, and reaching Leon, the Castilian nobles of his party eagerly thronged to render him homage.

On the 15th of October Ferdinand entered Valladolid, where he was received by the Archbishop of Toledo, and conducted to the apartments of Isabella.

When he entered her presence, Gutierrez de Cardenas, the first who pointed him out to the princess said, "*Ese es, ese es*,"—that's the one, that's the one! In reward for this, his family bears on their escutcheon the double SS, which sounds like his exclamation.

Ferdinand was at that time seventeen. His complexion was fair, though somewhat bronzed with exposure to the sun, his eye quick and cheerful, his forehead ample, and approaching baldness. His frame was muscular and well proportioned, for he was one of the best horsemen of his court, and excelled in field-sports of every kind. His health was ensured by his extreme temperance in diet, and by such habits of activity that it was said he seemed to find repose in being busy.

Isabella was a year older than her suitor. In stature she was somewhat above the middle size. Her complexion was fair, her hair of a bright chestnut color, inclining to red, and her mild blue eyes beamed with intelligence and sensibility.

She was dignified, modest, and reserved. She spoke the Castilian language with unusual elegance, and her intellectual cultivation was superior to that of Ferdinand, whose early education had been neglected.

The interview lasted more than two hours, and

CHURCH OF SAN JUAN DE LOS REYES.

was perfectly satisfactory to both parties. Among other things, the preliminaries of the marriage were adjusted. When the awkward question of expense came up, it turned out that both parties were so poor, they would have to borrow money for the wedding. On so small a basis did this young couple begin housekeeping.

The marriage took place four days afterwards, on the 19th of October, 1469, in the presence of about two thousand persons. A papal bull of dispensation was forthcoming to justify the union of cousins, as the bride and bridegroom were within the forbidden degrees. This document was forged by the old king of Arragon, aided by Ferdinand and the archbishop, because they knew Isabella would never consent to be married without it. The people knew nothing of it at the time, but, some years later, the dispensation was easily obtained from Sixtus the Fourth. Isabella was seriously offended when she heard about the deception.

When the marriage was fairly accomplished, messengers were sent to the king, Henry IV., to inform him of it. For the rest of his life he opposed the interests of his sister, but he was pining under an incurable malady, and died in 1474. Isabella was then twenty-three years old.

A numerous assembly of the nobles, clergy, and the public magistrates of the city of Segovia, where Isabella was at the time, then waited upon her, at the Alcazar, and, receiving her under a canopy of rich brocade, escorted her in solemn procession to the principal square of the city, where a broad scaffolding had been erected for the ceremony of proclamation. Isabella, royally attired, rode on a Spanish jennet, an officer preceding her on horseback, bearing aloft a naked sword, the symbol of sovereignty.

On arriving at the plaza, she alighted from her horse, and, ascending the platform, seated herself upon a throne which had been prepared for her. A herald, in a loud voice, proclaimed: "Castile! Castile for the king, Don Ferdinand, and his consort, Doña Isabella, queen proprietor of these kingdoms!" The royal standards were unfurled, bells pealed, and canons were fired from the castle.

Ferdinand was in Arragon, at the time of Henry's death, and had no share in these ceremonies. On his return, there was a little disagreeable discussion about the crown of Castile, which Isabella's friends regarded as hers exclusively, while Ferdinand's relatives, and especially the Henriquez, who had all the pugnacious qualities of his mother, one of their family, claimed his right to a share of it, as the nearest male representative of the House of Trastamara. The question was not easy; it had, of course, been expected, between the partisans of Isabella and the courtiers of Ferdinand. Could she, a woman, inherit the crown of Castile? It is the very question which has disturbed all Spain for the greater part of this nineteenth century. If she could not, her husband, Ferdinand, was the nearest male representative of the House of Henry the IV. The Cardinal of Spain and the Archbishop of Toledo determined that females could inherit the crown in Castile and Leon, though it was granted they could not in Arragon. Whatever authority Ferdinand might possess could be derived only through her. It is said that Ferdinand was so displeased with this arrangement, that he threatened to go back to Arragon; but Isabella soothed him, and persuaded him the distinction was only nominal. The images of both were stamped on the public coin, and the united arms of Castile and Arragon were emblazoned on the same seal, and she promised that his will should always be hers. All municipal and ecclesiastical appointments in Castile were, from that time, made in the single name of the queen. She ordered the issues from the treasury, and received the homage of commanders in the army. The king and queen both signed proclamations, the images of both were stamped on the coin, and from that day to this day the arms of both have been quartered together on the escutcheon.

Thanks to the good sense of Isabella, more than to any shown by her husband, the united kingdoms gradually gained in strength. But the young pair were not suffered to repose, for a war arose with Portugal about the succession, and they found it hard work, with their small purses, to maintain an army. Peace was effected in 1479, and, in the same year, Ferdinand received his own crown by the death of his father. Arragon, with its extensive dependencies, descended to him. Thus, the crowns of Arragon and Castile, after a separation of more than four centuries, became united, and the foundations were laid of the magnificent empire, destined to overshadow, in its time, every other European monarchy.

Isabella established her head-quarters in Seville, where she received the most loyal and magnificent reception. She held her court in the great hall of the Alcazar, still beautiful with the arabesque ornamentation of its Moorish architect, and devoted her time to the reformation of abuses licensed by her predecessors. Every Friday she took her seat in her chair of state, on an elevated platform covered with cloth of gold, and surrounded by her council. The queen herself examined the suits; and by extraordinary despatch, in the two months that she stayed in the city, a vast amount of plundered property was restored to its rightful owners, and so many offenders brought to prompt punishment, that it is said that no less than four thousand persons, with guilty consciences, fled from the place.

Such energetic conduct on the part of the queen, and the able assistance of her royal spouse, brought tranquillity into the country, such as had long been absent. When prosperity was thus restored, Ferdinand and Isabella, secure upon their thrones, with always increasing wealth and a good army, turned their eyes to that region of the Peninsula which was not theirs, although it should by natural position and ancient possession belong to the crown of Spain. It was then in 1481 that the war began which ended in the fall of Granada in 1492. All this time there was constant fighting going on, and deeds of the greatest prowess were performed on the Christian side as well as by the Moors.

Ferdinand was at the head of the Spanish troops, and fought with the greatest bravery on every occasion, while his coolness and excellent judgment pervaded every detail. Isabella threw herself into the contest with the greatest ardor, visiting the camp in person, encouraging the soldiers with gifts of clothes and money. She caused large tents, known as the "queen's hospitals," to be kept for the sick and wounded, and furnished them herself with medicines and attendants, thus herself originating the idea of camp-hospitals.

Isabella may be regarded as the soul of the war. She engaged in it with the exalted purpose of restoring the empire of the Cross over the ancient domain of Christendom. She never suffered her powerful mind to be diverted from this great and glorious object.

At the beginning of the long contest, the Spaniards were lower than most of the European nations in military science. Isabella took pains to avail herself of all foreign resources for their improvement. The soldiers were trained to act in concert and to obey authority, to patient endurance, fortitude, and subordination. It was in this school that were formed those celebrated captains who, in the beginning of the sixteenth century, spread the military fame of their country all over Christendom and the newly discovered world. It was in the war with Granada that the great Captain Gonsalvo de Cordova earned his first laurels, and it is said that Fernando Cortés, as a boy, thought of going to join his banner, but, instead, it happened when he was nineteen that he sailed for the West, and afterwards became the conqueror of Mexico.

While Ferdinand and Isabella were in their camp

Portrait of Columbus.

before Granada, the capitulation was signed that opened the way to an extent of empire compared to which the conquest of country on their own peninsula was insignificant.

Christopher Columbus, filled with faith in the existence of a new world, left Lisbon in disgust, where he had been trying to interest the king of Portugal in his plans of discovery, and came to submit his proposals to the Spanish sovereigns.

He arrived in the latter part of 1484, when the minds of the king and queen, and the heart of the whole nation were absorbed in the conquest of Granada, and it was long before he received the slightest notice. At last, however, he received an invitation to repair to Santa Fé, with money enough accompanying it to provide for his equipment and his expenses on the road.

Columbus arrived at the camp in season to witness the surrender of Granada, when every heart was swelling with triumph and exultation. Such success disposed the sovereigns to listen with favor to propositions leading to more glorious adventure. Columbus described to them the splendors of the Eastern kingdoms, which he fully expected to reach by sailing towards the setting sun; he held out to them the prospect of extending the empire of the Cross over these heathen lands, proposing to devote his own profits in the enterprise to the recovery of the Holy Sepulchre.

Ferdinand, from the first, regarded the scheme with cold distrust. It was Isabella who, won to it at last, said, in answer to his opposition:

" I will assume the undertaking, for my own crown of Castile, and am ready to pawn my jewels to defray the expenses of it."

This was no idle offer, for the treasury had been reduced to its lowest ebb by the Moorish wars. Funds were found, however, without the sacrifice of the royal gems. Arragon was not considered as

DEPARTURE OF COLUMBUS.

mixing in the scheme, the expense and the glory of which rested with Castile. As everybody knows, on the 3d of August, 1492, Columbus bade farewell to the Old World on his wonderful voyage of discovery.

The confidence of Isabella in Columbus was fully justified when, in the spring of 1493, letters were received from him announcing his return to Spain, after successfully achieving his great enterprise by the discovery of land beyond the Western Ocean.

The delight and astonishment raised by this news were in proportion to the scepticism with which his project had been looked upon at first.

The court was in Barcelona, when Columbus arrived—Admiral Columbus as he was now called. He at once hastened to present himself before the sovereigns; people thronged to meet him as he passed through the country, accompanied by several dark natives of the islands he had discovered, arrayed in their simple costumes, and decorated with collars and bracelets rudely fashioned of gold. He had with him several kinds of strange quadrupeds, and birds of gaudy plumage, unknown in Spain.

It was a proud moment for the discoverer, when the king and queen advanced from their throne, extending their hands for him to salute, and causing him to be seated before them. After a while the sovereigns requested him to tell his story, and then heard from his own lips the wonderful narrative of his adventures.

Immense wealth flowed into the coffers of the Spanish kings through the discovery of a new world; and Isabella might look back from the summit of her power and splendor with a smile upon the time when she had to borrow money for her marriage. The royal house of Spain had come to be one of the great powers of Europe, and its subjects, living in prosperity and harmony, were well governed and happy.

Ferdinand became involved in a long war in Italy,

COLUMBUS ON THE DECK OF HIS SHIP WITH AN ASTROLABE IN HIS HAND.

through his connection with the cause of Naples. He conducted his share in it with great sagacity and prudence, and aided by the genius of his chief commander, Gonsalvo de Cordova, the Great Captain, he accomplished brilliant results.

Queen Isabella had one son and four daughters, for all of whom she was careful to make good marriages. All her daughters lived to reign, but with little happiness added to their brilliant positions.

Prince John, the only son, and the heir to the kingdom, was married when he was not quite twenty years old, to the Princess Margaret, daughter of the Emperor Maximilian of Germany. The bride came by water from Flanders, escorted by a fleet of over one hundred vessels, large and small. She was met on her arrival on the coast, by the young Prince of the Asturias, for such was the title already given to the heir of the Spanish crown, and by his father, King Ferdinand.

They were married with great splendor; but in the midst of all the rejoicing, the young bridegroom was seized with a fever, of which he soon died, to the great grief of the country, by all the people of which he was greatly beloved.

The Infanta Isabella, the oldest child of the sovereigns, had married, one after the other, two princes of Portugal, for her first husband died soon after the wedding.

Not long after the death of Prince John, the young Isabella, Queen of Portugal, gave birth to a son, an event which would have occasioned great joy, for he would, as heir to Spain and Portugal at once, unite the two countries, which by their close connection ought naturally to be one.

But the rejoicing was brief, for scarcely an hour after the birth of the little prince his mother died.

The blow was heavy for Isabella, whose spirits had not had time to rally since the death of her only son.

The child, who was named Prince Miguel, was early confirmed in his rights to the three monarchies of Castile, Arragon, and Portugal, an act which was the culmination of all the grandeur of the reign of Ferdinand and Isabella. But this little prince also died—before he had completed his second year,— defeating the only chance which had ever occurred of bringing the three nations under one rule.

At his death the succession of Castile and Arragon came to the Princess Joanna, who married Philip, son of the Emperor Maximilian, at the same time that her brother married his sister.

The Princess Joanna survived her mother and all her immediate family. She became mad and incapable of government, and her father and husband settled between them, not always in the greatest harmony, the affairs of state. Her son Charles, as Charles V. of Germany, and Charles I. of Spain, inherited her kingdom and also attained the title of Emperor of Germany.

Catalina, the youngest daughter of the Castilian sovereigns, married Henry VIII. of England, known in English history as Catharine of Arragon. She was the second Spanish princess who married a prince of the royal house of England. The other was Constance, the daughter of Pedro the Cruel, from whom Queen Isabella was lineally descended.

So many domestic calamities, as well as the incessant fatigue and exposure of her life, had impaired the health of Queen Isabella. It was visibly declining in 1503, so that the Court of Castile begged her to make some provision for the government of her kingdom after her decease, for Joanna her daughter had already shown symptoms of insanity.

Ferdinand fell ill with a fever, and the queen was seized with the same disorder, increased by her anxiety for her husband, who, however, gradually threw off the attack, while she sank under it.

In her suffering the queen did not lose her care for the welfare of her people or the concerns of her government. Though she had to lie upon her couch a great part of the day, she there listened to the reading of what was taking place at home or abroad.

The deepest gloom overspread the nation. The superstitious Spaniards recalled ominous circumstances, an earthquake and a hurricane, which they were sure announced the great calamity of her death. Isabella herself felt the decay of her bodily strength, and resolved to perform what duties remained to her while her faculties were still vigorous.

She executed her will, which is a celebrated proof of the peculiar qualities of her mind and character. She appointed King Ferdinand, her husband, sole regent of Castile until the majority of her grandson Charles, being led to this, she says, "by the consideration of the magnanimity and illustrious qualities of the king, my lord, as well as his large experience and the great profit which will redound to the state from his wise and beneficent rule."

Three days after signing the last codicil to her will the queen died, surrounded by the friends of her childhood. As she saw them bathed in tears around

HALL OF THE TWO SISTERS (ALHAMBRA).

her bed, she said gently: "Do not weep for me, nor waste your tears in fruitless prayers for my recovery, but pray rather for the salvation of my soul." She was fifty-four years old, and had reigned thirty years. She died on the 26th of November, 1504.

One of the last requests of the queen was that she might be buried in Granada, the brightest pearl of her crown. Her body was transported there from a great distance, escorted by large numbers of cavaliers and priests. Scarcely had they set out when a tremendous tempest began, which continued during the whole journey; roads were made nearly impassable, bridges swept away, and the level land buried under a deluge of water. Horses and mules were borne down by the torrents, and their riders once or twice perished with them. The melancholy escort reached its destination on the 18th of December, and the remains of Isabella were laid in the Franciscan monastery of the Alhambra. Here, in the heart of the capital, which her determination had redeemed from the heretic, they reposed until after the death of Ferdinand, when they were removed to be laid by his side in the cathedral at Granada, built upon the ruins of the mosque which they destroyed after the conquest.

Charles V. called upon the best artists in the world to make designs for the royal sepulchres of his family. They lie in state in the chapel built for the purpose. Ferdinand and Isabella, Joanna, their daughter, and Philip her husband. Over the altar is a bas-relief representing the surrender of Granada, Isabella on a white palfrey between King Ferdinand and the great Cardinal Mendoza, who is riding on a mule, as is the fashion for dignitaries of the church in Spain. Boabdil presents the keys, behind are ladies, knights, and soldiers, and in the distance captives are seen coming out of the gates.

At each end of the altar, the Catholic sovereigns kneel in effigy, their faces, costumes, and forms exactly represented; behind the king is the banner of Castile.

TOMB OF FERDINAND AND ISABELLA.

In the centre of the chapel are two alabaster sepulchres, superby wrought by Italian artists, and decorated with delicate carving. Upon one are stretched the effigies of Ferdinand and Isabella; on the other, Philip and his wife, Joanna. Isabella lies, sleeping in marble, placid and beautiful, and, by her side, as she would have wished, lies Ferdinand, in marble as well. Here, also, is the royal standard, which flaunted on the hill when the Moorish flag went down before it. Here is what Isabella would have liked to call her talisman—the very mass-book which Francisco Florez made for her, that she might read her prayers. Here is a chasuble wrought by her own hand, and not far away is the portrait of Hernan Perez, who, in the heat of the siege, rode into Granada, and fixed an Ave Maria on the very wall of the Mosque, and retired safely. The mausoleum is one of the most interesting memorials in Spain.

CHAPTER XXI.

CHARLES I. OF SPAIN,—CHARLES V. OF GERMANY.

WITH the extraordinary reign of Charles, the grandson of Ferdinand and Isabella, begins a more intimate relation of Spain with the politics of Europe. Strange to say, and sad to say, in the same reign begins the visible decline of Spain from the prosperity and the strength which she had won and deserved, under the prudent and wise administration of Ferdinand and Isabella, and Cardinal Ximenes. It has been said that Charles had more power for good or ill in Europe than has been exercised by any man since the reign of Augustus; and that, on the whole, he probably did as much harm with it as could possibly be done. This is probably true, though it is hard to say how much harm a selfish bigot can do; and any one who has studied the history of Philip the Second, Charles' successor, will feel that Charles himself did not exhaust the resources of bigotry and selfishness.

There is preserved, in the Royal Library at Madrid, an exquisite missal-book, such as was made and adorned in those times for the personal use of princes. Nothing can be finer than are its paintings and other decorations. By a curious felicity of compliment, a series of royal contemporary portraits is introduced among the pictures of the illuminations, so that David, Solomon, and the Queen of Sheba are represented with the lineaments of the sovereigns who reigned in Europe in the beginning of the sixteenth century. But the highest value of this matchless book is not in its decorations or its art, though its covers blaze with gems and its pages display these beautiful paintings. An inscription in the beginning says that the gold used for the decoration, within and without, is absolutely the same gold which was brought by Columbus from the islands on his first voyage as the first fruits of his new discovery. Those very grains of gold were consecrated by Isabella, after the birth of her grandson, for the illumination of the most costly book which the art of her time could make—a book which was to be his book for use in worship, and with which, doubtless, she lavished her prayers that his administration of the wealth of the Indies might be worthy of the hopes with which all men welcomed the great discovery. But such hopes of hers were never fulfilled.

No! Spain and Charles were tried by prosperity, and they were not equal to the test. Indeed, that extension of empire which took Charles away from Spain for much of his life, and gave to him important duties elsewhere, may be said to have weaned him from the country in which he was born, and of which he was the absolute ruler. The excuse, rendered again and again, for some act of atrocious maladministration in Spain, is that

323   CHARLES THE FIFTH IN HIS 31ST YEAR.

Charles was absent when the thing was done. The land was governed, or it was not governed. It obeyed an absolute despot; and that despot was so engaged sometimes, as to think of it only as the treasury from which he should draw his revenue. The careful system of administration introduced by Ferdinand and Isabella would be, on the one side, stereotyped in hard forms, and on the other recklessly abandoned. From the end of the reign of Charles to the beginning of constitutional government in our own time, it may be said that Spain has been the worst-governed country in the world. Of such failures the beginnings are to be sought in Charles' absence from Spain, in his duties as Emperor of Germany, and arbiter of the destinies of Europe. Indeed, while Charles still reigned, the endless wars which he maintained in Europe, Africa, Asia, and America, drained from Spain the treasure which the newly discovered land poured in, and steadily exhausted the resources of the nation.

Ferdinand and Isabella had been unhappy and unfortunate in the death of their only son, Don John, and their eldest daughter, the queen of Portugal, neither of whom, as the reader knows, left any issue. Their only remaining child was Joanna, the princess whose after-career was so unfortunate, and who has given so many sad subjects to painters and poets. The daughter of the lords of the newly-discovered Indies would not lack for suitors whatever her personal attractions or deficiencies. Ferdinand and Isabella chose for the husband of Joanna, not unnaturally, the young Archduke of Austria, " Philip the Handsome," who was the son of the Emperor Maximilian, and of Mary of Burgundy, the only child of Charles the Bold. When, therefore, the baby was born, who was to be Charles the First of Spain, and Charles the Fifth of Germany, he was the grandson and heir apparent, on his mother's side, of the king and queen of Spain, and, on his father's side, of the princess to whom all Burgundy had descended, and also of the Emperor Maximilian. Although the title of the emperor was not transmitted by descent, still the claims of family were naturally considered in elections, and, in point of fact, when this baby prince had grown to be twenty years old he was elected emperor. We read of prospects like these surrounding a cradle, almost as we read the stories of the promises in a fairy tale. After the event we trace the misfortunes of Spain back to the very contingencies which, at the moment, seemed to promise so much for the glory of the child then born.

It will be a convenient aid to memory for the reader to recollect that Charles, who was to have so much to do with the drift of the sixteenth century, was born in the "even year" 1500, the year before that century began. His father, the Duke of Burgundy, resided at Brussels, which was his court and though he paid formal homage for these provinces to the French king, he reigned virtually as the sovereign. The reader must remember that Burgundy took in the districts which are more generally known now as Belgium, Burgundy, Dauphiny, part of Provence, and parts of what has made Languedoc,

Savoy, and Holland. His father died when he was but six years old, and he then inherited the crown of the Low Countries. He became king of Spain in 1516, and when his grandfather died, in 1519, Grand Duke of Austria.

The young prince Charles was born at Ghent, and brought up at his father's court in Brussels. Spain's first misfortune was that her sovereign for near forty years was not to be a Spainard. The boy showed an early interest in military exercises and the sports of the open air. While he was reputed to be somewhat dull of study, it was his pride to excel in the exercises of arms. The most interesting anecdote told of his life, is that in his first appearance at a public tournament, before a great assembly curious to see the young prince, and not prepossessed in his favor, he rode into the lists with a banner which bore the inscription, "*non demum*" "not yet." Even then, however, he had assumed the government of Flanders. When he was only fifteen years old, Chievres, his tutor, trained him to read public papers, to be present at his councils, and to propose himself the matters on which he needed its opinion. His grandfather, Ferdinand, died when he was sixteen years old. A voyage or a journey from Spain to Brussels was then a matter of many weeks, and by his will, Ferdinand left the Cardinal Ximenes regent until Charles could arrive in person in Spain.

This provision was the more necessary, because the old king had at times flattered his younger grandson, whose name also was Ferdinand, with the hope that the crown of Spain might be left to him.

But Ximenes boldly proclaimed Charles king of Castile in his absence, and, notwithstanding secret discontents, his title was recognized. From this time till Charles arrived, the administration of Spain was substantially in the hands of Ximenes. But the young king's Flemish ministers interfered, as far as they could, with his administration, and by their advice Charles sent associate councillors to his Spanish court, as if to assist the great cardinal. The Spaniard treated them with distinction, but maintained his own authority. He even carried on a war in Navarre from which he drove out John d' Albrecht. He dismantled all the fortresses except Pampeluna, and to this precaution Spain owes the possession of her part of Navarre to-day. He was constantly urging the new king to come to his kingdom, and, after a year, he succeeded. The voyage was dangerous, but Charles landed safely on the 13th of September, 1517, and was received with great magnificence and enthusiasm. But his first act was an insult to Ximenes. He took care not to meet his great minister. His abrupt message to that effect proved fatal, and, after a regency of twenty months, distinguished for sagacity, prudence, and boldness, Ximenes died. Thus did Charles begin on a false policy towards Spain, suggested by his Flemish courtiers, which alienated from him the nobility and the people of his kingdom. The Spainards thought, and thought justly, that the Flemings only cared for Spain so far as it supplied them with money. Peter Martyr declares that in ten months only they sent 1,100,000 ducats into Flanders.

So soon as Charles left them, therefore, each of the principal provinces rose in rebellion, not always against Charles' dignity, but against the government of the viceroys, whom he had left behind. In Castile, Padilla, a popular leader of great ability succeeded, at the head of an armed force, in obtaining possession of Joanna, the emperor's mother. She had been shut up as insane, as doubtless she was. But a sudden return of intelligence enabled this unfortunate lady to assure the people that she had been ignorant of their sufferings. She nominally held an equal share in the sovereignty with Charles, and in his absence, her co-operation with the insurgents was, of course, of the greatest importance.

Had the malcontents in the different provinces maintained any system of intelligent co-operation with each other, things would have gone hardly with the emperor's viceroys. But, in truth, the leaders of the several insurrections knew little and cared little in any case for what was going on in other provinces than their own. The viceroys, on the other hand, had at least the consciousness of imperial sympathy, they had the imperial finances to rely upon, and, to a considerable extent, they were sustained by the nobility in their respective provinces. For these reasons, they were able to act more promptly and with more decision than the insurgents, who were recruited, generally speaking, from the oppressed and discontented populace. To these causes, more than to any distant orders given by himself, Charles owed it that when he returned to Spain in 1522 he found the insurrections all suppressed. The people of the several provinces were dreading the punishment which might be meted out by an indignant master. The viceroy, in Castile, had punished twenty persons capitally. So cruel were those times, that this was considered, even by Dr. Robertson a hundred years ago, to be a very small number, in a province of which the population cannot have been two millions. It was supposed that on the emperor's arrival, his vengeance would sweep much more widely. But Charles showed his statesmanship, and we ought to say his generosity, by refusing to shed any more blood. He published a general order giving amnesty to all persons concerned in the insurrections,—an amnesty from which only eighty persons were exempted, and these, as it would appear, for a limited time.

At the time when Charles landed in Spain, with such cares before him, Adrian, who had been in his youth his preceptor, and afterward regent of Spain in his absence, was chosen Pope of Rome. The people of Rome were amazed by the austerity and humility of an old man, who showed none of the magnificence and splendor which, as they supposed, belonged to the head of the Church. The Pasquinades of the time, which took the privileges of *Punch* today, represented him as a schoolmaster with a bunch of rods, flogging the cardinals. Adrian did not forget to whom he owed his elevation. Still he tried to unite the warring princes of Christendom,—and proposed for them, as a common object, what might be called a crusade against Solyman the Magnificent who had conquered Rhodes. But here he did not succeed. Venice broke with Francis I. king of France, and joined Charles against him. The Pope, naturally enough, fell into the same alliance with his old pupil and master. At this time, the faithless Constable, Charles Duke of Bourbon, rebelled against Francis. Charles V. offered to this prince his sister in marriage,—the title of king of a kingdom to be made for him from Provence and Dauphiny. Henry VIII. of England was the third party in the treaty. The king of Spain was to invade France from the Pyrenees,—Henry on the side of Picardy,—and 12,000 German allies to attack the very heart of the kingdom with the forces of the treacherous Bourbon. This plot was detected by Francis before it could be executed. He prepared himself against it as well as he could, and then made his fatal push into Italy,—hoping that the success which in another generation Napoleon won, might relieve him from his complications. Alas for him!—when he might have had Bayard for his general he appointed a court favorite named Bonnivet, for no better reason than that he was the most accomplished gentleman at court, and an implacable enemy of the Constable, Duke of Bourbon.

Fortunately for his own reputation Pope Adrian died at this moment. So overjoyed were the people of Rome at this event, that they hung garlands on the door of his physician the night after it took place, with the inscription: "To the Deliverer of his Country." With his successor, Clement, Charles was not so closely bound.

The history of Charles' reign from this time to his

abdication is the history of the rest of Europe, rather than of Spain. At the end of his life, he said, as if with a certain self-approval, that he had visited Spain at six different times. So far did he refuse to regard it as his permanent home, or more indeed than a point to stand upon when he prepared for this or that enterprise for moving the world. But it was to the bravery of Spanish soldiers and the skill of Spanish officers that Charles owed his successes, and never have the noblest qualities of the Spanish nation stood out in a more distinguished way before the world than in Charles' reign.

It is difficult to believe in our time, that the suppression, for the moment, of the wretched business of Moorish piracy in the Mediterranean should have been one of the successes which reflected most personal credit upon Charles. But so long had the risk of piracy been accepted as a matter of course, and so arrogant were the Moors in maintaining it, that when Charles opened the business of punishing Barbarossa, the ruler of Tunis, he appeared in some sort as the champion of Christendom. When he succeeded, by the capture of Tunis, in dethroning Barbarossa, and establishing his rival on the throne, he liberated no less than twenty thousand Christian slaves, who had been captured in different piracies by the Moors. These men returned to their homes, eagerly sounding Charles' praises. Many of them—most of them probably—belonged to nations over which he did not rule. And thus, in a certain magnificence of his, in which he was apt to assert the position of ruler of

Europe, he had done for these unfortunates what their own sovereigns had failed to do. Charles deserved much credit. He had himself taken the charge of the expedition, and its motions by sea and by land were under his immediate direction. Another expedition, in which he attempted a similar success in Algiers, was an utter failure. He scarcely landed his men when his fleet, which was under Doria's command, was broken to pieces by a tempest, and Charles was glad to withdraw without even attacking his enemy. Of this unsuccessful foray the most interesting memory to-day is that Fernando Cortés, who knew how to lead men so well, was serving here as a volunteer in disgrace, after he had been recalled from Mexico. He had a horse wounded under him. He begged permission to stay, and offered to storm the city, but his proposal was ridiculed. Of Charles' military movements in other parts of Europe, by which he fairly earned the credit of a brave soldier and a far-seeing officer, we need not speak in a history of Spain.

Curiously enough it is the siege of Pampeluna in the year 1521, an event which to military historians is of no sort of importance, and which we have not even alluded to in our sketch of his reign, which has proved in the history of the world to have results more important than can be traced to any of the larger battles in which Charles had a share. Five years after Charles came to the crown, Francis, king of France, wishing at least to insult him, commissioned a young nobleman, named Henri d'Albrecht, to invade Spain. Henri's general took the Spanish frontier by surprise, and succeeded in taking the fortress of Pampeluna. The Castilians were at this time convulsed by those internal dissensions, which have been described. But so soon as news came to them of a French invasion, they turned the French out faster than they came in. The incident has not, therefore, the slightest military importance. But it

BATTLE OF PAVIA.

was in that siege of Pampeluna that Inigo Lopez de Recalde de Loyola, a Spanish gentleman of rank, was wounded and taken prisoner by the French. He had been a page of King Ferdinand's, and had served gallantly in his wars. With equal gallantry he was defending Spain, in defending Pampeluna, when he received the wound which has been so important in history. To while away his slow recovery, he read a book of Lives of the Saints, and in the contemplations to which it led him, he determined on what men called a "religious life." As soon as his health was restored he made a pilgrimage to the monastery of Montserrat, near Barcelona, and here remained nearly a year, concealing his name and rank. The next year he went to Jerusalem, travelling much of the way on foot. He had already formed the idea of an order of friends who should labor for the good of religion. Strange to say, Spain did not favor his earliest enterprises, and it was in the University of Paris that he found those companions, whose names have since been distinguished as the first members of the "Society of Jesus," founded by him. The new order was finally established in the year 1540. Loyola took for his "religious name" the name of Ignatius, and it was by that name that he was canonized a hundred years after he was wounded, and by this name he is generally known. He was born nine years before the Emperor Charles. He died two years before Charles, in the year 1556. This great leader, therefore, who has exercised an empire so wide over the minds and souls and society of men, now for more than two centuries, is almost exactly the contemporary of that king of Spain, who was born to empire, who thought his star never failed him, whose soldiers conquered, and whose banners flew in triumph in every quarter of the globe. The name and the work of Loyola are remembered today by hundreds of thousands who have never heard of the great sovereign in whose army he once served.

Even before Loyola died, Charles had ceased to reign. He seems to have seen the folly of his own life. It has been well said of him that he was too cunning to rule a world. Disgusted with his own intrigues, perhaps conscious of his own failures, he assembled a splendid company in Brussels on the 25th of October, 1555, and surrendered all his territories and authority in the Netherlands to his son, and abdicated his title to all his thrones. He retired to the monastery of Yuste and dragged along three more years of life there. They were spent in political complaints and gluttonous indulgence. The exposure made within this century of the pettiness of the interests of this prince, who was born to the empire of the world, has made men forget even what there was of courage and conduct in a life, which did so much to hold back civilization.

By the unfortunate result of the insurrections which had accompanied the beginning of Charles' reign, the people of Spain had lost the proud privileges which they had maintained ever since the times, when kings needed every day the arms and the lives of their subjects. Charles still maintained the Cortes in form, in one province or another. But it existed in form only, and in each case became little more than a Court of Registry, where the decrees of the emperor could be proclaimed and confirmed. The nobility may have supposed, at the outset, that they were to triumph by this subjugation of the commons. But in truth, as the people lost their power, the aristocracy, though somewhat more slowly, lost theirs. And, as Dr. Robertson implies, they found too late, when they had no power in council and were only a force to be used at arbitrary pleasure by their prince, that it was but a poor compensation for their old authority, that they might stand covered when they were in the presence of the king.

Meanwhile, through this reign, the soldiers of Spain, in those strange wars in which the customs of chivalry gave way before the arts of modern Europe, shed their blood and gave away their lives in every continent of the world. The reader has seen something of Charles' wars in Africa and in Europe. On Asiatic islands and in American discoveries his soldiers went in both directions round the world; they joined hands at the antipodes with their companions from whom they parted when they left Spain. For Charles' conquests at home he drew upon the treasury, matchless till now even in the Eastern romances, which his officers in America sent to him. And whatever may be thought or said of his failures at home, in his great charge of Europe, which was given so largely into his hands, it must be owned that he and his viceroys showed, on the whole, courage, skill, and address, in the enterprise, new to the world, which led to the immense Spanish empire in America and in Asia.

At the time when he became king of Spain, Cabot, Columbus, and Vespucius had discovered the continent of America. Not long after his accession to the crown, Fernando Cortes, with a handful of men, marched from the Gulf of Mexico upon the city of the same name, and, after terrible struggles, dethroned its sovereign, and reigned in his stead, as Charles' viceroy. He discovered the Pacific and California. Before Charles' death, Spanish officers pushed northward, and as early as the year 1540, Spanish establishments were made in what is now the State of New Mexico. Southward Charles' lieutenants established a regular line of communication from ocean to ocean across the Isthmus of Panama, not far from the very line at which M. de Lesseps hopes to cut the isthmus to-day. This line of communication was needed, indeed, for no less a purpose than to carry across the ingots of Peruvian silver to the Atlantic side on their way to Charles' treasury, and from the Atlantic to carry the stores for the arsenals and garrisons which Spain was establishing on the Pacific. Indeed, Spain regarded the Pacific Ocean as her own closed sea. And if, when Drake appeared there in 1574, he chose to think that he was at war with Spain because he was in the Pacific, he had this excuse, that Spain, at peace with England though she were, would have seized and imprisoned him, perhaps would have killed him, merely because she found him a trespasser on her waters. Meanwhile the islands of the West Indies calmly and peacefully became provinces of Spain, under her control as completely as were Valencia and Andalusia. Before the death of Charles V., Spain had taken possession of Florida, and her flag floated over New Mexico, Mexico, Guatemala, Peru, Chili, Paraguay, and Buenos Ayres, upon the continent, as over every large island of the Caribbean Sea. On the maps, indeed, Spain claimed wider dominion yet in America.

A Portuguese ship, on its way to the East Indies, had stumbled on the projecting Cape of Brazil. Before this, the Pope Alexander VI. had, in 1493, adjusted the claims of Portugal and of Spain to the extra-European world, by giving to Spain all which was west of an ideal meridian, and Portugal all which was east. No man then knew how wide the Pacific was. A generation after, even the eighteen men did not know who had crossed it, under Magellan at first, and afterwards under Sebastian Cano.

Well down in the sixteenth century, navigators of the American shores supposed that they were still feeling their way along the shores of Asia. Indeed it is quite probable that the first appearance of the coast of the United States on the map is due not to the observation of any adventurer who had really seen it, but to the certainty which Marco Polo had given two centuries before, that the coast of Asia trended in that direction. For the earliest coast maps of America had no Cape Cod, no Long Island, and no Chesapeake Bay. And in the fictions of those who pretend to be the discoverers, the natives pick lilies and roses in New Jersey, in the open air in May, and dry grapes for raisins in Block Island a month after. With the supposition that the Pacific was so narrow, the Philippines were brought twenty or thirty degrees nearer to America than they are. Really they belonged within the Portuguese half of the undiscovered world. But Magellan put them into the Spanish part, and there they have remained to this day. It was not till Anson's voyage of 1743 that this great error was exposed to Europe.

Government so extensive—more than imperial,— or any definition of empire which the world had known until now,-was administered by Charles,— while he was in the field perhaps, perhaps in fight, perhaps in his Mediterranean adventures, perhaps engaged in those perplexing diplomacies in which theology bore so large a part, and where, as it has proved, Charles bore himself so unwisely. No wonder, then, if in the details of the administration much went wrong. In that eventful half century between the reign of Ferdinand and the end of that of Philip, Spain had won, through most of the world, the reputation of the blackest cruelty. Her iron hand was on the inferior races. Arbitrary power did what it always does, and debased the men who used it. The people of our own race—such men, for instance, as Drake and Cavendish, and afterward such men as Essex and Hawkins and Raleigh and Sydney—regarded "Spaniard" as only another word for "child of hell," and the living Spaniard himself as the visible ally of the Devil. In their fierce warfare with him,—in such fighting as is described in Tennyson's ballad of "The Revenge," a deep religious horror of the author of lies and of his children gives dignity and strength to an Englishman's loyalty to his nation, his sovereign, and his Saviour. But, after granting this cruelty, yet making allowance for it, in memory of its sources, none the less is it true, that in discovery, in adventure, in colonization, in all that part of her work which fell outside of Europe, Spain showed the noblest courage, patience, and foresight. She illustrated some of the grandest qualities of man. It is not by cruelty and treachery that the people of a poor peninsula, just emerging from a long war of races, obtain possession of half the world. It is rather by such faith as led Columbus, by such manhood as gave Magalhaens his supremacy over discontented rivals. It is by that proud hospitality, in which Spain welcomed such leaders, and gave places of command to these two men, and to Cabot and Vespucius, who were only not their peers. It was by such prompt decision or heroic audacity as once and again saved Cortes,—it was by the wisdom of Ximenes, by the humanity of Las Casas, by the chivalric courage of thousands of unnamed soldiers, and the Christian constancy of thousands of unnamed confessors, that Spanish names were placed on half the headlands of the world. Everywhere the modern world, tracing back its recent history, looks with mysterious curiosity to that land which sent out such men as Columbus, and Balboa, and Cortes, and Magalhaens, in the age of Charles V., of Leo, of Michel Angelo, of Leonardo, of Loyola, and of Luther.

PART V.

CHAPTER XXII.

THREE PHILIPS.

AFTER the abdication of Charles V., Spain was ruled for a century by his direct successors, Philip II., III., and IV. This period is marked as the decline of the splendid fortunes of the country.

VALLADOLID.

No doubt Philip II. at one time had more power in his hand than had ever been held by a purely Spanish king. He was king of all the Spanish kingdoms and of both the Sicilies. He was titular king of England, France, and Jerusalem. He was Absolute Dominator in Asia, Africa, and America. He was Duke of Milan and both the Burgundies, and Hereditary Sovereign of the Seventeen Netherlands. These were his inheritance, and to them he himself added the crown of Portugal.

Cervantes, who lived in the time of Philip II., in his "Numantia," from which we have already quoted, makes the river Douro, coming upon the scene, "attired as a river," with several boys representing tributary streams, recite the prophetic tale of Spain's successes, culminating with the glories of his own sovereign.

> O Spain, my mother dear, thy piercing cries
>   Have struck upon mine ears for many an hour,
> And if I did not haste me to arise,
>   It was that succor lay beyond my power.
> That fatal day, that day of miseries,
>   Which seals Numántia's doom, begins to lower ;
> The stars have willed it so, and well I fear
> No means remain to change a fate so dear.
>
> Minuesa, Tera, Orvion as well,
>   Whose floods increase the volume of mine own,
> Have caused my bosom so to rise and swell,
>   That all its ancient banks are overflown.
> But my swift current will not break their spell
>   As if I were a brook, their pride has grown
> To do what thou, O Spain, didst never dream,
> To plant their dams and towers athwart my stream.
>
> But since the course of stern, relentless fate
>   Brings round the final fall, without avail,
> Of this, thy well-beloved Numantian State,
>   And closes up its sad and wondrous tale,

One comfort still its sorrows may abate,
  That never shall oblivion's sombre veil
Obscure the bright sun of its splendid deeds,
  Admired by all, while age to age succeeds.

But though this day the cruel Romans wave
  Their banners o'er thy wide and fertile land,
Here beat thee down, there treat thee as a slave,
  With pride ambitious, and a haughty hand,
The time will come (if I the knowledge grave
  Which Heaven to Proteus taught to understand)
When these said Romans shall receive their fall
From those whom presently they hold in thrall.

I see them come, the peoples from afar,
  Who on thy gentle breast will seek to dwell,
When to thy heart's content, they have made war
  Against the Romans, and have curbed them well.
Goths shall they be ; who, bright with glory's star,
  Leaving their fame through all the world to swell,
Will in thy bosom seek repose from strife,
And give their sturdy powers a higher life.

In coming years will Attila, that man
  Of wrath, avenge thy wrongs with bloody hands ;
Will place the hordes of Rome beneath the ban,
  And make them subject to his stern commands :
    *   *   *   *   *   *

And when the rightful Lord of heaven and earth
  Is recognized as such on every hand,
He, who shall then be 'stablished and set forth
  As God's vicegerent over every land,
Will on thy kings bestow a style of worth
  As fitting to thy zeal as it is grand ;
They all shall be of CATHOLIC the name,
In true succession to the Goths of fame.

But he, whose hand of vigor best shall bind
  In one thine honor, and thy realms content,

And make the Spanish name, too long confined,
  Hold place supreme, by general assent,
A king shall be, whose sound and thoughtful mind
  On grand affairs is well and wisely bent ;
His name through all the world he rules shall run,
The second PHILIP, second yet to none.

Beneath his fortunate imperial hand
  Three kingdoms once divided under stress,
Again beneath one single crown shall stand,
  For common welfare, and thy happiness.
The Lusitanian banner, famed and grand,
  Which once was severed from the flowing dress
Of fair Castile, will now be knit anew,
And in its ancient place have honor due.

What fear and envy, O beloved Spain,
  Shall bear to thee the nations strange and brave ;
Whose blood shall serve thy flashing sword to stain,
  O'er whom thy banners shall triumphal wave.

Cervantes himself took a part in the conquest that "knit anew" the Lusitanian banner to the stately robes of Castile. He had not cause for personal gratitude to Philip II., who allowed him to live in obscurity, without recognizng his services. Don Quixote was not published till 1603, after the death of this Philip, and it is his successor of whom the anecdote is told that, looking out of the palace window one day, he saw a man reading a book in the street, who had to keep stopping to strike his forehead, overcome with laughter.

"That student," remarked Philip III., "is either out of his mind, or he is reading Don Quixote."

And, indeed, it proved that this was the book in his hand.

The events of Philip the Second's reign relate in

great measure to his possessions outside of Spain, and are therefore not strictly matters belonging to this history. Philip was of a gloomy, stern character, bigoted in his zeal for his own religion. He not only allowed, but may be said to have enjoyed, the *auto-da-fé*, which was the burning of heretics who refused to abandon their religious creed. On his return to Spain, immediately after his father's abdication, at an auto-da-fé, in Valladolid, at which he was present, one of those condemned, who was an officer of distinction, asked the king how he could have the heart to behold the exquisite torments of his people. "Were my own son," replied the king, "such a wretch as thou, he should bear the same fate."

Philip was four times married, first to his cousin the Infanta, Mary of Portugal. He was then but sixteen years old, and she was nearly the same age, only five months younger. The princess came from Lisbon to Castile for the ceremony, and a splendid embassy was sent to meet her on the border. She was received at Salamanca, at the palace of the Duke of Alva, with all honors, by the duchess and a brilliant company of cavaliers and ladies.

But the young prince had already seen his destined bride, for he was so impatient that he sallied out with a few attendants, disguised like himself as huntsman, for five or six miles from the city, in order to see the Infanta unknown to herself. Philip wore a slouched velvet hat, and hid his face under a gauze mask, so that he could mingle in the crowd, and thus he accompanied the procession through the day, and after dark, when the blaze of ten thousand torches shed a light stronger than daylight.

It is pleasant to think of him as an impetuous youth, before he had become stern and moody. His young wife lived but two years, and her only child, Don Carlos, grew up to be a strange young man, a cause of trouble and anxiety, who died before his father.

We know how Philip looked as a young man from the wonderful portraits of Titian, who was painting at that time. At twenty-one, the king had a fair and even delicate complexion. His hair and beard were of a light yellow. His eyes were blue, with the eyebrows somewhat too close together. His nose was thin and aquiline. The bad feature in his face, conspicuous also in the portraits of all his family, was the heavy lower jaw. He was somewhat below the middle height, with a slight, graceful figure, and well-made limbs. His dress was rich and elegant, and his manners were a type of the old Castilian ceremonious dignity. His tastes were reserved and quiet, and he cared nothing for the chivalrous displays and athletic exercises of the time.

Philip's second marriage was with Mary Queen of England, commonly called "Bloody Mary." The match, on his side, was a matter of expediency, and on hers as well; yet it is said, that after the negotiations had begun, the queen became greatly enamoured of the prince, through a portrait of him, painted but two years before by Titian, sent her by Philip's aunt, regent of the Netherlands, which Mary was to return as soon as she had possession of the original.

The marriage was not a very happy one, for Philip spent but little time in England. He was drawn into resuming his father's quarrel with France, and invaded it with the help of Mary's army. The result to the English was the loss of their last possessions in France, including Calais, which the queen bitterly regretted.

She died before the end of the war, having said that "*Calais*" would be found stamped upon her heart. Little comfort did the English receive from their Spanish ally, for four months after her death Philip had made peace with France, and confirmed it with a new marriage with the daughter of the French king, Henry II.

This occasion, also, was a brilliant one with a sad ending. Henry II., tired of fighting, arranged a double marriage to take place at the same time; that of his sister, Marguerite, with Philibert Emanuel, and his daughter, Elizabeth, or Isabella, with the king of Spain. Another Spanish marriage had been talked of for this princess, with Carlos, the son of Philip, for the bridegroom, a match more suitable in the age of the parties, for Philip was now thirty and the bride only sixteen; Philip had already been twice married, and had lost the romantic spirit which led him disguised into the train of his first queen. But these considerations do not count in royal marriages.

The weddings were celebrated with the greatest splendor at the French court. Tournaments were then the fashion, and Henry II. displayed much skill at this sport, of which he was very fond. After several brilliant passages at arms, and when it was time to leave off, the king urged one more course. His opponent was his own captain of the guards, the

Count of Montgomery. Their two lances struck and flew into splinters, one of which entered the king's eye. He fell mortally wounded from his horse, and died eleven days afterwards. The wedding rejoicing was turned into mourning, and Philip of Spain silently withdrew from France with his young bride.

Much romance has been built upon the possible love between this French princess, and Carlos, the Spanish prince for whom she was at first intended. But he at this time was but fourteen; and there is no foundation for the tales of persecution and ill-treatment of his son by Philip. Carlos was of a moody, unhappy disposition, and died early. Justice must acquit his father of any thing more than extreme severity towards him.

The long struggle of Philip II. with his revolted subjects in the Netherlands, scarcely belongs here. The revolt of the Moriscos occupies for us a more important place.

The Moors who chose to become Christians, had been allowed to remain in the country; they were called Moriscos. Philip II. decreed that they should frequent the Christian Church, that they should give up the use of Arabic in writing, that both men and woman should wear the Spanish costume, that they should discontinue their ablutions, and no longer receive Mohammedan names.

In fact, however, the greater part of these Moors conformed only externally to the practices of the Christian religion. They went to mass only to escape the penalty of omitting it · they presented their children for baptism, but washed them afterwards with warm water, to show their contempt of the sacrament. They went to church to be married, but coming home after the service, with closed doors they celebrated the wedding with their own songs, dances, and ceremonies.

Communication was kept up with Turks and the Moors in Africa, always with the hope of deliverance. The Algerians, while they pillaged the sea-

BULL AND MATADOR, MADRID.

board towns, and carried off to slavery those Christians who fell into their hands, left untouched the villages and persons of the Moriscos. The restrictions of Philip exasperated them. Their enjoyments, their pleasures were taken from them; above all they resented the interdict of their use of the bath, which was a part of their religion, as well as a source of enjoyment.

The Moriscos took up arms in the mountains of

the Alpujarras, and were resisted by the flower of the Spanish army, led by Don John of Austria, brother of the king. Much blood was shed on both sides, before the insurrection was put down.

Philip was married for a fourth time, to Anne, the daughter of the Emperor Maximilian II. He died in 1598, in the palace of the Escorial, of which he was the founder. Philip III. succeeded him, his son by the last wife. It has been said that his father, fearing lest his heir should assert himself too much, had carefully trained him to be imbecile. If this was the case, he was only too successful. His son and heir allowed himself to be guided by worthless favorites, and exercised no force in the government of the kingdom. Its greatness ends with Philip II.

In the reign of Philip III. the Mohammedans were expelled from Valencia, Andalusia, and Granada. We have seen how, at this time, the beginning of the seventeenth century, this people, for eight hundred years the sovereigns of Spain, had successively lost their independence, their religion, and their manners and customs.

They had brought into Spain the cultivation of the sugar-cane, of cotton, and rice, and the mulberry, on which feeds the silkworm. Commerce owed them no less. The blades of Toledo, the silks of Granada, the leather of Cordova, the spices and sweets of Valencia, were renowned throughout Europe. At this period, the Moriscos had accustomed themselves to forget the past, and to seek no other successes than those of industry. They had made up their minds to pay the enormous taxes demanded of them, for the sake of mere peace and protection for their families and their industries.

It was decided by the councillors of the king that these good qualities were overbalanced by their heresy, and the dangers to be feared from insurrection. The king observed that he would rather be without subjects than rule over infidels; the foolish saying was applauded by his courtiers; and orders, dated September, 1609, were despatched to the captains-general to force the Moriscos on board the galleys prepared for them, and land them on the African coast.

Romance has found in the enforced departure of these poor exiles ample ground for tale and poem. Especially, stories of treasures hidden by them, which they could not carry with them, are still generally believed throughout Spain.

It is said that even in the time of Ferdinand and Isabella the Moors of Granada were persuaded that sooner or later they should return to the fair land which they had rightfully conquered, and which was, as they believed, unjustly wrested from them. So, many of them, before their departure, buried in secret places their most precious possessions.

Much of this treasure was discovered later by Spanish peasants, but other hidden places may have even yet escaped their greedy search. Legend says that the riches of one family of the Abencerrages, that brilliant race whose very name is regarded now as fabulous, were, and may perhaps still be, concealed in a cave reached by a subterranean passage, leading to a vast hall lighted by several lamps of silver. The ceiling of this excavated room was supported by eight columns of black marble, sparkling with gold and precious stones, like the scene of one of the Arabian Nights. Marble basins, placed between the columns, were heaped with gold pieces, stamped with the effigies of the first caliphs of Cordova or the kings of Granada; in coffers of cedar were masses of arms and ornaments incrusted with precious stones. Other vases held lumps of gold and silver, as they came from the mine. In cups of rock crystal, diamonds and topazes flashed with light, emeralds and rubies glowed.

Such retreats the Moriscos left behind them when they sailed for the shores of Africa. Those who had disembarked there were treated with inhumanity and underwent every suffering. Some, assuming the disguise of Christians, spread over Catalonia and Southern France, but as a nation they vanished.

In 1612, the double marriage was made, which was to strengthen the bonds of peace between France and Spain. The Prince of the Asturias, soon to become Philip IV., married Isabella of Bourbon, daughter of the late Henry IV. of France, and the young king of France, not twelve years old, Louis XIII., married Anna, the eldest daughter of the Spanish king, and then called Anne of Austria. This was the work of Marie de Médicis, after the death of her husband, and contrary to the advice of his wise counsellor, Sully, who had always disapproved of the scheme.

Philip III. died in 1621. He was the king who owed his death to the rigid etiquette of the Spanish court, because, being uncomfortably warm as he sat too near the fire, it took so long to send a messenger to tell a messenger to inform a gentleman in waiting to instruct a chamberlain to take the necessary steps to remove his majesty to a cooler distance, that he fell ill and expired.

Philip IV. was only seventeen when he began to reign on the death of his father. Like him, he surrendered the reins of government to worthless favorites. The first was the Count of Olivares, who had been his gentleman of the bedchamber.

Under such administration, Spain was steadily declining. The mass of the people were sinking into poverty, yet the court exhibited the greatest splendor; plays, pantomimes, and costly entertainments succeeded each other in the capital. Charles, Prince of Wales, afterwards Charles I. of England, visited the court of Spain, accompanied by the Duke of Buckingham, in disguise, though every one knew who he was,—with a view of obtaining the hand of Philip's sister, the Infanta Maria. He was received with the greatest splendor, but the project fell through, and Charles married later a French princess.

An insurrection of the Catalans gave the king and his minister something serious to think of. The rebels implored the aid of the French king, and Louis XIII. was proclaimed Count of Barcelona, and advanced himself to the frontier to direct his army. Philip intended to conduct the war in person, but his minister, Olivares, had not courage enough to meet the enemy; he was, instead, aiding, in the very heart of France, a conspiracy to assassinate the French minister, Cardinal Richelieu, and even to dethrone the French king. It was to this plot that the young Cinq-Mars, a favorite of the king of France, lent himself, and to which he was sacrificed, at the age of twenty-two.

The war lingered for years, with no decided success to either party; until the Catalans themselves grew tired of the French yoke. They were in the end pardoned, and their privileges, of which they had been always tenacious, recognized as inviolable.

The treaty which settled this and other things, was the celebrated treaty of the Pyrenees, by which was arranged the marriage of the Infanta, Maria Theresa, the daughter of Philip, with the youthful Louis XIV. On this occasion, to allay the opposition of Europe to the union of two powerful kingdoms, Louis solemnly renounced all claim to the Spanish crown, either for himself or for his sucessors; which renunciation, however, did not prevent, in the lifetime of Louis, the accession of his grandson, Philip V., to the Spanish throne.

From studying such a decline from the brilliant fortunes of the fifteenth century in Spain, it is pleasant to turn to the successes of the painter Velasquez, who was busy during the life of Philip IV. in painting those masterpieces which now make the picture gallery at Madrid so interesting. His portraits of

Philip and of the Duke of Olivares, as well as of other personages of the time, make us know how they looked, and give a reality to their lives, as books and dates fail to do.

Philip IV. died in 1665. He was married a second time, after the death of the French princess, to Maria Anna, the daughter of the emperor, Ferdinand III. She was his niece, for Ferdinand had married the sister of Philip. He left three children, Charles, Prince of the Asturias, who became, at the death of his father, Charles II. For Charles, the fifth emperor of the name, who was in his time king of Spain, was Charles I. of Spain, as there had been no other Charles on that throne before him. Philip's daughters were Maria Theresa, married to Louis XIV., and Margaret, Queen of Hungary.

With these descendants of Charles V. the line of real Spanish sovereigns may be said to end, for the next Philip was a pure Bourbon. With all their faults the Philips of this chapter displayed the virtues belonging to the Spanish character—devotion to their religion, due regard to the state of sovereigns, and grave dignity befitting royal birth. In them we have the type of the Spanish *hidalgo*,—*hijo de algo*, or " son of somebody."

CHAPTER XXIII.

THE BOURBONS.

CHARLES THE SECOND of Spain is the last of that House of Hapsburg of which we saw the first Spanish king, born at Ghent, in the convenient year 1500. In the equally convenient year 1700, Charles II. died. School-boys and school-girls will have little else to thank him for. But they may be grateful for that care by which he provided for flagging memories, that the Hapsburg rule of Spain should be measured exactly by two centuries.

The "Biographical Dictionary" dismisses him curtly with this sharp and brief biography: "He was the son of Philip IV. He was born in 1661, was proclaimed king in 1665, joined the coalition formed against Louis XIV., and in 1678 surrendered to this king Franche Comté and other provinces in the Low Countries. His last act was the leaving his crown to Philip, Duke of Anjou, the grandson of the same king."

The region thus surrendered to Louis XIV. by this weak descendant of the Emperor Charles, is the same region which, as Alsace and Lorraine, has been, in our own time, ceded by conquered France to the new-born German empire, of which the constitution

was completed in Versailles, when a German army
and a German emperor were encamped there. Such
are the compensations of history.

Readers of our race will find it convenient to remember that the Spanish King Charles II. and the
English King Charles II. were nearly contemporary.
Charles II. of Spain was born in the year 1660, the
same year in which England called her Charles II.

MALAGA.

to the throne. It is in the reigns of these two kings
that England and Spain, always in contest with each
other, if there were a European war, met in conflict
in America. St. Augustine had been established by
the Spaniards as early as the year 1565. It is therefore the oldest European establishment on the Atlantic seaboard of the United States. But in 1647
there were but three hundred families in St. Augus-

tine. Living with them were fifty Franciscan friars. This was almost the whole Spanish population of Florida. In 1663 Charles II. of England gave a charter for the settlement of Carolina, which bears his name. The limits of the patent ran so near St. Augustine, that Catholic and heretic felt the natural jealousy of each other, and in 1665 Captain John Davis, a buccaneer, landed at St. Augustine and destroyed the little town. But, in 1667, the two Charleses agreed by treaty to suppress buccaneering, and, indeed, from that time its decline as an institution may be said to begin. No English settlement was made in Carolina until 1670, and it was eventually agreed that the St. Mary's River should be the line of separation between the English and Spanish colonies. This river, therefore, to this day, divides Georgia and Florida, which in their English and Spanish names still bear the token of their origin.

In 1670 and 1686 the Spaniards attacked the English and burnt some of their houses. In 1687 negroes were first introduced as slaves into Florida. In 1696, still in the reign of Charles II. of Spain, the Spanish government established a fort at Pensacola, on the western side of the peninsula. They were induced to take this step by the establishment of the little French colony at the mouth of the Mississippi. For Spain, worsted in Europe, was unwilling, without some struggle, to surrender the control of the Gulf of Mexico.

Meanwhile, in Europe, Charles II. of Spain was engaged in the wretched series of falsehoods and intrigues, which led to what is known as the war of the Spanish Succession. Indeed, he is now remembered chiefly from his connection with these intrigues. The oldest sister of Charles, Maria Theresa, had married Louis XIV. of France. Charles himself had no children and no living brothers. His sister was his heir, and after her death her descendants were the heirs to the Spanish throne. But Louis and the Infanta had both solemnly renounced all claim to the succession at the time of their espousals. This renunciation had been confirmed by the Cortes. A younger sister of Charles had been the wife of Leopold, Emperor of Germany. She also had renounced her claims to the Spanish crown. But the Cortes had not sanctioned that renunciation. She had a daughter who married the Elector of Bavaria, and the Electoral Prince of Bavaria inherited her claim to the throne. A third claimant was Charles' first cousin, the Emperor Leopold. He was a son of a daughter of Philip III. No renunciation had been exacted from his mother when she was married. "The question," says Lord Macaulay, "was certainly very complicated. That claim which, according to the ordinary rules of inheritance, was the strongest, had been barred by a contract executed in the most binding form. The claim of the Electoral Prince of Bavaria was weaker. But so also was the contract which bound him not to prosecute his claim. The only party against whom no instrument of renunciation could be produced was the party who, in respect of blood, had the weakest claim of all."

The experience of Charles V. was enough to warn

Europe against the danger of giving the crown of Spain to any other monarch The emperor, out of deference to the opinion of Europe, waived his claim in favor of the Archduke Charles. The dauphin waived his claim in favor of Philip, Duke of Anjou. But, without consulting the king of Spain or the emperor, William of England, Louis of France, and the States of Holland made a treaty which stipulated that the Electoral Prince of Bavaria, the second of the claimants named above, should succeed to Spain, the Indies, and the Netherlands. Even the king of Spain agreed to this and made a will leaving the crown to the Bavarian prince. Hardly had this been done when the prince himself died and the question was again unsettled.

The same parties then agreed that Spain, the Indies, and the Netherlands should descend to the Archduke Charles. But to this treaty the Spaniards gave no consent. A quarrel ensued between the Spanish court and the English court. The king of France was utterly faithless to his share in the transaction and used his commanding influence to secure the crown for his own grandson Philip, the Duke of Anjou. As the reader sees, this was wholly in face of his own renunciation of the throne for any descendants of his, and the other renunciation made by his wife at the same time.

Whatever was the right or wrong between the two claimants to the throne, it is clear that the people of Madrid and, indeed, the people of Spain favored the French claimant. Charles died on the 3d of November, 1700. The Duke of Abrantes announced

CLOISTERS, TOLEDO.

that the king was dead, and proclaimed Philip his successor. The great news was sent to Paris as quickly as was possible. The new king hastened to Spain. "The Pyrenees," said his grandfather, Louis XIV., "have ceased to exist." Louis, indeed, knew that he should have to fight before the Pyrenees were made into a valley, but he was not unwilling to do so. Within a year he insulted the English in the keenest way by recognizing the son of James II. as king of England. King William of England still lived and was quite willing to measure swords again against Louis. War was proclaimed on the 15th of May, 1702. William had died meanwhile, but not before he had formed the great alliance of the European princes against the Bourbons, and the proclamation was made simultaneously at Vienna, at London, and at The Hague.

The young Philip was utterly incompetent for such a position. He was but nineteen years old, and his education had not at all fitted him for command. "He sat eating and drinking all night, lay in bed all day, yawned at the council table, and suffered the most important papers to lie unopened for weeks." Louis XIV., indeed, had so educated all the members of his family that they were unable, as they were unaccustomed, to act for themselves. Philip of Anjou, scarcely more than a boy, indeed, was little more than a puppet in the complications which followed. All he wanted was to have a wife, and Maria Louisa of Savoy, a beautiful girl of thirteen, was selected. From that time she ruled her husband, the Princess Orsini ruled her, and Louis, who had selected the Princess Orsini for this duty, found to his surprise that he could not rule her.

William III. of England died before hostilities began. But the English Government despatched the Duke of Ormond with a fleet, which seized the Spanish galleons at Vigo, where it had put in to escape him. Ormond took seven millions of dollars of treasure. Fourteen millions, or goods to that value, were sunk in six galleons that were lost. This was the beginning of a series of assaults which the English, Dutch, and Portuguese made upon Spain from one or another of its frontiers during the next six years. It is in this war that Lord Peterborough won those remarkable victories of which the story is almost like the stories of romance. It recalls memories of the Cid and of the conquest of the Moors. Poor Philip and his wife were driven hither and thither with no will of their own. Charles, the Austrian claimant, who was with Peterborough, seemed at one moment to be sure of success. But his inaction at one time and his quarrels with the great English leader at another, put an end to all such hopes. The Duke of Vendôme took command of the French king's forces and drove the adherents of Charles into Barcelona, which was the only place remaining to him after so many years of war. Of a sudden a change of parties in England brought about the Treaty of Utrecht, and with the Treaty of Utrecht the Bourbon dynasty was confirmed on the throne of Spain, with that hold which it has had, now with a strong grasp, and now with very feeble fingers, until this time.

Philip hated the cares of royalty, and in 1724 abdicated in favor of his son. But this boy died in the same year, and his name is not generally mentioned among the kings of Spain, for his father was obliged, however unwillingly, to resume the crown, which he held until his death in 1746. Ferdinand VI., his son, succeeded him, and died without children in 1759. His brother Charles, known as Charles III., succeeded him and reigned until 1788. His reign brought more good-fortune to Spain and less evil than that of any other prince of this wretched line of Bourbon.

It was in this reign that the Jesuits received that sudden blow from which this order has never recovered, either in America or in Europe. " A little before the break of day the decree for the expulsion of the Jesuits went forth, with the Great Seal itself, from the council-chamber of Charles III." This was on the morning of the 25th of June, 1767. The Jesuit writers and their enemies alike agree that the king was brought up to this point by proof which satisfied him that the Jesuits had circulated slanders regarding his birth. At that time Spain and Charles had the good-fortune that Aranda was his prime-minister. The decree against the Jesuits was the joint work of Aranda and Choiseul, who, fortunately for France, was the minister of Louis XV. Besides Aranda, Florida Bianca was one of the ministers of Charles III., who seems to have had either great good-fortune or good-sense in selecting his servants.

For a part of the time when these great statesmen administered his government for him, Vergennes

SAN SEBASTIAN.

another great statesman, was the prime-minister of France. In the same period there come in the eventful six years between 1776 and 1782, when the United States of America, an infant nation in its first struggles, needed the assistance of France and Spain against England. Spain moved very slowly in such things. Indeed it is one of the traditions of Spanish administration in these later times to move slowly. John Jay, who was the minister of the young republic to Spain, was sadly annoyed that he could not persuade them to move faster and to do more. But, if it were only that American vessels cruising in the Eastern Atlantic, and every now and then picking up an English prize, could run into the Spanish ports, that advantage was a very great one. There was, on our own side of the ocean, another way in which Spain gave great help to the new-born nation. It happened that from the year 1762 to the year 1803, the whole of the great region called "Louisiana," which included all the western half of the Mississippi Valley, beside that part to the east of it which is in the State of Louisiana to-day, was in the possession of Spain. To the great indignation of the French settlers there, their French king had abandoned them and ceded the whole magnificent province to Spain.

With the news of the battle of Lexington, the American traders in New Orleans went to the Spanish viceroy and urged him to come to the relief of their country. The American, Oliver Pollock, is always to be remembered as a friend in need at a time when America needed such friends. He persuaded the

THE PASS OF PANCORBO.

viceroy to let him have gunpowder from the stores of the king of Spain, which he might send up the Mississippi River to Pittsburg. Spain was nominally at peace with England, but the governor did not forget that England had snatched Florida from his king, and found this a good time for revenge. In the terrible stress of the first years of the Revolutionary war, the supply of powder thus received from an unexpected quarter proved to be of the greatest value. In the treaties of 1783, France and Spain repaid themselves for the losses which they had sustained in 1763. Spain then had lost Florida, and she now gained it again. The present possession of it by the United States dates back only to the year 1821, when the United States received it from Spain, having purchased it by a treaty which was made two years before.

Charles III., the best sovereign whom Spain has had till the present generation since the death of Ferdinand, died in 1788, in the fifty-seventh year of his reign. He was succeeded by his son, Charles IV., then a man of forty-eight years old. The wife of Charles, a woman who assumed an unfortunate pre-eminence in affairs was the Princess Maria Louisa of Parma. Unfortunately for Spain, a handsome guardsman appeared at court just before the king was crowned, who became a favorite both of king and queen. His name was Manuel Godoy, but he was afterwards known as the Duke of Alcudia, and the Prince of Peace. Four years were enough to advance him through all the stages of rank, from that of a private in the Life Guard up to prime-minister of Spain, and Knight of the Order of the Golden Fleece. He had obtained these dignities when he was twenty-five years old, in 1792. In 1795, when he had succeeded in making peace with France, he was made a grandee of the first class, and received a great grant of land with a very large income. In 1796 he concluded the offensive and defensive treaty with the French Republic, and the next year married Maria Theresa of Bourbon. This man was the evil genius of Spain. He handled both king and queen as he chose, and to the miserable intrigues of a miserable court we must look for such explanation as we need of the fall of Spain into the hands of Napoleon.

CHAPTER XXIV.

NAPOLEON.

FERDINAND, the son of Charles, in despair at some phase which these intrigues had taken, opened a secret correspondence with the French emperor. Napoleon, false to him as he was to almost every one, betrayed the son to the father, and took the occasion of the family quarrel, to begin that series of negotiations and assumptions which ended in his holding father and son both in captivity in France, while he established his brother Joseph at Madrid as king of Spain. All this was done so promptly and with such authority of force that the Spanish people had, at first, hardly any opportunity of resistance. Indeed, at that moment Spain was nominally in alliance with France, thanks to Godoy; and a large contingent from the Spanish army was holding Napoleon's fortresses in the north of Europe. Of this period of transition the critical event, so far as the fortunes of Spain were concerned, was the battle of Trafalgar.

By the treaty made by Godoy the French had gained the use of the Spanish fleet. In the battle of Cape St. Vincent of 1797 the English Admiral, Jervis, defeated them and took four line-of-battle

LEANING TOWER, SARAGOSSA.

ships. Peace was restored to Europe in 1802 by the short-lived treaty of Amiens, but on the 12th of December, 1804, Napoleon compelled Spain to join him in an alliance against England, and the Spanish court declared war. Napoleon was thus able to unite the fleets of France and Spain, and they took the sea under Villeneuve with some prospect of success. Nelson was the English admiral, quite as eager to find them as they were to find him. The French fleet had slipped the English blockade of Toulon on the 18th of January, 1805, and formed a junction with the Spanish fleet at Cadiz. Before Nelson was made sure of the junction, the combined French and Spanish fleets had sailed for the West Indies. Nelson followed. Again and again he missed them. On the 9th of June, he learned that they had taken under convoy a fleet of merchant vessels, and were on their way home. Nelson followed again. But this extraordinary pursuit, of one squadron by another, in which both parties crossed the Atlantic Ocean twice, ended in Nelson's failure. The French and Spaniards had passed through Sir Robert Calder's squadron, had proceeded to Ferrol, on the northwest of Spain, where a smaller squadron awaited them, and all returned to Cadiz in safety. Nelson landed for the first time, it is said, in two years, at Gibraltar, and then returned to England, almost inconsolable. It proved that he had passed his enemies on his way home from the West Indies, outsailing them.

So soon as he learned where they were, he offered his services again to the English Government, and was permitted by them to choose his officers from the whole list of the English navy. He set sail in the *Victory*, his old flag-ship, which had been refitted, and with the largest fleet which could be got together. He arrived off Cadiz again on the 29th of September, which was the very day when Villeneuve, the French admiral, had received peremptory orders to put to sea. Nelson was so afraid that Villeneuve would know his force, that he kept his station fifty or sixty miles west of Cadiz. Villeneuve, on his side, saw an American captain in Cadiz, who had left London but a few days before and had seen Nelson there. So that Villeneuve supposed he was not to meet his great antagonist. He sailed promptly, as ordered. On the 21st the French and Spanish fleets could be distinctly seen from the deck of the *Victory*. A little after daylight Nelson came on deck and made signal to attack the enemy in two lines. He led one, and Collingwood the other. They had twenty-seven ships of the line and four frigates. The French and Spanish fleet had six more ships of the line and three more frigates. They did not avoid the conflict, and were formed judiciously to meet his attack in a double line.

In the battle which followed Nelson was killed. The *Victory* was engaged on both sides, working both her batteries. Twice he gave orders to cease firing on the *Redoubtable*, because her great guns were silent, and he supposed she had struck. A musket ball from the mizzen-top of that ship struck his left shoulder, and he fell upon his face on the spot covered with the blood of his secretary, who had been killed a little before. Nelson died three hours after, but not before Hardy, his captain, announced to him a complete victory. His last words were: "I thank God I have done my duty."

Meanwhile Napoleon had been raging while waiting for the fleet at Boulogne to cover his invasion into England. But Villeneuve did not arrive. Greatly to Napoleon's mortification and annoyance, he was obliged to break up his camp at Boulogne and move eastward upon Vienna. The great battle was fought at Austerlitz, and not at Hastings on the English shore. When Napoleon heard of Trafalgar, he is said to have remarked: "I cannot be everywhere." On which remark of his, Sir Walter Scott grimly comments that it was quite as well for him that he was not under the guns of the *Victory*. The defeat of the allied fleet put an end to all projects of English invasion. Villeneuve was made a prisoner when his own ship surrendered, and remained a prisoner in England for several months. He knew the anger of his master so well that he dared not face it. After he was released and returned to France, he stabbed himself. It was said that the dagger entered his heart at the place indicated on an anatomical drawing, which was on the table before him, which he had pierced with a pin in studying for his successful suicide.

With the usurpation of the Spanish crown by Joseph, the pride and indignation of the Spanish people were aroused. It was one thing to march a French army to Madrid. It was quite another thing to keep a great and proud nation satisfied under a foreign rule. In each province the people rose in rebellion. There was even an insurrection in Madrid. At Baylen, Castaños, an old Spanish general, defeated Dupont, who was compelled to surrender with seventeen thousand men. This event was, as Napoleon afterward said, "his Caudine Forks." In truth it was the first serious reverse his arms had met with. The English writers say, and probably with truth, that it was due to Dupont's utter carelessness and the lack of discipline among his troops, more than to any military skill of Castaños. The battle, indeed, was a tangle of conflicting forces, arriving from one point and another, of which the result, probably fortunate in the end to Spain, was the surrender of an army corps.

"Probably fortunate!" One cannot speak too definitely. For the same English authors insist that the victory was in the end a great misfortune. They say that it gave a false confidence to the Spanish generals and to their guerilla bands, which, in the end, led them to their ruin.

The success had a more favorable influence on the national cause of Spain, by confirming the resolution of the English Government to maintain a large force in the Peninsula. Portugal had been for many generations the firm ally of England. England was now maintaining a strong force in Portugal, which was at last placed under the command of Sir Arthur Wellesley, who won for himself before long the title of Lord Wellington. Massena, one of Napoleon's marshals, with a force larger than Wellesley's threatened Lisbon. But Wellesley's combinations were so good, and his men fought so well, that he compelled Massena to withdraw, and even followed him into Spanish territory. In two terrible attacks he took by storm Ciudad Rodrigo and Badajoz, the fortified places which the French held on the Spanish frontier. In the battle of Salamanca he proved his superior generalship, and where the forces were fairly equal, he drove the French from the field. All this gave courage to the Spanish guerilla forces, and in some instances they achieved considerable successes. Whoever reads a modern Spanish history might imagine that the Spaniards themselves drove the invaders out of Spain, and that a few English soldiers were there looking on. Whoever reads an English history might suppose that "Lord Wellington," as he then was, marched serene from victory to victory, only now and then varying the course of conquest by a masterly retreat, to show the world how a retreat should be carried on, but with the final result of the evacuation of Spain. The last great battle was fought at Victoria, a place so named in honor of a victory won five centuries before, of which "Ingles mundi" (the English mound) is a memorial of the Englishmen who then beat the French there. In the battle under Wellington's orders the French were completely broken, and fled. The losses of the allied nations show fairly enough, to whom belongs the honor of the victory. Of the English 3,308 fell, of the Portuguese 1,049, and of the Spaniards only 553. The English could not follow their victory as promptly as Wellington wished, because they were fairly demoralized by the extent of their plunder. King Joseph fled with only one Napoleon in his pocket. His carriage and his "loot" from the galleries of Madrid fell into English hands.

Now came the fall of Napoleon.

PART VI.

CHAPTER XXV.

THE NINETEENTH CENTURY.

AN ODE.

WRITTEN, OCTOBER, 1819, BEFORE THE SPANIARDS HAD RECOVERED
THEIR LIBERTY.

    Arise, arise, arise !
There is blood on the earth that denies ye bread ;
    Be your wounds like eyes
To weep for the dead, the dead, the dead.
What other grief were it just to pay ?
Your sons, your wives, your brethren, were they :
Who said they were slain on the battle day ?

    Awaken, awaken, awaken !
The slave and the tyrant are twin-born foes ;
    Be the cold chains shaken
To the dust where your kindred repose, repose !
Their bones in the grave will start and move,
When they hear the voices of those they love,
Most loud in the holy combat above.

    Wave, wave high the banner !
When freedom is riding to conquest by ;
    Though the slaves that fan her,
Be famine and toil, giving sigh for sigh.
And ye who attend her imperial car,
Lift not your hands in the banded war,
But in her defence whose children ye are.

> Glory, glory, glory,
> To those who have greatly suffered and done ;
> Never name in story
> Was greater than that which ye shall have won.
> Conquerors have conquered their foes alone,
> Whose revenge, pride, and power they have overthrown :
> Ride ye, more victorious, over your own.
>
> Bind, bind every brow
> With coronals of violets, ivy, and pine ;
> Hide the blood-stains now
> With hues which sweet nature has made divine ;
> Green strength, azure hope, and eternity ;
> But let not the pansy among them be ;
> Ye were injured, and that means memory.
> —SHELLEY.

Ferdinand VII., who had been in theory king of Spain ever since the abdication of Charles in his favor in 1808, returned to his capital to assume his crown. He had been living meanwhile in an honorable captivity in France. He now took up his residence in Spain in 1814.

Two years before, a constitution had been drawn for Spain in the king's absence. It was the work of the Cortes on which all the real government of Spain had depended in the absence of its kings. It remodelled the whole administration, so that Spain, which had been the most absolute monarchy in Europe, would become, under this constitution, the monarchy most severely limited. But Ferdinand returned on the wave of absolutism, and he took advantage of it, as sovereigns did, who had more sense than he. It was not long before he promulgated a decree, by which the Cortes were declared illegal, and all their acts rescinded, the constitution among

PALACIO REALE, MADRID.

the rest. The Inquisition had been abolished since the king's departure, but it was now restored, and the most arbitrary bigotry reigned triumphant. The constitution was publicly burnt. The king promised, indeed, to grant one with liberal principles, but did nothing to fulfil his promise in six years. The government, which one would have said was as bad as it could be, passed from worse to worse. Numerous conspiracies were quenched in blood, and the rebellion of all the American colonies made the condition of things desperate.

In the autumn of 1819, a considerable army had been brought together at Cadiz, for the subjugation of America. But officers and troops refused to embark. They joined the disaffected people of Cadiz, and proclaimed the constitution of 1812. Soon after, Mina, a patriot who had been exiled, proclaimed it in Spanish Navarre, and a series of insurrections through the whole country, compelled the king to acknowledge the constitution in March of 1820. A short interval of liberal government ensued. But, in 1822, other conspiracies broke out in the interests of absolute government, which were generally sustained by the Catholic clergy. Under the direction of the Holy Alliance, a French army of 100,000 men moved into Spain, took possession of the capital, and appointed a regency. Ferdinand, with the Spanish army, maintained a separate government for some months, but in October, 1823, without resistance from them, the Duke d' Angoulême took possession of Spain and reinstated Ferdinand with absolute power. From this time forward for five years, a

French army of occupation was in Spain. All credit was destroyed at home and abroad. The contests between the two parties were of the bitterest description, and the government oppressed the liberals with the hardest hand. Ferdinand, himself, was more moderate than the most bitter of his supporters. They made a plot to compel him to abdicate in favor of his brother Charles. This is the beginning of the Carlist plots, always in the interest of absolutism, and of the most extreme bigotry, which have desolated Spain, with but little intermission from that time to this.

Don Carlos, as this brother is always called, was presumptive heir to the throne. As long back, however, as 1789, Charles IV., his grandfather, had issued a "Pragmatic Sanction," establishing the succession to the crown of Spain in females as well as males. On the 6th of April, 1830, King Ferdinand confirmed this decree. On this decree and his confirmation depend the rights to the throne of the king who has so lately died, and, of course, of his infant daughter, and infant son, who since his death have been proclaimed queen and king of Spain.

Ferdinand had no children by either of his first three wives. His fourth wife, Christina, was a Neapolitan princess, as was Carlotta, the wife of Don Francisco, a younger brother of the queen. The wife of Don Carlos was a Portuguese princess, and between the Neapolitan princesses and their Portuguese sister-in-law there was a constant palace war. The Neapolitan ladies persuaded Calomarde to suggest the abrogation of the Salic law to the king, and the decree was executed without the knowledge of the other ministers.

When, therefore, the princess Doña Isabella was born to the king, on the 10th of October, 1830, she was the heiress to the throne, if only Spain recognized the authority which had made a change so radical in the succession. It was a coincidence curious and interesting, especially to those who were children in those days, that there were then three princesses awaiting the death of old men before they should mount three of the oldest thrones in Europe—Victoria in England, who was then eleven years old; Doña Maria in Portugal; and Doña Isabella in Spain. In Spain, the change in the Salic law was not made without a protest. Ferdinand's brother, Carlos, vehemently denied the right of the king or the Cortes to take from him the succession. Ferdinand himself was weak, and in a fit of illness on September 18, 1832, he instituted again the Salic law. But as soon as he began to recover, he revoked this decision. He then banished his brother, Don Carlos, to Portugal, and soon afterwards ordered him to reside in the Papal States. But before the younger brother could sail for Italy, Ferdinand died on the 29th of September, 1833. Isabella the Second was proclaimed queen when she was not two years old, her mother, Maria Christina, of the two Sicilies, being appointed regent. Don Carlos, the child's uncle, with such assistance as he could receive from Dom Miguel, the uncle of the queen of Portugal, whose position was not very different from that of Don Carlos, led an insurrection

MADRID. GENERAL VIEW.

against her in the northeastern provinces. The most extreme of the Catholic party and the most conservative of the mountaineers sustained him. It can hardly be said that the fires of that insurrection are extinct at the end of half a century. But the little queen, all unconscious as she was of wars and rumors of wars, had stout allies. For her cause was regarded almost by common consent as the cause of liberalism. So the new government of Louis Philippe in France and the reform administration in England, with Dom Pedro, the liberal regent in Portugal, who had to maintain another niece against another uncle, all made a quadruple alliance with the Queen Regent of Spain. A force so strong as theirs, in the field and in reserve, overpowered Don Carlos, and he was obliged to flee his country. But he returned once and again. And when he died, his son, who bore the same name, renewed the attempt, always supported by the more rigid Catholics, by the mountaineers on the southern slopes of the Pyrenees, and always affecting to have the support of the priesthood of the Roman Church. To this hour, in any overthrow of parties or in any attempt at a revolution in Spain, there will be a rumor of "Carlist" influence among the insurgents. But the last military movement of the Carlists was crushed when Amadeo was king of Spain in 1876. It must be understood that these Carlist movements have been headed by three different princes named Carlos. The first of these was Don Carlos, the brother of Ferdinand VII. He died in 1855. The second was his son, the Count of Montemolin, who died in 1861. Before his death, he signed a renunciation of all his claims to the throne of Spain. The Carlist cause is now represented by his nephew, also named Don Carlos, who is the son of his brother Juan, and was born in 1849. In 1868 Don Juan renounced all his rights to his son, Alfonso *Carlos* Ferdinando Juan Pio, who was born on the 12th of September, 1849. His wife is Maria, the daughter of the late Dom Miguel of Portugal, whose life, as has been said, has run somewhat on parallel lines with that of the first Don Carlos.

The little princess came to the throne with the title thus seriously challenged before she was two years old. Her mother, Christina of Naples, was appointed regent, and when one remembers the wretched failure of the daughter's life it is but fair to reflect that she was the child of such a mother. There were two children, the young queen, Isabella, and Maria Louisa, who has since been known as the Duchess Montpensier. By Ferdinand's will, Christina was made both guardian of the children and regent of the kingdom; and regent she was in a fashion for seven years. For those seven years, Spain was desolated by civil war. As for the regent, all that people knew of her was her shameless passion for her chamberlain, Hernando Muñoz, an officer of the body-guard, whom she made her chamberlain. Muñoz was of insignificant rank, his father having kept a tobacco shop in Taroncon. She contracted with him a Morganatic marriage in December, 1833, but this was kept a secret, and by him she had ten children. A conspiracy of men determined to give Spain liberal institutions, compelled her in 1836 to give a new constitution to the kingdom and to concede some of the rights of constitutional government. But in 1840, the scandals of her administration had become so odious, that she was compelled to resign her office of regent.

To the great good-fortune of Spain, Espartero, a military officer of great ability, was high in command when Ferdinand died, and pronounced unequivocally for Isabella. Among the wretched intrigues of the court, and the constant changes of ministers, Espartero retained the favor of the army and of what may be called the Spanish people. Twice he saved the capital when it was imperilled by the Carlists. His campaign of 1839, drove the Don Carlos of the day from Spain, and he was honored by the title of Grandee of Spain and Duke of Victory. In 1841, after Christina had been compelled to give up the regency, he was named regent until the princess should have reached the age of eighteen, and in this capacity, which was really that of a sovereign, he administered the affairs of poor Spain with dignity and ability.

But the student of modern Spanish history must remember all along that Spain is the prey of unceasing partisan dissension. By a combination of parties, which had nothing in common but their hatred of Espartero, he was dethroned, in 1843. He lived in England for four years, then returned to Spain, and lived there in private until 1854. The miserable despotism of which Christina had been the moving spirit, whether she were nominally in power or no, then roused an insurrection which drove her from the kingdom, and Espartero was again called to the head of the government. Isabella was by this time queen, and he served as her prime-minister.

The queen had been declared by the Cortes to have attained her majority in 1843, when she was but thirteen years old, and in 1846 she married her cousin Don Francisco d' Assisi, the son of the Don Francis, Ferdinand's brother, whose wife's intrigues in 1833 have been spoken of. At the same time her sister married the Duke of Montpensier, Louis Philippe's fifth son. These marriages were to a considerable extent the fruit of Louis Philippe's personal and selfish policy, and they did much to make him unpopular among the powers of Europe, when the French people ejected him in 1848. But whatever might have been the dictates of public politics or of family intrigue, Queen Isabella's history was apt to be a wretched story of personal passion, in which she followed the example of her mother. In all changes of party, in the pendulum swings of administrations from pure absolutism to constitutional freedom and back again, personal intrigue and personal passion were always intervening. At last, in 1868, the nation would bear no more. A revolution broke out in September. The people of Madrid turned against her. Isabella fled to France, and a provisional government was appointed. In November, 1870, the Cortes, finding the impossibility of agreeing upon any candidate from the family of their rulers at home, attempted as a measure of compromise to introduce a wholly new dynasty. They offered the crown to Amadeo, the second son of King Humbert of Italy. They thus avoided all decision between the Carlist candidates and their cousins. They secured a king from an old house, and from a dynasty that was popular at that moment among the Liberals of Europe.

Amadeo Ferdinand Marie, Duke of Aosta, was born on the 30th of May, 1845. He was married on his twenty-second birthday, three years before he was called to the Spanish throne, to Marie, daughter of Charles Emmanuel, Prince of Pozzo della Cisterna. He brought to his new position a certain popularity; but the problem was too hard a one to be solved by his ingenuity, and early in 1873 he abdicated in his turn.

His reign had been long enough to show what had been, indeed, well enough known before, that the people of the two peninsulas do not like each other. This short reign is likely to be remembered in history, for a visit which Amicis, the brilliant Italian traveller, made in Spain at that time, and the entertaining book of travels which he wrote then and afterwards.

When Amadeo returned, the Republican party, who were responsible for his fall, attempted to organize Spain as a republic. The present French Republic was then just born, and the Spaniards had the sympathy of France. Castelar, a pure and intelligent statesman, the friend of Garibaldi, Mazzini, Kossuth, and other leading Republicans of

Southern Europe, led this movement. Castelar showed dignity and resource, which received, as they deserved, the admiration of the intelligent world.

But the problem was not to be solved by him, and at the end of 1874 a new combination brought back the legitimate Bourbon line.

The younger Don Carlos, the Count of Montemolin, had led an insurrection in the northern provinces from the moment of the abdication of Amadeo.

The friends of constitutional government would not trust him and did not trust the republic. They now proclaimed Alfonso the son of Isabella, a young man seventeen years old. He was the prince whose recent death seems so unfortunate for Spain, and has called forth the general regret of Europe and America.

Alfonso XII., Francis d' Assise Ferdinand Pius John Marie-de-la-Concepçion Gregory, etc., etc., was born November 28, 1857. His education in early life is said to have been entrusted, as was that of his sisters, to Madam Calderon de la Barca, a lady of English birth, long resident in America, who had married one of the more distinguished Spanish diplomatists. Her entertaining book on Mexico is well remembered. In later years the young prince had the great advantage, for a prince, of the school of exile. For in the fall of his mother, he also was banished from Madrid, and when, at seventeen years of age, he came back to that city, he had been away from it more than half his life. It was familiarly said in Spain, that when his partisans offered him the crown and he accepted it, he did so saying that he wished them to understand that he was the first Republican in Europe, and that when they were tired of him, he hoped they would tell him so, and that he would leave as Amadeo had done.

Whether he said this or not, the speech was well invented by any one who wished to earn for him popularity among Spaniards. Their loyalty is certain; but it is loyalty which, as the reader has seen, is accompanied with a decided self-respect. Alfonso's throne was all the more secure, that it was at least supposed that he had not intrigued for it. From that moment until he died, eleven years after, the Spanish people were generally disposed to think good things of their young prince. It was freely said, while he was on the throne, that while there were but sixteen million people in Spain there were sixteen million and one political parties. And there is but little exaggeration in the epigram.

King Alfonso seemed to show courage and discretion. He, at least, maintained the forms of constitutional government. As soon as a new ministry came into power, all other factions have, almost of course, united against it. Such terms as the "Democratic Monarchic" combination have been usual phrases in Spanish politics. The king changed his ministers when he was compelled to. But he has been fortunate in some of them. And Sagasta, who is at the moment when we write at the head of the government, has approved himself to the world looking on, and to at least a considerable part of Spain, as a prudent, brave, and wise man.

The young king won popular enthusiasm more than once. When the cholera attacked Eastern Spain in 1885, he insisted on visiting the places stricken by the disease, to encourage those who were contending against it. But his constitution was not so strong as his friends tried to believe. He died on the 25th of November, 1885. His oldest child. Marie de la Mercedès, succeeded him. She was five years old when she came to the throne. Her mother is regent.

But, as these sheets pass the press, the telegraph announces the birth of a boy, brother to Marie de la Mercedes,—who inherits, as the son of the late king, the throne which for five months has been filled by his sister.

THE DIRGE OF LARRA.

(Imitated from the Spanish of Zorilla.)

On the breeze I hear the knell
Of the solemn, funeral bell,
Marshalling another guest
To the grave's unbroken rest.

He has done his earthly toil,
And cast off his mortal coil,
As a maid, in beauty's bloom,
Seeks the cloister's living tomb.

When he saw the future rise
To his disenchanted eyes,
Void of love's celestial light,
It was worthless in his sight;
And he hurried, without warning,
To the night that knows no morning.

He has perished in his pride,
Like a fountain, summer-dried;
Like a flower of odorous breath,
Which the tempest scattereth;
But the rich aroma left us,
Shows the sweets that have been reft us,
And the meadow, fresh and green,
What the fountain would have been.

Ah! the poet's mystic measure
Is a rich but fatal treasure:
Bliss to others, to the master
Full of bitterest disaster.

Poet! sleep within the tomb,
Where no other voice shall come
O'er the silence to prevail,
Save a brother poet's wail;
That, if parted spirits know
Aught that passes here below,—
Falling on thy pensive ear
Softly as an infant's tear,
Shall relate a sweeter story
Than the pealing trump of glory.

If, beyond our mortal sight,
In some glorious realm of light,
Poets pass their happy hours,
Far from this cold world of ours.
Oh, how sweet to throw away
This frail tenement of clay,
And in spirit soar above
To the home of endless love.

And if in that world of bliss
Thou rememberest aught of this,—
If *not Being's* higher scene
Have a glimpse of what *has been*,—
Poet! from the seats divine,
Let thy spirit answer mine.

INDEX.

A

Abbasides, 157 ; governor of, 158 ; in Damascus, 163
Abdallah ben Yassim, 189
Abdelmumen, 196
Abderahman I. at Tours, 156
Abderahman II., the Omeyyad, 157–162
Abderahman III., 65; tribute to, 240; cures Sancho, 243
Abencerrages, 203; quarrels of, 206; at the lists, 208; riches of, 353
Abenhamet, prince of the Moors, 210
Abjuration of Arianism by Goths, 123
Abrantes, Duke of, 362
Abu Abdalla (Boabdil), 220–227, 318
Abu Bekir, Emir, 189–192
Adrian VI., Pope, 329
Aduba, birthplace of Lucan, 62
Æmillius Paulus, 38
Ætius, 86
Agmat, Fortress of 193
Agramonts and Beaumonts, 285
Aixa, Moorish princess, 206
Alabez, Moorish tribe, 208
Alans, 76; disappear from Spain, 84
Alarab, the African, 201
Alaric, the Goth, 76; wife of, 77; court at Toulouse, 94
Albrecht, John of, 327
Alcazar of Seville, 270, 307
Alcudia, Duke of, 370
Alexander VI., 338

Alfaqui of Fez, 188
Alfonso II., el Casto, 233
Alfonso V., 283, 286
Alfonso VI., 187–192, 247
Alfonso IX., 200
Alfonso X., el Sabio, 262–266; sister of, 276
Alfonso XI., children of, 271
Alfonso XII., 393
Algalif, 182
Algazali, Abu Hamed, 195
Alhama, taken by Christians, 223
Alhambra, The, 203, 214, 221 ; keys of, 226
Almanzor, regent at Cordova, 168, 246
Almohades, 187, 199
Almoravides, 187, 195
Alorcus, 25
Alphabet, Phœnician, 17
Alpujarras, 226, 352
Alsace, 358
Amadeo, King, 388, 392
Amadis of Gaul, 249
American colonies, Rebellion of, 384
Amiens, Treaty of, 374
Amphitheatre at Nismes, 130
Andalusia, name, 74; fertile fields of, 90; subdued, 193 ; accepts Henry of,
Angoûleme, Duke of, 384
Anjou, Philip, Duke of, 356, 362
Anjou, Margaret of, 296
Anjou, Réné, King of, 294, 296
Anne of Austria, 354
Anne, daughter of Maximilian II., 352

397

Antæus, grave of, 46
Antiquera, Governor of, 217
Arabs, Spanish, 164, 166
Aranda, Duke of, 366
Arianism, gift to Spain, 100; religion of Leovigild, 106; faith of Goswinda, 111; abjured by their sons, 112, 121; by Goths, 123
Arians, 92; simple creed, 95; battle with Catholics, 98
Arles, Goths at, 75
Arragon, Blanche of, 285; Catharine of, 315
Arragon, kingdom of, under St. Ferdinand, 264; in arms against Pedro, 276; united to Castile, 279; story of, 281–297
Arsilla, 140
Arthur, King, Myths of, 249
Ascalis, 46
Assisi, Don Francisco de, 391
Astronomical tables of Alfonso, 266
Asturias, 8 ; possessed by Goths, 233 ; at war with Leon, 244
Asturias, Prince of, 314, 354, 357
Ataulphus, King of the Goths, 73–80
Athens, 282
Atlas, Mountain chain of, 188
Attila, King of the Huns, 85 ; death, 86
Augustus Cæsar in Spain, 58
Aurrich, Don, 252
Austerlitz, 376
Austria, Anne of, 354
Austria, Don John of, 352
Austria, Grand Duke of, 326
Azhera, palace of, 165

B

Bacon, Roger, time of, 266
Badajoz, 378
Bætis, river, 44
Barbarossa, Emperor of Germany, Frederick I., 33
Barca, Governor of, 158
Barca, Hamilcar, 28
Barcelona, 79, 283, 287, 290, 296, 312

Barcelona, Louis XIII., Count of, 355
Basques, 9 ; language of, 10 ; at Roncesvalles, 172
Bavaria, Elector of, 361
Bavieca, horse of the Cid, 258
Bayard, Chevalier, 330
Baylen, Battle of, 377
Beaumonts and Agramonts, 285
Bedouins, wandering tribes, 158
Belgium, 325
Bermuez, Peter, 259.
Bernardo del Carpio, 234
Bilbilis birthplace of Martial, 62
Bivar, Rodrigo del, 249
Blanche of Arragon, 285
Blanche, princess of France, 285
Blanche of Navarre, 284, 291
Boabdil, 220, 225, 227, 318
Bonaparte, Joseph, 372
Bonnivet, General, 330
Bordeaux, burned by Goths, 79 ; birthplace of Black Prince, 276
Boulogne, French fleet at, 376
Bourbon, Blanche of, 272
Bourbon, Constable of, 330
Bourbon, Isabella of, 354
Bourbon, Peter of, 272
Bourbons, 358
Braga (Bracata-Augusta), 60
Brazil, Cape of, 338
Brunhilda, the wicked princess, 111
Bucar, brother of Yussef, 256
Buckingham, Duke of, 355
Buenos Ayres, 337
Bull-fights, 8
Burgos, birthplace of Cid, 247 ; Cid at, 254
Burgundy, Mary of, 325
Burgundians, Vandal tribe, 93

C

Cabot, Sebastian, 336
Cadiz, 15, 37, 374, 384
Cæcias, northerly wind, 50
Cæsar-Augusta (now Saragossa) 60
Cæsar, Augustus, in Spain, 58–61
Cæsar, Julius, in Spain, 54–58 ; in Seville, 262

INDEX.

399

Calabria, John of, 296
Calais lost to the English, 349
Calderon, Plays of, 104
Calder, Sir Robert, Squadron of, 374
California, 251, 337
Caliphate of Cordova, Story of, 155-170
Callagurris, now Callahorra, 62
Calomarde, 385
Campeador, the Cid, 249
Carlists, 385, 389
Carlos, Prince of Viana, 284, 285, 290, 299
Carlos, son of Philip II., 348
Carlos, Don, head of Carlists, 385, 388
Carlotta, wife of Don Francisco, 385
Carrion, Count of, 251
Carthagena, New Carthage, founded by Hamilcar, 21; seized by Scipio, 34
Carthaginians in Spain, 19; merchants, 20; under Hannibal, 22; at Saguntum, 24, 26; possess Southern Spain, 33; expelled, 37
Castaños, General, 377
Castelar, 392
Castile, Catalonia of, Counts of, 244; kingdom of, extent, 281; Ferdinand of, 283; Henry of, 288, 291; Isabella of, 298; defrays expenses of Columbus, 311
Catalans, 282, 289, 301, 355
Catalaunian plains, 85
Catalina of Castile, 315
Catalonia subdued, 38
Catalonians, 14, 281, 294
Catharine of Arragon, 315
Catharine, daughter of John of Gaunt, 280
Catholic, faith declared, 123; sovereigns, 319; party, 388
Cato the Elder in Spain, 38
Celts in Spain, 5; habits of, 6; religion, 12
Cerda de la Ferdinand, 268; Infantas, 277

Cervantes, tragedy of Numantia, 40; writings of, 104, 250, 344
Ceuta, Gothic garrison, 140; pillar of Hercules, 142
Châlons, Battle of, 85
Characitanians, 49
Charlemagne, at Paderborn, Legend of, 171; at Saragossa, 177; invasion of, 235
Charles, Arch-Duke, 362
Charles the Bold, 325
Charles, Prince of Wales, 355
Charles II. of England, 359
Charles V. of France, 277
Charles V., Emperor of Germany, 315, 321
Charles I. of Spain, 315, 321; Charles II., 358; Charles III., 365; Charles IV., 370
Chièvres, tutor of Charles V., 320
Chili, 337
Chilpéric of France, 107
Choiseul, Duke of, 366
Christendom, domain of, 308
Christianity, conversion of Goths to, 94
Christians, captives, 204; friendly with Moors 215, 217; before Grenada, 224; after defeat of Goths, 231; at Clavigo, 239; spreading in Spain, 244; take Seville, 264; formerly Moors, 350
Christina, Queen, 385
Christina of Naples, 389
Chronicle of the Cid, 250, 261
Chronicle of Spain, 266
Cid, the birth-place of, 247; story of, 248-261
Cinq Mars, Plot of, 356
Ciudad Rodrigo, 378
Clavigo, Battle of, 238
Code of Alfonso, 266
Coimbra, 274
Collingwood, Admiral, 375
Columbus, at Granada, 310; voyage of, 311; discovery of America, 336
Campostella, St. Jago de, 238
Constance, daughter of Peter the

Cruel, 280; ancestress of Isabella, 316
Constantinople, 282
Constantius, lover of Placidia, 81
Cordova, taken by Tarik, 148; caliphate of, 155; academy of, 164; mosque, 165; centre of Arabic learning, 167; palace at, 243; rivalled by Seville, 264
Cordova, Gonsalvo de, 225, 314
Corduba (Cordova), 60
Corneille's Sertorius, 53
Cortes, Fernando, 251, 322, 326
Cortes, Spanish, 382
Cotta, beaten by Sertorius, 47
Couching eyes of John of Arragon, 296
Cross, Empire of, 308
Crowns, united, of Castile and Leon, 264; of Castile and Arragon, 279, 306

D

Damascus, Caliphate of, 157, 163
Damascus, sovereigns of, 163; rivalled by Cordova, 170
Dante, Time of, 266
Darro, river, 211
Dauphiny, 325
Davis, Captain John, 360
Diaz, Sancho, Count of Soldaña, 234
Dido, 27
Dominic, 75
Doria, Fleet of, 332
Druids, 11, 12
Dupont, Carelessness of, 377
Durindana, sword of Roland, 178
Dwarf assassinates Ataulphus, 80

E

Early tribes, 1; coast trade of, 6; different names of, 8
Edward III. of England, 276
Egypt, Sultan of, 265
Eleanor of Arragon, 285; Countess of Foix, 292; daughter of Henry II., 265

Elections of Visigoth chiefs, 90
Elizabeth of France, 349
Emerita-Augusta, 60
England, William the Conqueror of, 250; Henry II. of, 265; Henry III. of, 268; Henry VIII. of, 330; William III. of, 362, 365; Victoria of, 386
Enrique, Prince, 271, 277
Ervigius, successor of Wamba, 135
Espartero, 389, 390
Esplandian, 251
Esquera, or Basque language, 10
Erminigild, Story of, 106-119
Evaric, founder of the Gothic kingdom in Spain, 87; death of, 89

F

Fadrique, Prince, 271, 274
Ferdinand of Arragon, Story of, 298-320
Ferdinand of Castile, 283
Ferdinand de la Cerda, 268
Ferdinand of Naples, 286
Ferdinand III. (Saint) of Spain, 264; tomb, 265; VI., 265; VII., 382
Ferdinand and Isabella, marriage of, 298; invest Grenada, 225, 307; receive Columbus, 310; grandeur of, 315; tombs, 318
Fernando, King of Castile, 251, 252
Ferrol, port of Spain, 374
Fez, Kings of, 204
Flanders, Government of, 326
Flor, Roger de, 282
Florez, Francisco, 320
Florida, Bianca, 366
Florida, Spanish population of, 360
Foix, Count and Countess of, 292
France, losses of England in, 349; marriage of Isabella of, 354; conspiracy of Cinq Mars, 356; assistance to United States, Francis I., 330, 332
Francisco, Don, 385
Frega, Insurrection at, 289
368

INDEX. 401

Frere, Hookham, translation of the Cid, 261
Froissart, 292
Fuero Juzgo, Foundation of, 87

G

Galiana, Palaces of, 252
Galicians, 11
Gallio, 62
Ganelon, 175
Garibaldi, 392
Geber, Arabic architect, 264
Geierstein, Anne of, 294
Georgia, 360
German empire, 358
Germany, Emperor of, 268, 314, 331, 352, 361
Ghent, 326, 358
Gibraltar, Straits of, 1, 4, 142, 374
Giralda of Seville, 264
Godoy, Manuel, 370, 372
Gold and silver mines of Spain, 16
Gomélez, Moorish tribe, 208
Gonsalvo de Cordova, 225, 314
Gonzalez, Fernan, 244
Goswinda, queen of Leovigild, 111
Gothic architecture, 137
Goths, at Narbonne. 75; burn Bordeaux, 79; elect Wallia, 81; resist Attila, 85; civilized, 87; triumphant, 89; origin, 92; christianized, 95; Arians, 97; Catholics, 123; in Toledo, 126; betrayed, 141; conquered, 147; after Guadalete, 231 ; in Seville, 262
Grandee of Spain, 389
Greek, explorers 16; emperor, 282
Granada, Moorish kingdom, 203; divided, 220; fall of, 307; Isabella's tomb at, 318; wealth of Moors of, 353
Granada, city of, 213; invested, 225; surrender, 226
Guadalete, Battle of the, 146
Guadalquivir, 264

Guatemala, possessed by Spain, 337
Guesclin, Bertrand du, 277
Guienne, War-cry of, 278
Gutierrez de Cardenas, 302

H

Hamilcar in Spain, 21; builds new Carthage, 21
Hannibal, a boy in Spain, 21; at Saguntum, m, 24; terror of Rome, 27
Hapsburg, House of, 38
Hardy, Captain, 375
Hauteclerc, sword of Olivier, 182
Henriquez, Joan, 284
Henry of England, II., 265; VIII., 330
Henry of France, II. 349; IV.; 354
Hercules, Cave of, 142
Heruli, Vandal tribe, 93
Hieronymo, 257, 260
Hilderic, Count of Nismes, 128
Hispalis (Seville), 262
Hixem, III., 169, 170
Holland, States of, 362
Honorius, Roman emperor, 77
Horn of Roland, 181
Hostages in ancient warfare, 35
Huesca, University of, 47
Huns, invasion of, 84; resisted at Châlons, 85; vanquished, 86

I

Iberians, 1, 4
Ibn-el-Arabi, 171
Ildefonso, Legend of 126
Ingunda, French princess, 107
Isabella, queen of Spain, marriage of, 220; suitors, 299; at Valladolid, 301; good sense of, 306; in camp, 308; confidence in Columbus, 311, children of. 314; death, 317 ; tomb at Granada, 318
Islands of the Blest, 34
Ismail of Granada, 216

J

Jaca, walls built by Cato, 38
James, Saint, 126
Janus, Gates of, 58
Jay, John, 368
Jerusalem, in possession of the Mohammedans, 156; visited by Charles V., 334
Jervis, Admiral, 372
Jesuits, Expulsion of, 366
Jesus, Society of, 334
Jewish physician restores the sight of John of Arragon, 295
Jews in Toledo, 126; bargain with Cid, 254
Jezebel, 27
Joanna, Queen of Naples, 283
Joanna, Princess, 315, 324
John of Arragon, 283–297
John of Castile, 283
John, Prince, son of Isabella, 314
Joseph, King, 378
Julian, Count, 140–147
Julius Cæsar, 54–58, 262

K

Kartah-tuba (Cordova), 28
Koran, 196
Kossuth, 392

L

Lamp-lighter, Son of the, 195
Lancaster, Duke of, 280
Lancaster, Red-rose of, 296
Lancelot, 249
Language, Gothic, 93
Language, Spanish, 30, 38, 68, 88, 100, 302
Languedoc, 325
Larra, Dirge of, 395
Las Casas, 340
Latin customs and language in Spain, 38
Laynez, Diego, 260
Leander, Saint, 113, 124
Leo, Pope, 127

Leon, captured by Christians, 233; at war with Asturias, 244; Ferdinand at, 302
Leopold, Emperor of Germany, 361
Leovigild, 106, 120
Lexington, Battle of, 368
Library of Cordova, 167
Licianus, 62
Lions, Court of, 211
Lisbon, 377
Literature of Spain, 28, 101, 104
Lorraine, Duke of, 296, 358
Louis IX., of France, 265
Louis XI., 294
Louis XIII., 354
Louis XIV., 356
Louis Philippe, 388
Louisiana, 368
Low Countries, Crown of, 326
Loyola, Inigo Lopez de, 333; canonized, 334
Lucan, 62
Lusitanians, 11; capital of, 60; summon Sertorius, 46; banner of, 346

M

Madrid, 362; insurrection in, 377; galleries of, 378
Magellan, 338
Mago, Carthaginian general, 34
Mahdi, Title of, 197
Mahomet, see Mohammed
Majorca, Minorca, and Ivica, 281
Malaga, 224
Marcella, wife of Martial, 62
Margaret, Princess of Germany, 314
Margaret, Queen of Hungary, 357
Marguerite of France, 349
Maria de las Mercedes, 395
Maria, daughter of Charles Emmanuel, 392
Maria, Princess of Portugal, 386
Maria de Médicis, 354
Maria de Padilla, 272, 328
Maria Anna, daughter of Emperor Ferdinand III., 357

INDEX. 403

Maria Christina, 386
Maria, Infanta, 355
Maria Louisa of Savoy, 364
Maria Louisa, Duchess of Montpensier, 389
Maria Louisa of Parma, 370
Maria Theresa, daughter of Philip IV., 356
Marius against Sylla, 44
Marsillius, King of Saragossa, 173
Martial, born at Bilbilis, 62
Martel, Charles, 156
Martin, King of Arragon, 283
Martyr, Peter, 327
Mary, "Bloody," of England, 348
Massena, Marshal, 377
Mauritania, Sertorius in, 46; Morocco, part of, 140; town in, 160
Maximilian, Emperor of Germany, 314
Mazzini, 292
Médicis, Maria of, 354
Mendoza, Cardinal, 318
Merida, capital of Lusitania, 60
Metellus, 47
Mexico, 337; Gulf of, 360
Miguel, Dom, 386
Miguel, Prince, 315
Mina, General, 384
Mir, King of Sueves, 115
Miramolin Almançor, 141
Mithridates, treaty with Sertorius, 52
Missal-book of Charles V., 321
Mississippi, 360; river, 370
Mistletoe, 12
Mohammed, the prophet, 140, 155
Mohammed V. of Granada, 216
Mohammed ben Abdallah, 195
Mohammed ben Alhamar, 213
Mohammed, ruler of Almohades, 201
Mohammedans in Spain, 157; Almohades sovereigns of, 200; driven from Andalusia, 201; finally expelled, 352
Monkeys at Gibraltar, 4
Montemolin, Count of, 388
Montgomery, Count of, 350
Montpensier, Duke of, 391

Montserrat, 334
Moorish, court, 204; maidens, 207; king, retreat of, 226
Moors, in Spain, 206; baths of, 214; friendly with Christians, 215, 217; take Zahara, 223; against Cid, 258; win Seville, 264; arabesques of, 271; prowess of, 307; piracy of, 331; Christianized, 350; in Africa, 351
Morocco, capital of Yussef, 193; besieged, 188; king of, 269
Moriscos, 350
Moslem, belief, 215; quarrels, 216; power dwindling, 244
Munda, Battle of, 54
Munificence of Omeyyades, 165
Muley Ali Abul Hassan, 220
Munoz, Hernando, 389
Murabitins, or Almoravides, 189
Murcia, 38
Murillo, 126
Mur-viedro, 22; siege of, 24; surrender of, 26
Muse, Saracen leader, 141
Mustapha, general of Almanzor, 168

N

Naples, Kingdom of, 283, 314
Napoleon, 372
Narbonne, Goths at, 75
Narvaez, governor of Antiquera, 217
Navarre, 291; kingdom of, 243; aggressive, 281; bone of contention, 284; renounced by Blanche, 291; taken by Ferdinand, 292; attacked by Charles V., 200.
Navarrete, Battle of, 277
Navas de Tolosa, Battle of, 200
Nelson, Admiral, 374
New Testament in Gothic, 94
Netherlands, 335
New Carthage, 21; blockaded, 34
New Mexico, possessed by Spain, 337
Nismes, Rebellion of, 128
Northern invaders, 73
Numantia, Siege of, 40, 344

O

Ode, Shelley's, to Spaniards, 381
Omeyyades, House of, 157, 163, 284
Oppas, bishop of Toledo, 140
Olivares, Count of, 355
Orleans, resists Huns, 85
Ormond, Duke of, 365
Orosius, Spanish historian, 88
Orthes, Chateau of, 292
Orthodoxy of Recared, 121
Orsini, Princess, 364
Osca (Huesca), 47
Ostro-Goths, 92
Oviedo, capital of Goths, 233

P

Pacific Ocean discovered, 337
Padilla, Maria de, 272, 328
Palm, transplanted to Spain, 163 ; sign of palma, 340
Pampeluna, 243, 327, 332
Panama, Isthmus of, 337
Paraguay, 327
Parma, Maria Louisa of, 370
Paul, Duke, letter of, 128 ; at Nismes, 129 ; scized, 131 ; life spared, 132
Pax Augusta (Badajos), 60
Peace, Prince of, 370
Pedro the Cruel, 270 ; rightful heir, 271 ; marriage, 273 ; crimes of, 276 ; daring, 278 ; slain, 279
Pedro, Dom, regent of Portugal, 388
Pelayo, 150 ; leader of the Goths, 231
Pensacola, 360
Perez Hernan, 320
Peru, 337
Peter, Saint, 246
Peterborough, Lord, 365
Philadelphia, Siege of, 283
Philibert Emmanuel, 349
Philip the I., of Spain, 315, 319, 325 ; II., 247, 321, 343 ; III., 346, 352, 355 ; IV., 355 ; V., 356

Phœnicians, 1, 14, 262
Piracy, Moorish, 331
Pittsburg, 370
Placidia, sister of Honorius, 77
Plutarch, story of Sertorius, 44–48
Pollock, Oliver, 368
Pompey, 47–57
Pope, Adrian VI., 329 ; Alexander VI., 338 ; Leo, 127 ; Sixtus IV., 304
Portugal, 11 ; ruler of, 51 ; borders of, 264 ; story separate from that of Spain, 279 ; king of, 310 ; princess of, 314 ; crown possessed by Philip II., 343 ; Mary of, 347 ; ally of England, 377 ; regent of, 388
Portuguese, Losses of, 378
Pragmatic Sanction, 385
Prince, Black, 276
Provence, 74, 75, 325
Prudentius, Poem of, 62
Ptolemy, System of, 270
Publius Scipio, 37
Punic war, 20
Pyrenees, 1 ; spurs of, 5 ; Jaca in, 38 ; northern site of, 75 ; crossed by Gothic princess, 110 ; by Charlemagne, 171 ; by Black Prince, 277 ; "ceased to exist," 364

Q

Quintilian, 63
Quixote, Don, 104, 346

R

Ramiro, 238 ; II., 244
Rebellion of Nismes, 129
Recared, 106 ; died, 124
Redoubtable, 275
Regeb (October), 192
Remond, 252
René, king of Anjou, 294
Republic, French, 370
Republic in Spain, 292
Rhodes, 329
Rhodians, 16
Richard, Cœur de Lion, 250 ; brother of Henry III., 268

INDEX. 405

Richelieu, Cardinal, 356
Roderick, last of the Goths, 139; legend of, 142; courage, 146; drowned, 147
Rodriguez Diego, 260
Roland, Song of, 171
Romans, in Spain, 30; customs, 32; routed by Sertorius, 47; language of, 88; monuments of, in Seville, 262
Rome, opposed by Hannibal, 22, 27, 30; Sylla master of, 44; dark period of, 51; subjugates Spain, 61; domination of, 67; end of power in Spain, 87
Roncesvalles, 171, 277
Ronda, Alcalde of, 218
Roumania, Admiral of, 282
Ruy Diaz, the Cid Campeador, 256

S

Sabio el, Alfonso, 266
Saguntum, 22, 24
Saint Aignan, 85
Saint Augustine, 359
Saint Ferdinand, 264
Saint Jago de Campostella, 238
Saint Lazarus, 260
Saint Louis of France, 265
Saint Mary's river, 360
Saint Peter, 246, 260
Saint Vincent, Cape, Battle of, 372
Salamanca, 347
Saldaña, Count of, 234
Sancha of Navarre, 244
Sancho, 268; the Fat, 243; Don, 249, 252
San Martin, Bridge of, 125
San Milan, vida de, 241
Santa Maria, Church of, 125
Santiago, 238, 247, 280
Saracens, 140, 155, 180, 238
Saragossa (Cæsar Augusta), 60, 177
Sardinia, 281
Savoy, 326
Scallop, mark of pilgrim, 240
Scandinavia, 92

Scipio Africanus, 32; Publius, 32
Scipios, The, 30; in Seville, 262
Scourge of God, Attila, 85
Segovia, 304
Seneca, Lucius, 62
Senecas, The two, 62
Sermon on the mount, in four languages, 101
Sertorius, Quintus, 44; civilizer of Spain, 48; resources of, 49; in Portugal, 51; assassinated, 52
Seville, 149, 262, 307; surrenders to Musa, 149; prosperity of, 262
Shelley, ode to the Spaniards, 381
Sicily, 281, 287; Isabella at, 307
Sigeric, 80
Sixtus IV., Pope, 304
Soleyman the Magnificent, 329
Sos, birthplace of Ferdinand, 284
Southey's Roderick, 150, 250
Spain, subjugated by Rome, 61; Roman domination of, 67; reduced to province, 149; Arabs in, 164; invaded by Almoravides, 192; under Almohades, 200; importance of, 265; cardinal of, 305; prosperity of, 312; dominions in America, 337; occupied by French, 385; civil war, 389
Spaniard, The true, 265
Spanish language, 30, 38, 68, 88, 100, 302
Spanish war of succession, 361, 364
Stilicho, 75
Sueves in Galicia, 76
Sully, 355
Sylla against Marius, 44
Sword, of Olivier, 182; of Roland, 178; of Yussef, 257

T

Tagus, river, 49, 125
Tangier, Gothic garrison of, 140
Tarifa, 1, 4
Tarik, 142; attack of, 146; at Toledo, 148; reviled by Musa, 149

Tarraco (Tarragona), 58, 61, 117
Tarshish, Ships of, 19
Tartessus, 19
Taxfin ben Ali, 198
Theodemir, Bishop, 238
Theodofred, father of Roderick, 139
Theodoric the Visigoth, 84
Theodosia, first wife of Leovigild, 113
Ticinus, Battle of, 32
Tingis, City of, 46
Titian, Portraits by, 348
Tizona, sword of Yussef, 257
Toledo, schools of, 100 ; Goths at, 107–137 ; taken by Tarik, 148 ; fast at, 200 ; regained by Christians, 247
Toledo, Archbishop of, 302
Torres Bamejas, 222
Toulon, Blocade of, 374
Toulouse, 75, 77
Tours, Battle of, 156
Trance of King Wamba, 134
Trastamara, Henry of, 277, 279, 283
Trastamara, House of, 283, 305
Treachery of Ganelon, 176
Treasures of Moors, 354
Triumvirate, Civil wars of, 58
Tubal, in Spain, 10
Tunis Capture of, 331
Turpin, Archbishop, 179

U

Ulfilas, 93–95
Unitarians, the Almohades, 198
United States, 338, 359, 370
Utrecht, Treaty of, 365

V

Valdabrun the Saracen, 180
Valencia, 38 ; attacked by Cid, 251 ; governed by Cid, 256 ; possessed by Ferdinand III., 264 ; Moors expelled from, 352
Valentinian, son of Placidia, 81
Valladolid, 301, 347

Vandals, in Bœtica, 76 ; at war with Goths, 78–84 ; court at Seville, 262 ; Heruli, tribe of, 93
Vascones (Basques), 9
Veillantif, the horse of Roland, 183
Velasquez, 356
Vendôme, Duke of, 365
Venice, joined to Charles V., 330
Vergennes, 366
Versailles, 359
Vespucius, 336
Viana, Carlos, Prince of, 285
Viceroys in Castile, 328
Victoria, Battle of, 378
Victoria, Princess, of England, 386
Victory, Nelson's flag-ship, 375
Vigo, 365
Villeneuve, Admiral, 374
Visigoths, king of, 77 ; princes, 84 ; monarchs, 89 ; government, 90 ; name, 92 ; deteriorated, 232
Vincæ, 24
Vivarambla, 207

W

Wahit, sheik of the Arabs, 160
Wallia, King of the Goths, 80
Wamba, Story of, 125–135
Wellington, Lord, 378
West Indies, 337
Wellesley, Sir Arthur, 377
White hind of Sertorius, 46, 53
William the Conqueror, 250
William III. of England, 362
Witiza, 139, 146
World, History of, by Orosius, 88

X

Xanas, 9
Xeres, Battle of, 146
Ximena, sister of Alfonso el Casto, 234
Ximenes, Cardinal, 326
Xucat, river, 256

Y

Yahia ben Ibrahim, 188
Yussef, Emir of Abbasides, 161

INDEX.

Yussef ben Taxfin, 188 190, 257
Yuste, Monastery of, 335

Z

Zagat, governor of Malaga, 188
Zahani, El, 141
Zahara, taken by Moors, 223
Zaineb, sister of Abu Bekir, 190
Zama, Battle of, 32
Zamora, Lorenzo de, 28
Zante currants, 24
Zegris, Moorish tribe, 204 ; quarrels of, 207 ; at the lists, 208
Zoraïde, Moorish princess, 210
Zoraya, 222, 223

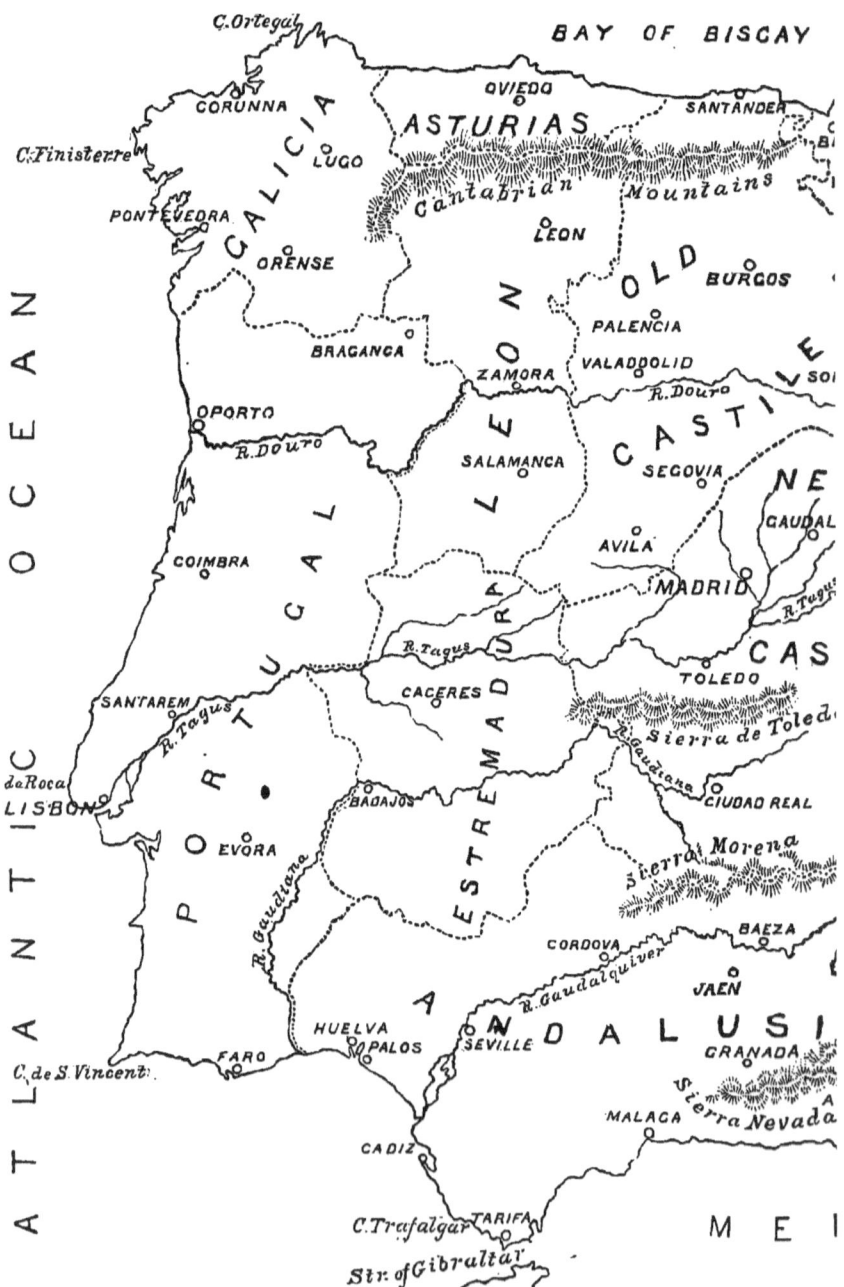

The Story of the Nations.

Messrs. G. P. PUTNAM'S SONS take pleasure in announcing that they have in course of publication a series of historical studies, intended to present in a graphic manner the stories of the different nations that have attained prominence in history.

In the story form the current of each national life will be distinctly indicated, and its picturesque and noteworthy periods and episodes will be presented for the reader in their philosophical relation to each other as well as to universal history.

It is the plan of the writers of the different volumes to enter into the real life of the peoples, and to bring them before the reader as they actually lived, labored, and struggled—as they studied and wrote, and as they amused themselves. In carrying out this plan, the myths, with which the history of all lands begins, will not be overlooked, though these will be carefully distinguished from the actual history, so far as the labors of the accepted historical authorities have resulted in definite conclusions.

The subjects of the different volumes will be planned to cover connecting and, as far as possible, consecutive epochs or periods, so that the set when completed will present in a comprehensive narrative the chief events in the great STORY OF THE NATIONS; but it will, of course, not always prove practicable to issue the several volumes in their chronological order.

The "Stories" are printed in good readable type, and in handsome 12mo form. They are adequately illustrated and furnished with maps and indexes. They are sold separately at a price of $1.50 each.

The following is a partial list of the subjects thus far determined upon :

THE STORY OF EARLY EGYPT. Prof. GEORGE RAWLINSON.
"   "   " *CHALDEA. Z. RAGOZIN.
"   "   " *GREECE. Prof. JAMES A. HARRISON,
                         Washington and Lee University.
"   "   " *ROME. ARTHUR GILMAN.
"   "   " *THE JEWS. Prof. JAMES K. HOSMER,
                         Washington University of St. Louis.
"   "   " *CARTHAGE. Prof. ALFRED J. CHURCH,
                         University College, London.
"   "   " BYZANTIUM.
"   "   " THE GOTHS. HENRY BRADLEY.
"   "   " *THE NORMANS. SARAH O. JEWETT.
"   "   " *PERSIA. S. G. W. BENJAMIN.
"   "   " *SPAIN. Rev. E. E. and SUSAN HALE.
"   "   " *GERMANY. S. BARING-GOULD.
"   "   " THE ITALIAN REPUBLICS.
"   "   " HOLLAND. Prof. C. E. THOROLD ROGERS.
"   "   " *NORWAY. HJALMAR H. BOYESEN.
"   "   " *THE MOORS IN SPAIN. STANLEY LANE-POOLE.
"   "   " *HUNGARY. Prof. A. VÁMBÉRY.
"   "   " THE ITALIAN KINGDOM. W. L. ALDEN.
"   "   " EARLY FRANCE. Prof. GUSTAVE MASSON.
"   "   " ALEXANDER'S EMPIRE. Prof. J. P. MAHAFFY.
"   "   " THE HANSE TOWNS. HELEN ZIMMERN.
"   "   " ASSYRIA. Z. RAGOZIN.
"   "   " *THE SARACENS. ARTHUR GILMAN.
"   "   " TURKEY. STANLEY LANE-POOLE.
"   "   " PORTUGAL. H. MORSE STEPHENS.
"   "   " MEXICO. SUSAN HALE.
"   "   " IRELAND. Hon. EMILY LAWLESS.
"   "   " PHŒNICIA.
"   "   " SWITZERLAND.
"   "   " RUSSIA.
"   "   " WALES.
"   "   " SCOTLAND.

* (The volumes starred are now ready, January, 1887.)

G. P. PUTNAM'S SONS

NEW YORK   LONDON

27 and 29 WEST TWENTY-THIRD STREET   27 KING WILLIAM STREET, STRAND